HANDBOOK OF SYNAGOGUE ARCHITECTURE

BROWN UNIVERSITY
BROWN JUDAIC STUDIES
Edited by
Jacob Neusner
Wendell S. Dietrich, Ernest S. Frerichs,
Alan Zuckerman

Number 29

HANDBOOK OF SYNAGOGUE ARCHITECTURE

by Marilyn Joyce Segal Chiat

HANDBOOK OF
SYNAGOGUE ARCHITECTURE

by
Marilyn Joyce Segal Chiat

Scholars Press

Published by
Scholars Press
101 Salem Street
P.O. Box 2268
Chico, California 95927

HANDBOOK OF SYNAGOGUE ARCHITECTURE

by
Marilyn Joyce Segal Chiat

Publication of this book has been made possible in part by The Tisch
Publication Fund of Brown Judaic Studies.

Library of Congress in Publication Data

Chiat, Marilyn Joyce Segal
  Handbook of synagogue architecture.

  (Brown Judaic Studies ; no. 29) (ISSN 0147–927X)
  Includes bibliographical references and index.
  1. Synagogue   architecture—Palestine.   2. Palestine—
Antiquities. I. Title. II. Series.
NA5977.C5   726'.3'0933   81–9419
ISBN 0–89130–524–6 (pbk.)   AACR2

Printed in the United States of America

TABLE OF CONTENTS

List of Tables

List of Map and Plans

Plan

Preface and Acknowledgments

Over the past several decades, scholars have become
increasingly aware of the historic importance of ancient synagogue art and architecture. With their growing awareness came
the realization that no one source was available that contained
all the pertinent data related to these buildings. With the full
support and encouragement of my advisor, Professor Carl D.
Sheppard, Department of Art History, University of Minnesota, I
have attempted to fill this void. The Handbook of Synagogue
Architecture is the result. To Professor Sheppard goes my
gratitude for all his assistance.

The research undertaken for the handbook indicates that the
remains of synagogues uncovered in Israel, the West Bank and the
Golan Heights offer important evidence of provincial Roman and
Byzantine art and architecture as it developed in Syria and
Palestine during the first seven centuries of the common era.
Such evidence augments and enriches that of neighboring contem-
porary monuments, surveyed in such publications as H. C. Butler's
series on Syria and J. B. Ward-Perkins and Richard Krautheimer's
studies of Roman, Early Christian, and Byzantine architecture.[1]
By virtue of their dates and locations, synagogues further our
knowledge of the extent and depth of Greco-Roman influence in the
Middle East, particularly its impact on the ordinary people.
They provide data regarding the intermingling of cultures of the
Orient and the West, the legacies of which are often exotic and
important artistic monuments. Synagogues contain elements of
the style that was to influence the development of art and
architecture in the later Byzantine world as well as in the Latin
West.

Archaeological evidence of synagogues and churches uncovered
in the same or neighboring territories reflects the architectural
and decorative elements shared by Jews and Christians. The
handbook contains data for further investigation of the recipro-
cal relationship between church and synagogue development in
Palestine. The evidence enhances our knowledge of the religious,
cultural and social relationships between the two religious
communities. This area of study must be furthered by scholars
well versed in religious studies and art history. Such a study
requires a willingness to approach complex and often

contradictory material in an objective manner, free of precon-
ceived notions. It must be based on studies of appropriate
historical, archaeological, and literary data.

It is hoped this handbook will fill, at least in part, the
need for more insight into the ". . . religious and aesthetic
sensibilities of the Jews in antiquity."[2]

A task such as this cannot be undertaken without the support
and cooperation of many others. Professor A. Thomas Kraabel,
Chairman of the Classics Department, University of Minnesota,
must be singled out for a very special thank you. Professor
Kraabel went far beyond that required of him in counseling me on
many facets of my research. I was able to reap a harvest of
benefits from his expertise in the fields of synagogue archaeology and religious studies. Professor Kraabel has, in
addition, tirelessly read several versions of this manuscript and
his suggestions have contributed a great deal to its final form.

Professor Jacob Neusner of Brown University and Professor
Jakob Petuchowski of Hebrew Union College, Cincinnati, patiently
read and listened to my theories and concerns regarding my
research and contributed comments and criticisms that have proved
invaluable. A very special acknowledgment must be accorded
Professor Neusner who displayed great patience during the
preparation of the manuscript for publication.

Staff members of the Israel Department of Antiquities and
Museums graciously provided me with their time and assistance
during my visits to Israel to do research. I would like to thank
Claire Epstein, Fanny Vitto, Gideon Foerster, and in particular,
Ze'ev Yeivin. Professors Dan Barag, Bezalel Narkiss, Joseph
Naveh and Avram Negev of Hebrew University, Jerusalem, also made
themselves available to discuss questions and problems related
to my research, for which I am grateful.

Professor Eric Meyers of Duke University generously shared
plans and photographs of the four synagogues in Israel where he
was the director of excavations. His publication, <u>Ancient
Synagogue Excavations at Khirbet Shema', Upper Galilee, Israel</u>,
co-authored by A. Thomas Kraabel and James F. Strange, sets the
standard of excellence for work in the field of synagogue
archaeology.

I would like to thank those who have contributed so much to
the preparation of the final manuscript. Professor Arthur
Merrill of United Theological Seminary of the Twin Cities for

his careful reading of the manuscript and his eagle eye for
errors, my editor, Carol Masters, my typist, Nancy Smith, and my
patient sister-in-law, Mrs. Rose Chiat Pickman, who assisted me
in proof-reading.

Professional considerations aside, I must now take note of
the personal side of the ledger. I would like to thank my mother,
Mrs. Taube Segal Horwitz and mother-in-law, Mrs. Mary Chiat, for
their good and practical advice. My son, William Segal Chiat,
and daughter and son-in-law, Penny and Paul Svenkeson, have
always eased the burden of my responsibilities so I could under-
take and complete this task. But it is to my dear husband,
Harvey Jay Chiat, that this book is dedicated.

24 June 1981   Marilyn J. Chiat
22 Sivan 5741

Notes

[1] A. Boethius and J. B. Ward-Perkins, _Etruscan and Roman
Architecture_ (Harmondsworth, Middlesex: Penguin Books, 1970),
chapter 18. Richard Krautheimer, _Early Christian and Byzantine
Architecture_, 2nd ed. (Harmondsworth, Middlesex: Penguin Books,
1975). H. C. Butler, _Early Churches in Syria_, edited and completed by E. Baldwin Smith (Amsterdam: Hakkert, 1969); _Archi-
tecture and other Arts_, 2 vols. (New York: Century Co., 1903);
Syria, 4 vols. (Leyden: Brill, 1914, 1919).

[2] Eric Meyers, "Synagogue," _IDBS_, 1976.

Introduction

The Handbook of Synagogue Architecture is a digest of the evidence from all known synagogue remains uncovered within the boundaries of ancient Palestine. Its purpose is to provide a research tool for archaeology, history and religious studies.

Organization of the Handbook

The handbook is divided according to the following seven regions and forty-four city-territories (or districts) formed by the Romans in the province of Palestine.[1]

A. Phoenician cities

    1. Tyre
    2. Ptolemais

B. Galilee

    1. Tetracomia (district)
    2. Sepphoris/Diocaesarea (includes Helenopolis and Exaloth-Nain)
    3. Tiberias
    4. Beth She'an/Scythopolis
    5. Legio/Maximianupolis

C. Coastal cities

    1. Dora
    2. Caesarea
    3. Apollonia
    4. Antipatris
    5. Joppa
    6. Jamnia
    7. Azotus
    8. Ascalon
    9. Gaza
  10. Raphia

D. Samaria

    1. Sebaste
    2. Neapolis

E. Judaea

    1. Aelia-Capitolina (Jerusalem)
    2. Lydda/Diospolis
    3. Nicopolis/Emmaus
    4. Bethgabra/Eleutheropolis

F. Limes Palaestinae (district)

    1. Saltus Constaniniaces
    2. Sycomazon
    3. Saltus Gerarticus
    4. Jericho

G. East of the Jordan River

    1. Caesarea Philippi/Paneas
    2. Gaulanitis (district)
    3. Batanaea
    4. Hippos/Susitha
    5. Trachonitis
    6. Auranitis
    7. Dium
    8. Gadara/Umm Qeis
    9. Abila
  10. Pella
  11. Gerasa
  12. Philadelphia/Amman
  13. Heshbon
  14. Medeba
  15. Peraea (district)
  16. Rabbath Moab/Areopolis
  17. Charachmaba

All entries are placed in one of three categories:

I. Validated: The ruins of a building bear Jewish inscriptions and/or motifs.

II. Attested: Architectural or decorative fragments bear Jewish inscriptions and/or motifs from a synagogue; location of the building is unknown.

III. Disputed: Two subcategories are given.

    A. Attributed: The ruins of a building or fragments lack Jewish inscriptions or motifs but are identified as the remains of a synagogue by some scholars.

    B. Not Accepted: The ruins of a building or fragments lack Jewish inscriptions and/or motifs; attribution is questionable on the basis of present evidence.

To qualify as a synagogue (category I and II) a building or its architectural/decorative fragments must be decorated with common motifs, such as the image of the Torah Shrine, menorah, lulab, ethrog, and shofar, or contain inscriptions that establish its identity as having been constructed and used by a Jewish community for a form of assembly. Neither a building's plan nor its location within a presumed Jewish village can qualify a ruin as a synagogue. Only rarely is it possible to identify a building as a synagogue solely on the basis of its architectural form or location (category III A). The available archaeological and literary evidence has in only a few instances been analyzed to the extent that it can be used to verify a building's identi- fication. The Khirbet Shema' publication is a rare example of the validation of a site and synagogue that has used all the available literary and archaeological evidence; it is a model for future endeavors of this kind.[2]

The entries are arranged according to the numbered list below. If no information for an entry-section is available, that section is omitted. Each entry contains a bibliography; citations of those references are given in parentheses. The letter (A) refers to the present author. The form of the data entries is:

1. Name of site and map reference. The accepted name is followed by its variations; the map reference is for the 1:100,000 map edited by the Survey of Israel, 1967- 1972. Map coordinates are for the synagogue site (4 numbers), or if that is unknown, the village or ruin. The map number is placed in parentheses.
2. Survey of site.
3. Character and sections of the building as suggested by extant and identifiable remains.
4. Measurements (as published, length followed by width).
5. Orientation.
6. Character and form: apse, niche, Torah Shrine, bema, chancel.
7. Auxiliary rooms and structures.
8. Ornamentation.
9. Coins, ceramics, and other artifacts found within the building complex.
10. Inscriptions.[3]
11. Donors and patrons.
12. Date, as suggested by excavator or documentor of entry.
13. Bibliography. A selected rather than exhaustive biblio- graphy is given for each site. The major source is listed first, the remainder chronologically. Abbrevia- tions are used for commonly cited sources. (See: List of Abbreviations, pp. 365 ff.)

Each entry is given a catalogue number. For example, the number of Kefar Bar'am A is: B:1, I-2. This breaks down as follows:

> B -- Galilee (region)
> 1 -- Tetracomia (city-territory)
> I -- validated (category)
> 2 -- entry listed alphabetically within its category
>   and city-territory (or district).

Each entry, regardless of category, is listed alphabetically in the index, followed by its catalogue number. Entries beginning with Horvat, Kafr, Kefar, Kfar, Khirbet, are alphabetized under the first word of their names, so that Kefar Bar'am would be under the letter K̲. Transliterations of Hebraic and Arabic terms and place names are written according to the system approved by the American Library Association and Library of Congress, bulletins 43 and 91.

Parenthetical numbers following the descriptions of certain mosaic pavements refer to the system developed by the Association Internationale pour l'Etude de la Mosaïque Antique.[4]

Israel Department of Antiquities and Museums chronological table has been used in this handbook unless otherwise indicated.[5]

Hellenistic I	332-152 B.C.E.
Hellenistic II (Hasmonean)	152-37 B.C.E.
Roman I (Herodian)	37 B.C.E.-70 C.E.
Roman II	70-180 C.E.
Roman III	180-324
Byzantine I	324-451
Byzantine II	451-640
Early Arab	640-1099

Although Samaritan synagogue data are problematic because the relationship among Jews, Christians, and the Samaritans during the Roman and Byzantine periods is uncertain, Samaritan entries are catalogued in their appropriate city-territory.[6]

Several prior attempts have been made to organize and systematize synagogue data. Heinrich Kohl and Carl Watzinger, in their monumental study of synagogues published in 1916, gave the name "Galilean" to a type of synagogue they uncovered in Galilee.[7] This was a basilica with two or three rows of interior columns and a monumental facade facing toward Jerusalem. Buildings of this type often were decorated with reliefs and paved with flagstone. For a time this was believed to be the standard architectural form of the ancient Palestinian synagogue; further discoveries, however, proved this conclusion wrong. The dramatic finds at Na'aran, Beth Alpha, and Hammat Gadara almost a

half-century ago led scholars to add a second category of
Palestinian synagogues. Eliezer Sukenik referred to these as
"new," as compared with the "earlier" Galilean type.[8] The "new"
synagogue was dated to the Byzantine period, and was characterized
by its mosaic pavement and an apse or niche facing toward Jerusalem. Later discoveries in Palestine showed these two categories
to be inadequate. The changes apparent in the orientation of the
synagogue at Beth She'arim, the discovery of the "broadhouse"
type in Palestine, at Eshtemoa and Khirbet Sūsīya in Judaea and
Khirbet Shema' in Galilee, required a third category. Thus,
Michael Avi-Yonah postulated three types of synagogues, which
were grouped into three related chronological periods: 1. Early
(Galilean); 2. Transitional (broadhouse); 3. Fifth century
(Byzantine).[9] E. R. Goodenough adopted a similar division:
A. Galilean; B. Broadhouse; C. Synagogues with mosaic pavements.[10]
Nevertheless, Avi-Yonah, in one of his last writings on the sub-
ject, realized the shortcomings of such a rigid typological-
chronological categorization and cautioned against the use of
these "types" as a basis for determining chronology.[11]

Problems created by the indiscriminate use of such a rigid
method are manifold. Only a few synagogues are dated by
inscription and equally few are dated through the use of stratigraphic evidence. The ongoing controversy regarding the dating
of the synagogue at Capernaum serves only to illustrate the
problems that may arise if one insists on a rigid typological or
stylistic categorization of synagogue architecture.[12] Furthermore, the category "transitional" soon became a catchall for
synagogue types that did not conform to the other two categories.
It became apparent that the evolutionary concept of an early,
middle, and late form of synagogue was untenable and a new
system would have to be proposed.

The two most recent catalogues listing synagogue sites have
chosen to avoid the typological-chronological issue entirely,
by listing the entrants alphabetically. S. Saller's catalogue
must be used with great caution owing to numerous errors and
questionable attributions.[13] The effort of Frowald Hüttenmeister
and Gottfried Reeg is more accurate and complete.[14]
Hüttenmeister and Reeg have elected to list synagogue sites for
which actual archaeological evidence exists with those known
solely through references in ancient literature. This arrangement can lead to confusion on the part of the reader. Furthermore,
buildings they consider "uncertain synagogues" are included in

their catalogue with those considered "certain." On closer
examination of all available evidence, the attributions of a
number of their "certain" synagogues are in reality unconfirmed.

The most recent publication on the subject, edited by Lee
Levine, Ancient Synagogues Revealed (Jerusalem, 1981) arrived too
late to be included in this publication.

All studies of Palestinian synagogues have ignored the
important evidence that the related field of historical geography
can provide. The diversity of the Jewish communities within
Roman and Byzantine Palestine has finally begun to be recognized.
The long held concept of "normative" Judaism, as posited by
George Foot Moore, has now been rejected.[15] Morton Smith,
writing of Judaism in first century Palestine notes " . . . the
different parts of the country were so different, such gulfs of
feeling and practice separated Idumea, Judea, Caesarea, and
Galilee, that even on this level [the religion of the average
people] there was probably no more agreement between them than
between any one of them and a similar area in the Diaspora."[16]
One other factor that must be considered along with historical
geography is the material culture of the community, that is, the
evidence uncovered by archaeology. To ignore this evidence is
in effect to "speak in vacuo."[17] Furthermore, to date synagogues
solely on the basis of typological observations, without con-
sidering the related data, is inaccurate.[18]

In this handbook, unlike the catalogues and surveys
described above, synagogue sites are listed within the boundaries
as they existed in Palestine during the Roman and Byzantine
periods (Map 1). These limits are those of the city-territories
formed by the Romans following their conquest of the country,
not boundaries derived from Talmudic or Biblical sources. Rome's
division of Palestine accurately reflects the religious, social,
and cultural configurations of the province.

Historical Summary

The following brief summary of historical events that
occurred in Palestine during the time in which the synagogues
were built is taken from the standard works on the subject by
Avi-Yonah, Jones, Neusner, and Smallwood; all are cited in notes
and in the bibliography.

Palestine was divided by the Romans into city-territories, each of which possessed distinctive traditions and character- istics.[19] The locations of the majority of city-territories can be determined by the use of literary sources, archaeological evidence, and epigraphy, although their actual territorial extent is often less certain.[20] The Romans instituted a territorial division following the first Jewish revolt (which ended 70 C.E.) as an effective method of controlling the province's Jewish population, which had settled in two compact regions: Judaea, including Jerusalem, and Galilee. Up to the time of the first revolt, the Jewish people living within the Province of Judaea had easy access to one another and, through Galilee and adjoining Gaulanitis, to the large Jewish population residing under Parthian control in Babylonia.[21] The Jewish rebels had hoped that with the cooperation of Babylonian Jewry they could force Rome and Parthia into a conflict in which the Parthians would support the rebels' cause.[22] The large number of Jews in Babylonia, although outside the Roman Empire, when included with those of Judaea and Galilee, rendered the Jewish people poten- tially more powerful than their number within the Roman Empire would imply. The Palestinian and Babylonian communities formed in fact one national body separated by an artificial political boundary.[23] That many Jews resided in the westernmost provinces of the Parthian Empire and were in such close contact with their Palestinian neighbors was of major political and military impor- tance to the Romans.

The Roman emperors had tried several times to conquer Babylonia to prevent a Parthian conquest of Syria that would inhibit Rome's expansionist policies in the east.[24] Rome had to find ways of keeping the three areas of concentrated Jewish population separate, so as to alleviate the threat of a second uprising that would involve Parthia. The Romans were no doubt aware that the Greek cities within Jewish territory had generally remained passive during the rebellion, probably for economic as well as political reasons. Three of these cities, Caesarea, Sebaste, and Scythopolis, controlled territories that reached from the Mediterranean Sea to the Jordan River, strategically separating the two large Jewish population centers--Judaea to the south and Galilee to the north. In light of the passive role played by the Greek cities during the rebellion, the Romans decided to extend the municipal system over much of the remainder of the province. The Romans' attempt to confine the Jewish population within certain districts did not, however, prevent a second revolt in 132 C.E.; it lasted for three years before the rebels capitulated. This revolt was confined primarily to the region of Judaea; the Jews residing in Galilee and Babylonia did not participate actively.[25]

The emperor Hadrian, angered by the revolt, instituted radical measures against the surviving Jewish population in Judaea. They were expelled not only from Jerusalem, but also from Judaea, and were replaced by Syrians and Arabs. Several Jewish villages were allowed to exist along the fringes of the Judaean Hills: in the Jordan Valley, in the Daromas, and along the Coastal Plain.[26] Rome expanded its policy of urbanizing Palestine and only three areas were left without city-status. These were the imperial estates around Jericho, which included the three districts of Peraea, the two adjoining territories of Tetracomia and Gaulanitis, and the Daromas. Tetracomia and Gaulanitis had large conservative Jewish populations, which may account for Rome's unwillingness to provide them with city-status.[27] The Daromas became part of the Roman _limes_ and was administered by the military.[28]

The territorial division of Palestine remained essentially unchanged throughout the reigns of the Antonine and Severan emperors. Diocletian, assuming imperial power in 284 C.E., initiated an administrative and military reorganization of the Roman provinces. The diocese of the Orient included the province of Palestine. Its territorial extent was enlarged by the acquisition of the area between Idumaea and the head of the Red Sea, together with Moab, located south of the Arnon River and east of the Dead Sea. The date of this transfer is unknown; however, the earliest evidence from Eusebius speaks of copper mines between Petra and the Dead Sea that belonged to Palestine during the period of Diocletian's persecution of Christians.[29] In the north, the counterbalancing transfer of Auranitis, Trachonitis, and Batanaea from Syria to Arabia is dated ca. 295 C.E., according to the adoption of the era of Bostra in those districts.[30] The transfer of the coastal city of Dor from Phoenicia to Palestine may have occurred at this time.[31] In 357-358, Palestine was divided into northern and southern halves along the line of the Roman _limes Palestinae_. The southern half, _Palestina salutaris_, had its capital at Petra. The remainder of Palestine was further divided into two provinces in ca. 400 C.E., _Palestina prima_ and _Palestina secunda_. The former consisted of Judaea, Idumaea, Samaria, the Coastal Plain, and Peraea; its capital was at Caesarea. Palestina secunda was composed of Galilee, the Decapolis, and Gaulanitis; Scythopolis was made its capital. Palestina salutaris was renamed Palestina tertia. Two edicts of Theodosius II (7.4304, dated 424, and 16. 8. 29, dated 429) are addressed to the Jewish Sanhedrins of the two Palestines, prima and secunda; this evidence suggests that by the fifth century few, if any, Jews resided in the southeastern region known as Palestina tertia.

Citations of Literary Evidence

Citations from the New Testament are numbered according to the Revised Standard Version of the Bible (Nazareth: Luke 2:51). The Holy Scriptures, according to the Masoretic text, is used for quotations from the Hebrew Bible (Beersheba: Judges 20:1; I Kings 4:25). Often-cited rabbinic sources include the Mishnah, Tosefta, and two talmudim, Yerushalmi (Jerusalem or Palestinian) and Bavli (Babylonian). References to the Yerushalmi Talmud include the abbreviated name of the tractate, chapter and section of Mishnah, followed by folio number and columns (Meron: JT Sheb. 9:2).[32] The Bavli Talmud, because of its standard pagination, uses only the folio number and page side (Chorozain: BT Men. 85a, 85b). Tosefta citations have the letter T preceding the tractate's abbreviated name and the numerals designating chapter and section within the tractate (Gush Halav: T. Sheb. 7:15). The same system applies to Mishnah: the letter M followed by numerals (Khirbet Shema': M. BB:2).

Josephus produced four works following the first Jewish revolt: Antiquitates Judicae, Contra Apionem, Bellus Judaicum and Vita. The translation referred to is the Loeb Classical Edition[33] (Giscala: BJ II:575).

Eusebius of Caesarea wrote his Onomasticon sometime between 326-330. It is a dictionary of some six hundred names of towns, mountains, rivers, and districts mentioned in the Torah and New Testament. The reference numbers refer to the numbering system used in Klostermann's edition (Chorozain: Onom. 74:23).[34]

Notes

[1] Avi-Yonah, Holy Land, pp. 127-180. Map 1.

[2] Eric M. Meyers, A. T. Kraabel, James F. Strange, Ancient Synagogue Excavations at Khirbet Shema', Upper Galilee, Israel 1970-1972 (Durham: Duke Univ. Press, 1976).

[3] P. J. B. Frey, Corpus Inscriptionum Iudaicarum II (Rome: Pontificio Instituto di Archeologia Cristiania, 1952). B. Lifshitz, Donateurs et Fondateurs dans les Synagogues Juives, Cahiers de la Revue Biblique 7 (1967). Joseph Naveh, 'Al Pesifas wa-Even (On Stone and Mosaic: The Aramaic and Hebrew Inscriptions from Ancient Synagogues) (Tel Aviv: 1978).

[4] M. Blanchard et al., eds., Repertoire Graphique du Décor Géométrique dans la Mosaïque Antique. Bulletin de l'Association Internationale Pour l'Etude de la Mosaïque Antique (May, 1973).

[5] Chronology used in The Encyclopedia of Archaeological Excavations in the Holy Land, 4 vols. (Jerusalem: Kedem, 1975-1978).

[6] Reinhard Plummer, "New Evidence for Samaritan Christianity," Catholic Biblical Quarterly, 41, 1 (Jan. 1979), 98-117. See Handbook: Beth She'an A B:4, I-2), Ramat Aviv (C:3, IIIA-1), Salbit (E:3, I-1).

[7] Heinrich Kohl, Carl Watzinger, Antike Synagogen in Galilaea (Leipzig: J. C. Hinrichs'sche Buchhandlung, 1916).

[8] E. L. Sukenik, Ancient Synagogues in Palestine and Greece (London: Oxford University Press, 1934), pp. 27-28; 68-69.

[9] Michael Avi-Yonah, "Synagogue Architecture in the Late Classical Period," in Jewish Art: An Illustrated History, eds. Cecil Roth and Bezalel Narkiss, 2nd ed. (New York: New York Graphic Society, 1971), pp. 65-82.

[10] E. R. Goodenough, Jewish Symbols in the Greco-Roman Period I (New York: Pantheon Books, 1953), pp. 181-267.

[11] Avi-Yonah, "Ancient Synagogues," Ariel, 32 (1973), 38-42.

[12] See: Capernaum (B:3, I-1) for review and bibliography of dating controversy.

[13] S. J. Saller, Second Revised Catalogue of Ancient Synagogues of the Holy Land (Jerusalem: Franciscan Printing Press, 1972). Reviewed by Gideon Foerster, Journal of Jewish Art, 3/4 (1977), 133-135.

[14] Frowald Hüttenmeister, Gottfried Reeg, Die Antiken Synagogen in Israel, 2 vols., Beihefte Zum Tübinger Atlas des Vorderen Orients, Reihe B, Nr. 12/1. (Wiesbaden: Dr. Ludwig Reichert, 1977).

[15] George Foot Moore, Judaism in the First Centuries of the Christian Era I (Cambridge: Harvard University Press, 1927), p. 109. According to Moore's hypothesis, "normative" Judaism

was a development of the Babylonian and Palestinian rabbinic
academies, and was to be distinguished from other so-called non-
normative, or fringe sects of Judaism. Jacob Neusner has
commented on the problems associated with Moore's hypothesis.
See: "Judaism in Late Antiquity," Judaism, XV, 2 (Spring, 1966),
231-240; "The Demise of Normative Judaism," in Early Rabbinic
Judaism: Historical Studies in Religion, Literature and Art
(Leiden: Brill, 1975); his review of E. R. Sanders, Paul and
Palestinian Judaism, in History of Religions, 18 (1978), 178-191;
and most recently "'Judaism' after Moore: A Programmatic State-
ment," Journal of Jewish Studies, XXXI, no. 2 (Autumn, 1980),
141-156.

[16] Morton Smith, "Palestinian Judaism in the First Century,"
in Israel: Its Role in Civilization, ed. Moshe Davis (New York:
Harper and Brothers, 1956), p. 81. It should be noted that
Smith's theory did not receive immediate acceptance. Recent
scholarship, cited herein, has since proven him to be correct.

[17] Eric Meyers, "Galilean Regionalism as a Factor in
Reconstruction," BASOR 221 (Feb., 1976), 93.

[18] Ibid., 99.

[19] Avi-Yonah, "Palestina," PW Supplement, band XIII, p. 322.

[20] Avi-Yonah, The Holy Land, rev. ed. (Grand Rapids: Baker
Books, 1977), p. 127.

[21] According to Jacob Neusner, the Jews formed minority
communities in almost every city of the Euphrates Valley and
throughout the western satrapies of Parthia. Jews also occupied
large tracts of farmland outside the major cities in Babylonia,
forming a minority but still significant group. A History of the
Jews in Babylonia I, 2nd ed. (Leiden: Brill, 1969), pp. 13-15.
By the Sassanian Period, Neusner states, the Jewish population of
Babylonia and its surrounding territories was approximately
860,000, or a tenth to an eighth of the local population. A
History of the Jews in Babylonia II, p. 250.

[22] Avi-Yonah, The Jews of Palestine (Oxford: Basil Blackwell,
1976), p. 11.

[23] Ibid.

[24] Ibid.

[25] Ibid., p. 18. Avi-Yonah notes that seven Jewish villages
in Galilee disappeared following the second revolt. However, in
The Holy Land, p. 113, he states there is no evidence of the
uprooting of the Jewish population in Galilee during the period
of the second revolt, which suggests that it was not included
in the rebellion. Smallwood, Jews, pp. 442-443, states that it
is barely conceivable that the Jews of Galilee held aloof from
the revolt completely, and cites evidence of land confiscations
in Galilee following the revolt.

[26] Following the second revolt, Jews formed three-quarters
of the population of Galilee and one-quarter of the population
of the Coastal Plain and lands east of the Jordan River. Avi-
Yonah, Jews in Palestine, p. 19.

[27] Avi-Yonah, Holy Land, p. 112.

[28] Ibid., p. 163.

[29] Eusebius, Onom. 142:7 as quoted in E. Mary Smallwood, The Jews Under Roman Rule (Leiden: Brill, 1976), p. 533.

[30] Ibid.

[31] Ibid.

[32] Talmud Yerushalmi (New York: Talmud Yerushalmi Publishing Company, 1959-1969).

[33] Josephus Flavius. Complete works, trans. by H. St. Thackery, et al., The Loeb Classical Library, 9 vols. (Cambridge: 1926-1965). The references give the work's name (in its abbreviated form), followed by the book number in Roman numerals, and sentence number in Arabic numerals.

[34] E. Klostermann, Die Griechischen Christlichen Schriftseller, Eusebius Werke, iii.I (Leipzig, 1904).

A. PHOENICIAN CITIES

Although Tyre was considered by rabbinical authorities to lie outside the halakhic borders of Eretz Israel, Josephus (AJ XIV: 313-322) records the existence of a Jewish community in the city that may have settled there at the time of Hasmonean expansion along the Coastal Plain. Only scant archaeological evidence has been uncovered attesting to its presence. A capital decorated with a menorah was found at Mi'ilya (A:1, II-1); two other sites, Abrikha (A:1, IIIB-1) and Siddikin (A:1, IIIB-2), have remnants of buildings considered to be possible synagogues.

MI'ILYA
A:1, II-1

1. Name of site and map reference.
    Mi'ilya
    174.270 (1.108)
2. Survey of site.
    The site is located 21 km. northeast of Ptolemais, south of the Wadi Qarn.
8. Ornamentation.
    Several capitals were found in the area of Mi'ilya; one was decorated with a menorah. Fragments of white mosaic pavement also were reported in the courtyard of Yūsuf Qassis. [1]

13. Bibliography.

    1. Avi-Yonah, M. QDAP 3 (1934), p. 35, no. 262.

    2. Hüttenmeister, F. Antiken Synagogen. Vol. I, p. 319.

ABRIKHA
A:1, IIIB-1

1. Name of site and map reference.
    Abrikha, Qabrīha, Kŭbrīkhah, Rubrika, Kubûka.
    1937.2953 (2.119)
2. Survey of site.
    Abrikha is an unexcavated site situated in southeastern

Lebanon, east of Sidon, 11 km. northwest of the modern Israeli town of Kiryat (Qiryat) Shemona. In 1856, Robinson reported finding a "temple" oriented east to west with evidence of two rows of columns on the interior; seven columns are in situ.[1] In 1870, Warren wrote that much of the building had been destroyed by the inhabitants of the area except for several columns and a bas relief of what appeared to be a pot of manna. He identified the ruins as a "synagogue."[2] Guérin later found fragments of a wine press and a stone decorated with a conch.[4] The evidence is too inconclusive to make an attribution.

13. Bibliography.

1. Robinson, Edward. Later Biblical Researches in Palestine. 11th ed. Boston: Crocker & Brewster, 1874. Vol. III, pp. 55f.

2. Warren, Charles. PEFQS I (1870), 230.

3. Conder, Kitchener. SWP. Vol. I. 1881, pp. 107 f.

4. Guérin, V. DGHA. Vol. VII. 1880, p. 273.

5. Goodenough, E. Jewish Symbols. Vol. I. 1953, pp. 214, 224.

6. Hüttenmeister, F. Antiken Synagogen. Vol. I, p. 355-356.

SIDDIKIN

A:1, IIIB-2

1. Name of site and map reference.
   Siddikin, Saddīqīn, Sadikin.
   1795.2874 (1.132)

2. Survey of site.
   The site is located 14 km. southeast of Tyre. In 1880, Guérin reported finding the ruins of a building oriented north-south. He described its columns and pillars as similar to those found in the "early Galilean synagogues," suggesting to him that the ruins were of a "synagogue."[1] The evidence is too inconclusive to make an attribution.

3. Bibliography.

1. Guérin, V. DGHA. Vol. VII. 1880, p. 389.

2. Goodenough, E. Jewish Symbols. Vol. I. 1953, p. 224.

3. Hüttenmeister, F. Antiken Synagogen. Vol. I, p. 380.

Ptolemais was considered outside the halakhic boundaries of Eretz Israel, but this did not discourage Jewish settlers. Vespasian, during the first Jewish revolt against Rome, transformed the city into a base for launching strikes against Jewish rebels in Galilee. Many of the Jews fled Ptolemais, but a number returned after the rebellion, establishing what became a large, prosperous Jewish community (Smallwood, Jews, p. 19).

A stone decorated with a menorah and a mosaic pavement, now lost, were reported uncovered in the village of Kefar Yāsīf. They are all that remains of the territory's Jewish population.

KEFAR YĀSĪF
A:2, II-1

1. <u>Name of site and map reference.</u>
   Kefar Yāsīf.
   165.262 (1.84)

2. <u>Survey of site.</u>
   The village is 9.5 km. north-northeast of the port of Ptolemais. According to local tradition, the village was founded by the Jewish historian and general Josephus who was given the land as a gift from the Emperor Vespasian; the village's name, Kefar Yāsīf (Joseph), reflects this tradition. Josephus (BJ II:573) records a village named Kafr Acco located in this area. This may have been the village's name before the first Jewish revolt.

   Records stored in the archives of the British Mandatory Government report the discovery of mosaic pavements, foundations, rock-cut cisterns, tombs, architectural and decorative fragments, and press stones in Kefar Yāsīf.[1] The building material, reused in modern dwellings, includes a stone decorated with a seven-branched menorah.

   Braslavsky and Ben Zvi visited the village in the early 1920s and reported the menorah stone missing.[2,3] They uncovered a mosaic pavement, which has since disappeared.

8. <u>Ornamentation.</u>
   According to the description of Braslavsky and Ben Zvi, the

border of the mosaic pavement was decorated with an inter-
woven geometric pattern and ornaments that framed a field
strewn with figures of doves, serpents, glasses, fruit, a
"Star of David," and other "symbolic" images. Several inter-
twined crosses are described as "betraying" the hand of a
Christian restorer.[2,3] The lack of Jewish motifs and/or
inscriptions makes an attribution difficult. The "Star of
David" was not an exclusive Jewish motif in the Roman and
Byzantine periods.[A]
The missing stone was decorated with a seven-branched menorah
flanked by a lulab and enclosed within a "circle" (wreath?).
A shofar, outside the "circle," was to the menorah's left.[1]

13. Bibliography.

1. British Mandatory Government of Palestine. Archives.
        Jerusalem: Rockefeller Museum.

2. Ben Zvi, I. JPOS, V, 2 (1925), 204 ff.

3. Braslavsky, I. JJPES, I, 2 (1925), 139.

YIRKĀ
A:2, IIIB-1

1. Name of site and map reference.
   Yirkā, Yerka, Helkath.
   170.262 (1.165)

2. Survey of site.
   The site is located 14 km. east-northeast of Ptolemais.
   V. Guérin reported the discovery of an ancient dressed stone
   and column base reused in a modern dwelling in the village.
   He suggested the fragments may have come from an ancient
   synagogue or church.[1] The source of the fragments is
   uncertain.[A]

13. Bibliography.

1. Guérin, V. DGHA. Vol. VII. 1880, p. 16.

2. Hüttenmeister, F. Antiken Synagogen. Vol. I, p. 516.

B. GALILEE

TETRACOMIA
B:1

Josephus (BJ III:35) refers to two sections of Galilee, the
Upper and the Lower, separated by the almost straight Beth
ha-Kerem Valley and the deep gorge of the Amud Stream. The
Romans took advantage of the natural topographic differences
between the regions to establish two distinct political units:
the southern urbanized Lower Galilee, and the rural, more reli-
giously conservative Upper Galilee, known in ancient sources as
Tetracomia (Georgii Cyprii, Descriptio Orbis Romane, ed. H.
Gelzer, Lypsiae, 1890, no. 1040).

Comparatively little archaeological activity had been undertaken in the mountains of Tetracomia until a team led by Eric M.
Meyers conducted a surface survey of ancient sites in the territory (1970-). This same group also is responsible for excavating
at four of the region's five known synagogue sites: Gush Halav A
(B:1, I-1), Khirbet Shema' (B:1, I-3), Meron (B:1, I-4), and
Nabratein A (B:1, I-5); Kefar Bar'am A (B:1, I-2) had been cleared
and restored earlier by the Israel Department of Antiquities.
Fragmentary evidence of synagogues has been reported at seven
other sites: 'Alma (B:1, II-1), Beersheba (B:1, II-2), Dalton
(B:1, II-3), er-Ramah (B:1, II-4), Jassud-Hamma'le (B:1, II-5),
Kefar Bar'am B (B:1, II-6), and Peqi'in (B:1, II-7). Two sites
have long been considered to have evidence of synagogues--Gush
Halav B (B:1, IIIA-1) and Kefar Hananyah (B:1, IIIA-2)--but the
ruins are too meager to make attribution certain. Twelve other
sites are in the rejected category.

GUSH HALAV A
B:1, I-1

1. Name of site and map reference.
   Gush Halav, Giscala, El Jîsh.
   1923.2703 (2.60a)
   Plan 1.
2. Survey of site.
   The village of Gush Halav is located about 8 km. north-
   northeast of modern Safed at the summit of the region's
   highest hill. The site was visited by Charles Wilson in
   1869[3] and by H. Kitchener in 1877.[4] Both explorers

reported finding the ruins of two ancient synagogues in the
vicinity of the village.[3,4] Gush Halav A, the smaller of
the synagogues, is located in a valley on the west slope of
the Wadi ed-Dśiche. The ruins were first surveyed and
cleared by H. Kohl and C. Watzinger in 1905.[6] Intensive
excavations were undertaken in 1977 and 1978 under the
direction of Eric M. Meyers.

The name Gush Halav, "milk clod," may refer to the production
of milk and cheese for which the village has been famous
since the Medieval period, or to the light color of the local
limestone used in the construction of the two
synagogues.[9]

The village is called Giscala in Josephus' BJ (II:575, 585-
590, 593-594, 614-625) and Vit. (44-45, 84-103, 122-123, 132).
It was the home of John (Johanan), son of Levi, a dealer in
oil, and the leader of 400 zealots who opposed Josephus'
policy of nonprovocation of Rome.

The community continued to exist following both ill-fated
Jewish revolts. According to Mishnah (M Ar. 9:6), the town
folk produced a high quality of olive oil, second only to
that of Khirbet Shema'.[9]

In the second century C.E., the Romans may have made Gush
Halav the administrative center and head village of Tetracomia. This idea is based in part on evidence from a coin
hoard allegedly found in 1948 in a clay jar set in the
foundation of a village dwelling.[8] The hoard consisted of
337 coins: 280 Syrian Tetradrachms dated from Nero (54-68
C.E.) to Macrinus (217 C.E.), 22 Roman Denarii dated from
Septimius Severus (193-211) and Geta (212), and 35 coins from
provincial cities, mainly Tyre, dated to Alexander Severus
(222-235) and Philippus (244-249). H. Hamburger has suggested
that the hoard may have been assembled by someone who was in
the military himself or who dealt directly with troops. Tyre
is believed to have been the major marketplace for goods from
Tetracomia, the avenue for trade being the road located near
Gush Halav, which led north into Lebanon.

A surface survey of Gush Halav conducted in 1975, suggests
that the city may have been very wealthy.[1] This conclusion
is based on finds of Late Roman fine wares from Cyprus, North
Africa, and Antioch. Tombs and mausoleums cleared on the
west slope of a hill below the village further attest to the
people's wealth. A well-preserved mausoleum, dated from the

second to fourth centuries, is composed of fine ashlar
stones.[10,11] The walls of the burial chamber are decorated
with incised circles, rosettes, and other simple geometric
patterns. A large double sarcophagus, found in the burial
chamber, was cut from a single limestone block into two
loculii. Each is covered by a gabled lid with four acroteria.
Glass bottles, cosmetic sticks, gold and bronze jewelry, and
a bronze vessel decorated with four animals and some stylized
plants were found within the tomb. Ossuaries, found in a
nearby tomb indicate the Jewish ritual of secondary burial
was practiced in the village. One of the tombs has recently
been identified by E. W. Sanders as Jewish-Christian;[14]
however, this attribution is by no means certain.

Excavations initiated in 1977 under the direction of Eric
Meyers, have completely revised the earlier plan of synagogue
A as published by Kohl and Watzinger in 1916.[1,6] One of
Meyers' major discoveries was that the ancient synagogue was
constructed on a tell. Over five meters of debris had
accumulated in several of the excavated sections, and in no
place was either virgin soil or bedrock reached. The earliest level thus far reached is Stratum I, LB II/Iron I, 13th
century B.C.E. The synagogue occupied Stratum VI, Late Roman,
250-362, and Stratum VII, Byzantine, 363/5-551. The synagogue's foundations were sunk deep into the tell material,
often incorporating elements of earlier architecture into
its foundations or underground supports.

3. Character and sections of the building, as suggested by
    extant and identifiable remains.

The exterior and interior walls were built of roughly hewn
fieldstone, save for the facade wall, which was constructed
of large, finely trimmed ashlar blocks.[1] The building
underwent several renovations and repairs, apparently after
damage caused by earthquakes.[1]

PLAN

The external walls of the synagogue form an almost square
building; the sanctuary, however, is rectangular, bounded
on three sides, west, north, and east, by corridors and
rooms (see below, no. 7).

The sanctuary is divided by two rows of columns, standing on
pedestals resting on stylobates, into a central nave and two
aisles.

Two nearly intact capitals and columns with heart-shaped
cross-sections were found near the north end of the building.
At other synagogue sites in Tetracomia (Kefar Bar'am A, B:1,
I-2, and Meron, B:1, I-4), they provided support for a north
transverse colonnade; however, here they are not the rear-most
columns; those (one _in situ_) are not heart-shaped. Meyers
suggests that the heart-shaped columns may be related to the
use of the space at the north end of the building, possibly
to help support a gallery.[1]

ENTRANCES

South: A single, large double-hung door is placed in the
center of the facade wall. North: An entrance opens onto
four external stairs that descend toward the north.

BENCHES

Parts of benches were found along two of the interior walls:
north and west. Indications are that they were added at
different times. The benches vary in size and bear evidence
of plaster.[1]

PAVEMENT

The pavement consists of flagstone slabs.

4. _Measurements_.[1]

Over-all dimensions: 17.5 N-S x 17.5/18.0 m. E-W.

Main Hall: 13.75 x 10.6/11.0 m.

South portal: 1.7 m. jamb-jamb.

North portal: 1.15 m. wide.

5. _Orientation_.

The long axis is north-south; the facade is on the south,
facing Jerusalem.

6. _Character and form: apse, niche, Torah Shrine, bema, chancel_.

Evidence has been uncovered of two superimposed bemas built
against the western portion of the south wall.[1] Bema I
(Stratum VI) was a large rectangular structure extending two
meters out from the south wall, and one meter eastward from
the stylobate. It has a rectangular depression approximately
50 x 75 cm. deep, possibly a genizah, sunk against the
southern wall. Bema II (Stratum VII) was smaller, 1.46 x
1.17 x 3 m., and was partially built over the western stylobate.[1]

Small architectural fragments found in the debris suggest an
aedicula or Torah Shrine may have been built atop bema II.[1]

7. <u>Auxiliary rooms/structures</u>.

West: A corridor, possibly used for storage, also may have functioned as a retaining or terrace wall. It was entered from the sanctuary's west aisle at a point between the second and third columns, through a small doorway, 85 cm. wide.[1]

North: An exterior door and stairway opened directly into the sanctuary. East of the stairway is an enclosed corridor whose function is unknown; it lacks any form of access. Meyers has suggested it may have formed part of the support for an upper gallery (see above, no. 3).[1]

East: Two small rooms. The southern room could be entered from the sanctuary; the northern room lacked any access.[1]

8. <u>Ornamentation</u>.

A large number of architectural fragments were uncovered; they include columns, various types of moldings and cornices, window jambs, capitals, and "arrows" whose place and function remain unknown. Meyers will publish further details in the site's final report.

The massive lintel over the main entry was first reported by Kohl and Watzinger.[6] It is decorated on the underside with an eagle enclosed within a garland, which can be seen only if one looks directly overhead when passing through the doorway. Meyers cites an analogous occurrence on the eagle doorway at the Temple of Bacchus at Baalbek.[1]

9. <u>Coins, ceramics and other artifacts found within the building complex</u>.

Approximately 225 coins were reported found.[1] Late Roman coins predominate, as in coin finds at Meron (B:1, I-4) and Khirbet Shema' (B:1, I-3); however, Byzantine coins were found in Gush Halav in greater relative quantity than at the other two sites.[1]

A pot of 1,943 small coins was unearthed in the north end of the building's west corridor. It was not concealed, suggesting that it was some form of depository rather than a hidden hoard. The find consisted entirely of coins of the lowest possible value, spanning a period of 188 years. The identifiable coins date from 330-518, with most clustering around the later dates.[1] Pottery finds will be published in the final report. Ceramics uncovered in probes in and around the building appear to confirm the proposed dates (see below, no. 12). Other finds include a bronze finger ring engraved in Greek with the name Domitila, a Latin name unknown in Jewish epigraphy;[1]

sherd, dated to the first century B.C.E. to the first century
C.E., inscribed in Greek letters with the name Arist. . . ,
possibly the name of the artisan;[1] and a fragment of a
Herodian lamp decorated in relief with a bunch of grapes and
a grape leaf.[1] A number of glass lamps, with solid cylindrical bases, were possibly meant to be suspended as candela-
bra.[1] Large quantities of tesserae, uncovered in the north
end of the east corridor, and fragments of painted plaster,
found in the foundations of the eastern stylobate, were
probably from a fine earlier building in this area of the
tell, dated to some time between the Hellenistic and Middle
Roman periods.[1]

10. Inscriptions.
A four line Aramaic inscription on a column reads:

> Jose, son of Nahum/ made this [column?]/
> may it be for him/ a blessing.[1]

The Aramaic term "ha-aron" has been translated as column,[5,7]
or ark.[6]

11. Donors and Patrons.
Jose, described in the inscription as the maker of the column,
more likely was the donor. The term "made" occurs again at
Capernaum, B:3, I-1.[A]

12. Date.
On the basis of his excavation, Meyers proposes the following
stratigraphic history of the synagogue:[1]

Stratum VI: Late Roman (250-362)

    Phase A: ca. 250 -- Synagogue constructed.

                306 -- Damaged by earthquake.

    Phase B: 306 -- Synagogue repaired.

                362 -- Damaged by second earthquake.

Stratum VII: Byzantine (362/5-551)

    Phase A: 362 -- Synagogue repaired.

                447 -- Damaged by third earthquake.

                447 -- Synagogue repaired.

                551 -- Destroyed by major earthquake;
                       site taken over by squatters.

13. Bibliography.

1. Meyers, E. M., J. F. Strange, Carol Meyers. "Preliminary
    Report on the 1977 and 1978 Seasons at Gush Halav."
    BASOR, 233 (June 1979), n.p.

2. Hanson, Richard. "Numismatic Report." BASOR, 233 (June
    1979), n.p.

3. Wilson, Charles. "Notes on Jewish Synagogues in Galilee." _PEFQS_, I (1869), 37-45.

4. Kitchener, H. "Lieutenant Kitchener's Reports." _PEFQS_, (1877), pp. 116-125.

5. Dalman, K. O. _PJB_, X (1914), 48.

6. Kohl, Watzinger, pp. 107-111.

7. Klein, Samuel. _Corpus Inscr._, p. 78.

8. Hamburger, H. "A Hoard of Syrian Tetradrachmae and Tyrian Bronze Coins from Gush Halav." _IEJ_, IV, 3-4 (1954), 201 ff.

9. Avi-Yonah, M. _Holy Land_, pp. 203, 205.

10. Vitto, Fanny. "Gush Halav." _IEJ_, XXV, 3-4 (1974), 282.

11. Idem. "The Mausoleum at Gush Halav." _Qad._ VII, 49-55.

12. Meyers, Eric. "Meiron and Gush Halav, 1977." _ASOR Newsletter_ (Nov. 1977), pp. 6-9.

13. Idem. "Gush Halav (el-Jish), 1977." _IEJ_, XXVII, 4 (1977), 253-254.

14. Saunders, E. W. "Christian Synagogues and Jewish Christianity in Galilee." _Explor._, 3 (1977), 70-78.

15. Hüttenmeister, F. _Antiken Synagogen_, Vol. I, pp. 144-146.

KEFAR BAR'AM A

B:1, I-2

1. Name of site and map reference.

Kefar Bar'am, Kafr Bir'im, Kefr-Berein.

1891.2721 (2.16)

Plan 2.

2. Survey of site.

The ruined village of Kefar Bar'am is located 11 km. northwest of modern Safed near the ancient border with Tyre. E. Robinson visited the site in 1852 and reported finding the ruins of two synagogues.[2] The smaller of the two (Kefar Bar'am B) had already disappeared by 1905 when Kohl and Watzinger surveyed the village and cleared the larger synagogue.[1] Further excavations and restorations were undertaken in the 1950s by the Israel Department of Antiquities under the supervision of A. S. Hiram. Kefar Bar'am is not mentioned in any ancient sources. The economy of the village remains unknown; however, the villagers must have enjoyed a degree of prosperity in order to construct and support two synagogues.[A]

3. <u>Character and sections of the building as suggested by extant and identifiable remains</u>.

The synagogue was constructed of local limestone ashlars set without mortar. The exterior faces of the walls were finished, the interior left rough to receive plaster.[3] The present reconstruction is not considered accurate in all details.[A]

NARTHEX

A prostyle hexastyle narthex, with a single column on each side is adjacent to the synagogue's south facade. The narthex pavement, 38 cm. below ground level, is reached by three broad steps. Its unfluted columns, with Attic-type bases, rest on high pedestals. The columns support an architrave that curved up in the center without interruption to form an arcuated lintel surmounted by a pediment.

The inner angles of the two corner pedestals were cut away to form two half-pedestals; the bases and column shafts are heart-shaped in cross-section.

PLAN

Two longitudinal rows of columns (6 per row) and a north transverse colonnade (two columns) divide the sanctuary's interior into a central nave surrounded on three sides by aisles. Unfluted columns, bases, and pedestals (the pedestals are reconstructions), similar to those of the narthex, rest directly on the pavement (no stylobate). The corner columns, bases, and pedestals also are similar to those of the narthex.

ENTRANCES

There are three entrances on the south, a large central portal flanked by two smaller doors. On the east, a small door opens onto the east aisle.

BENCHES

Double-tiered benches are built along the east and west walls.[1]

WINDOWS

A large semicircular window is over the central portal; smaller, square windows are over each flanking portal.

PAVEMENT

The pavement consists of large flagstone slabs.

GALLERY

The existence of a gallery has been postulated on the basis of fragments of smaller capitals and columns found inside the sanctuary.[1]

4. Measurements.
   Main hall: 18.44 x 14.17 m.[3]
                 18.10 x 13.35 m.[1]
                 18.10 x 13.95 m.[6]
   Nave: 6.20 m. wide[3,1,6]
   Aisles: 2.14 m. wide[3,1,6]
   Narthex: 4 m. wide[1,6]
   Main portal: 1.42 wide x 2.65 m. high[1,6]
   Flanking portals: 1.12 wide x 1.95 m. high[1,6]

5. Orientation.
   The long axis is north-south; the facade is on the south,
   facing Jerusalem.

6. Character and form: apse, niche, Torah Shrine, bema, chancel.
   No evidence has been found of any of the above; however, it
   has been postulated that a shrine of some form may have stood
   inside the nave, blocking the central portal.[1] This theory
   is supported by the discovery of a three-dimensional lion
   conjectured to be part of the shrine (see below, no. 8).[1]

7. Auxiliary rooms/structures.
   A small room is indicated on the plan to be off the northwest
   corner of the hall; it appears to lack direct access into the
   main hall.[1] No evidence of the room survives.[A]

8. Ornamentation.
   Only the synagogue's external ornamentation survives. It
   consists of finely executed reliefs that bear evidence of
   possible iconoclastic mutilation.
   FACADE
   The molding of the facade's second story echoes the arcuated
   lintel of the narthex, curving up and over the large central
   semicircular window.[1]
   CENTRAL PORTAL
   This most elaborately decorated door has well-cut moldings
   distantly derived from classical models, such as the Attic and
   Ionic moldings described by Vitruvius, IV: 6. The door's
   lintel is broader than its aperture; its moldings frame a
   relief depicting two winged genii (defaced) carrying aloft a
   crown of olive leaves tied with a Hercules knot. Two consoles
   flank the lintel and hang down to its bottom level.[1] Above
   the lintel, carved from the same stone, is a pulvinated frieze
   decorated with a stylized vine scroll issuing from a gadrooned
   amphora. The cornice is unadorned. The central window is
   surmounted by a relieving arch. The architrave of the arch

is decorated with a series of moldings similar to the door jambs. Blocks on either side of the arch were carved with figurative reliefs, now effaced.

FLANKING PORTALS

Their moldings are similar to those of the central portal, but their lintels do not project beyond the aperture. A pulvinated frieze over the east portal is decorated with a "bay" leaf pattern similar to one decorating a frieze at Palmyra.[11]

WINDOWS

The windows are surmounted by elaborate acroteria; plant tendrils and a rosette decorate each tympanum. Scars on either side of the acroteria suggest some form of figurative motif now effaced.

MISCELLANEOUS DECORATION

Lion's head:[1] Only the head of one lion is found here, but the hindquarters of three-dimensional lions were found at Capernaum (B:3, I-1) and Chorozain (B:3, I-2). It has been proposed that the lions flanked a screen or shrine located inside the synagogue's central entrance (see above, no. 6)[1,8] or that they stood as acroteria on the roof.[6]
Meander relief: A double-lined meander pattern peopled with various figures and decorative motifs used as decoration on this synagogue has close parallels to patterns found in Syria, at Inkhil, Naveh (G:3, I-1), and Horvat Rimmon (E:4, I-3). The decoration may have been part of a frieze[6] or a lintel.[9]

10. Inscriptions.

A fragment of a Hebrew inscription, now badly damaged, is cut into a stone set under the window over the east portal of the facade.

Architect: Eleazar bar Yudan.[5]

The name "bar Yudan" (son of Yudan) occurs again in a fragmentary inscription found at Naveh (G:3, I-1).[9]

11. Donors and patrons.

It has been suggested that Eleazar was the synagogue's builder or architect and was also responsible for building the synagogue at Naveh; this theory would explain the similarity in meander motifs.[5,9]

12. Date.

Kohl and Watzinger dated the Galilean synagogues they uncovered to the reigns of Septimius Severus (193-211) and

Caracalla (211-217), the same period in which the Mishna was redacted and that they were destroyed in the mid fourth century possibly during a Jewish uprising that began in Sepphoris.[1] Recent discoveries at Capernaum and elsewhere, however, have placed this early date in doubt (see B:3, I-1).[A]

13. Bibliography.

1. Kohl, Watzinger, pp. 89-100.

2. Robinson, Edward. ZDMG, 7 (1853), 42.

3. Wilson, Charles. PEFQS I (1869), 37-42.

4. Masterson, E. Studies, pp. 14, 16, 18, 116-118.

5. Klein, Samuel. Corpus Inscr., pp. 79 f.

6. Sukenik, E. L. Ancient Synagogues, pp. 24-26.

7. Frey, J. B. CIJ, #975.

8. Goodenough, E. R. Jewish Symbols. Vol. I (1953), pp. 201-203. Vol. III, figs. 511-515.

9. Amiran, Ruth. "A Fragment of an Ornamental Relief from Kefar Bar'am." IEJ, VI (1956), 239-245.

10. Hüttenmeister, F. Antiken Synagogen. Vol. I, pp. 31-34.

11. Klengel, Horst. The Art of Ancient Syria. (New York, 1972), p. 165.

KHIRBET SHEMA'
B:1, I-3

1. Name of site and map reference.
    Khirbet Shema', Teqoa'.
    1915.2646 (2.139)
    Plan 3

2. Survey of site.
    The ruined village of Khirbet Shema' is located about 10 km. west of modern Safed and south of the Wadi Meron, on one of the eastern spurs of Mount Meron, 760 m. above sea level. The Wadi Meron separates Khirbet Shema' from its nearest neighbor, ancient Meron (B:1, I-4), 1.5 km. to the north. The site of Khirbet Shema' is virtually inaccessible except from the southwest. Excavations were carried out at Khirbet Shema' from 1970-1972 by Eric Meyers, A. T. Kraabel, and J. F. Strange.

The name Khirbet Shema' is fairly recent. It may be based on a late tradition attributing the tomb of Rabbi Shammai to the site. Arabs refer to the site as Shema', "candle." Most scholars now agree that Khirbet Shema' is synonymous with Galilean Teqoa', mentioned in ancient sources. It was probably founded as a Jewish village in the years immediately following the second Jewish revolt. The village prospered during the late third and fourth centuries, only to be destroyed by a devastating earthquake in 419, and subsequently abandoned. The Mishnah (Men. 8:2) refers to Teqoa's ritually pure, high-quality olive oil.[1]

Ceramic and numismatic evidence suggests that Teqoa' had close cultural ties with regions as far west and north as Tyre, and east to Gaulanitis. The avenue for trade may have been the trans-Galilean route that passed nearby.[1]

The village's necropolis is built along the eastern incline of a hill near the southwest edge of the village, not far from the synagogue. This placement is contrary to rabbinic law, which states that graves are to be situated downwind and beyond a city's limits (M. BB 2:9). The tombs are contemporaneous with the village, and their architectural form can be paralleled to the major Jewish necropolis at Beth She'arim (p. 70). Both sites show evidence of the Jewish practice of secondary burial in ossuaries.[1]

Two miqvahs were uncovered in the village; one, predating the synagogue, is located under the synagogue's northeast corner. It was covered over when the synagogue was built, and a new miqvah was installed on the east slope of the hill, in the vicinity of the tombs.[1] The synagogue was built in the center of the village on a site spanning a series of three terraces. The entire floor is set on bedrock, except for the eastern sector, which extends over the lower terrace; the west wall is on the third, or highest, terrace.[1]

3. Character and sections of the building as suggested by extant and identifiable remains.

The synagogue underwent two stages of construction.[1]

STAGE I

It was constructed of roughly dressed local fieldstone with ashlars used around the north entrance. All the interior walls were plastered.[1]

PLAN

The synagogue was in the form of a rectangular hall divided by two rows of columns (four per row) into three aisles.

The unfluted columns rest on pedestals. The northeast and southeast pedestals stand on a fieldstone stylobate; the others stand directly on bedrock.

ENTRANCES

On the west, the main entrance, located in the southwest corner of the third terrace, opens onto a broad staircase that descends over two meters to the synagogue pavement. On the north, a secondary entrance is located in the west quadrant of the north wall.

GALLERY

A gallery is situated against the synagogue's western wall at the same level as the upper terrace (and west entrance). The north end is founded on an outcropping of bedrock; the south end abuts the landing of the first step east of the west entrance's threshold. The gallery is supported on the west by a mortared wall. Its entrance may have been on the south near the west entrance into the synagogue. [1] The gallery is angled so as to be slightly directed toward the synagogue's south wall.

BENCHES

The surviving benches are in the southeast corner of the hall, behind the second stage bema, in the northwest corner of the hall, and in a section against the north wall east of the north entry. They were made of roughly dressed ashlars covered with plaster and laid tightly against the walls.

PAVEMENT

The form of the pavement is unknown.

STAGE II

After its destruction by an earthquake, the synagogue was rebuilt of roughly dressed fieldstone, and some reused ashlars. [1]

PLAN

The plan remains essentially unchanged from Stage I, except for the following modifications. [1]

ENTRANCES

On the west, no change is noted, except that it no longer appears to be the main entrance into the synagogue. This modification may be due to changes in pedestrian traffic (see below, no. 7). [1] On the north, the entry is now raised three steps above the synagogue pavement. The exterior wall around the doorway was plastered and a new lintel decorated

with a menorah was added. The changes suggest that the north
was now considered the synagogue's main entrance.[1]

GALLERY

A new entrance, added on the north replaced the west entrance
to the gallery.

BENCHES

West of the stylobate wall, parallel to the north wall, a
second row of benches was added; the height of the original
bench was doubled. A second section of bench extended east
from the stylobate wall to the corner of the hall. The
benches were built of unplastered limestone blocks, and were
not attached to the walls.[1]

PAVEMENT

Large quantities of white and gray tesserae were recovered;
the pavement's pattern is unknown.[1]

4. Measurements.
   Both stages:[1]
   Main hall: 11 x 15 m. wide.
   Frescoed room: 2.25 x 3.5 m.
   Genizah: 3.3 x 3.25 m.

5. Orientation.
   Both stages: The broad southern wall faces Jerusalem.

6. Character and form: apse, niche, Torah Shrine, bema, chancel.
   STAGE I
   Torah Shrine: The benches contiguous with the broad southern
   wall may have been covered, in part, by a Torah Shrine.
   Fragments attributed to such a shrine were used as fill for
   Stage II; they include parts of a small capital(s) decorated
   with acanthus leaves that fits a column 22-24 cm. in diameter,
   half the diameter of the columns of the main hall. Also
   uncovered were about a dozen badly damaged pieces of small
   columns and bases.[1]

   STAGE II
   Bema: The Torah Shrine was destroyed by the earthquake and
   was replaced by a large stone bema raised nearly 70 cm. above
   the hall's pavement. The bema was constructed with a solid
   exterior and an earth and rubble core. The lower course on
   the exterior is decorated with a heavy, convex molding.

7. Auxiliary rooms/structures.
   A doorway in the center of the hall's west wall leads into a
   small plastered room, cut into the bedrock, directly under the
   gallery. Used during Stage I as a storage room, it had

direct access into a genizah (?) located under the west staircase. An unplastered stone bench was built against the north end of the room's west wall. During the synagogue's second stage, the room was plastered and frescoed. The excavators suggest it may then have served as a Torah Shrine, replacing the one in the hall destroyed by the earthquake.
North building: Located northwest of the synagogue, the north building, in its present form is contemporary with the synagogue's Stage II.[1] The building is almost square (6.55 x 6.50 m.) with its main entrance on the east. Stairs along the building's south wall lead to an alley located on the west terrace, which has access into the gallery (see above, no. 3). A second stairway along the building's north wall joins the middle and upper terraces, forming the Stage II east-west pedestrian route (see above, no. 3). Additional rooms have walls in common with the synagogue, but none communicates directly with it.[1]

8. Ornamentation.
   STAGE I
   An eagle, set within a garland, was incised on the south doorpost of the west entrance.
   Capitals: Two of the capitals are "Doric," two "vaguely Ionic," two "simple Corinthian," one similar to an unfinished Byzantine basket capital, and one decorated with rosettes carved on one end of each of two cylindrical projections.[1]
   STAGE II
   A lintel added over the north entrance is decorated with a menorah crudely carved in high relief.[1] The west room is frescoed with red and white geometric designs.

9. Coins, ceramics and other artifacts found within the building complex.[1]
   1. In the genizah were five substantial pieces of glass and many glass fragments. Coins are dated to the mid fourth century.
   2. The fill sealed under the bema contained late Roman pottery, a coin of Constans (337-341), and a Hasmonean coin (103-76 B.C.E.).
   3. Sealed in the northwest declivity under the hall pavement was some pottery dated from the mid to late Roman period, a smaller quantity of earlier Roman pottery, a coin of Gratian (373-383), and a coin of Hadrian (119-138).
   4. Sealed below the pavement west of the stylobate was early and late Roman pottery, two coins of Alexander Jannaeus

(Hasmonean, 103-76 B.C.E.), a coin of Nero (58 C.E.), and a coin of Trajan (104-107 ?).

5. Found in the southwest corner of the synagogue, one meter above the pavement, was a ceramic lampbase decorated with a five-branched menorah.

6. In a dwelling adjoining the synagogue, a red carnelian gem of a popular Roman type was discovered.

12. Date.
    According to published final report.[1]

    Stage I: The synagogue was constructed in the latter part of the third century, and destroyed by an earthquake in 306.

    Stage II: The synagogue was immediately rebuilt, then destroyed by an earthquake for a second, final, time in 419.

13. Bibliography.

1. Meyers, Eric M., A. T. Kraabel, J. F. Strange. Shema'.

2. Conder, C. R. SWP, I (1881-1883), p. 246.

3. Macalister, R. A. S. "Remains at Khurbet Shem'a, near Safed." PEFQS, II (1909), 195-200.

4. Bull, R. J. "Khirbet Shema'." IEJ, XX (1970), 232-234.

5. Idem. AJA, 75 (1971), 196-197.

6. Kraabel, A. Thomas. "Khirbet Shema', 1972." Archaeology of the Mediterranean: Exhibitions from the University of Minnesota. Univ. of Minnesota: Jan.-Feb., 1972.

7. Meyers, Eric, A. T. Kraabel, J. Strange. "Archaeology and Rabbinic Tradition at Khirbet Shema': 1970-1971 Campaigns." BA, XXXV (1972), 1-31.

8. Meyers, Eric. "The Ancient Synagogue of Khirbet Shema." In Perspectives in Jewish Learning, V. Chicago: Spertus College of Judaism, 1973.

9. Idem. IDBS.

10. Idem. EAEh. Vol. IV.

11. Hüttenmeister, F. Antiken Synagogen. Vol. I, pp. 387-390.

MERON

B:1, I-4

1. Name of site and map reference.
    Meron, Meiron.
    1915.2654 (2.104)
    Plan 4.
2. Survey of site.
    Meron is located 5 km. northeast of modern Safed, north of
    Wadi Meron on one of the eastern foothills of Mount Meron.
    Its nearest neighbor is the village of Khirbet Shema' (B:1,
    I-3), 1.5 km. to the south. Meron is mentioned in Talmudic
    sources with regard to its production of olive oil (JT Sheb.
    9:2). It is one of the villages mentioned in the list of
    Priestly Courses (I Chron. 24). The town prospered and grew
    in the years following the second Jewish revolt, only to be
    abandoned in the middle of the fourth century.[2]
    The synagogue at Meron was first surveyed and reported on by
    Charles Wilson in 1869.[5] In 1905, Kohl and Watzinger
    excavated the building, publishing their findings in 1916.[6]
    Soundings were begun in the village in July, 1971 by Eric
    Meyers, who then directed a full-scale excavation of the site
    in 1974 and 1975.
    The village was built on a series of terraces descending the
    east slope of a cliff (Jebel Jurmuk); the synagogue was con-
    structed on the topmost terrace, level III. Seven strata of
    occupation were uncovered, dating from Stratum I, 88-1 B.C.E.,
    to Stratum VIIb, 14th century C.E. The heyday of the village
    appears to have been Strata III-IV, 135-360 C.E. Major
    buildings were constructed in Stratum III, and expansion
    peaked in Stratum IV, when the large and imposing synagogue
    was built.[1,3]
    Meron I, the lower city, has evidence of a large building
    complex spanning Strata III and IV, the full dimensions of
    which are not yet known. One of the rooms may have been used
    as a cooperage, since remains of a workbench, bronze plane,
    and assorted metal fittings were found within it.[1,3]
    Excavation south of this complex's courtyard, and to the west
    of the main building area, revealed a series of cuttings or
    declivities in bedrock that appear to be earlier in date than
    the main buildings. The cuttings are two large cavities
    immediately adjacent to one another; one is entered by

descending seven rock-cut steps and then stepping through a
well-cut stone doorway. The interior of this chamber is
coated with plaster. The adjacent, but not connected, chamber
has a small opening in its eastern wall leading toward the
east and may have been used to heat water for the plastered
chamber. Meyers suggests that the plastered cavity was a
miqvah. [1]

Numerous coins from Tyre were uncovered in Meron, indicating
that the port city was the town's major center for trade.
Ceramic types are similar to those found at locations west
and north of the village, and east toward Gaulanitis. [4]
The synagogue was built into the eastern slope of the cliff;
its western wall and pavement are bedrock.

3. Character and sections of the building as suggested by extant
    and identifiable remains.

The entire building, other than its west wall and pavement,
are constructed of local limestone ashlars set without mortar.
The exterior faces of the walls were finely dressed, but the
interior was left rough to receive plaster. [5] An additional
wall, built against and parallel to the basilica's eastern
wall, was intended to strengthen the foundations. [3]

NARTHEX

Four broad stairs, cut out of bedrock, ascend to a prostyle
hexastyle narthex; half columns are attached to its northeast
and northwest corners. The unfluted columns rest on square
pedestals. The inner angles of the two corner pedestals are
cut away, forming two half-pedestals; their bases and column
shafts have heart-shaped cross-sections. The narthex extends
on the west to the cliff wall, which has been cut away to
receive a bench.

PLAN

Two longitudinal rows of columns (eight per row), and a
transverse colonnade (two columns) on the north, divide the
main hall into a central nave surrounded on three sides by
aisles. The unfluted columns and bases are set on high
pedestals that rest on stylobates. The corner columns, bases,
and pedestals are similar to those of the narthex.

ENTRANCES

South: Three entrances include a large central portal,
flanked by two smaller ones. The entrance to the east is not
extant. [6] East: A small door opens onto the east aisle from
an adjoining room (see below, no. 7).

BENCHES

Kohl and Watzinger's plan shows benches along the east and west walls. [6]

GALLERY

It is believed that a gallery was located above the three aisles. [3]

PAVEMENT

Limestone slabs are set on the bedrock.

4. Measurements.

Main hall: 27.43 x 13.61 m. [5,6]

Central door: 1.75 wide x 1.95 m. high. [5]

West door: 1.27 wide x 1.96 m. high. [5]

Annex A: 4.90 x 6.00 m. [3]

5. Orientation.

The long axis of the hall is north-south; the facade is on the south, facing Jerusalem.

6. Character and form: apse, niche, Torah Shrine, bema, chancel.

Evidence was reported of an aedicula that stood inside the main hall between the central and western doors. [3] It is shown in Meyer's reconstruction as having a pedimented facade supported on two columns that rest on a platform raised one step above the hall's pavement. [3]

7. Auxiliary rooms/structures.

Annex A, a two-storied structure bonded to the eastern wall of the synagogue, was built at the same time as the synagogue. The walls are similar to the lower courses of the synagogue's eastern wall. Because of its 50 to 80 cm. thick walls, it has been proposed that the annex could support a second story; however, no evidence survives to confirm this theory. [3] The annex had a single entry opening off the synagogue's eastern aisle. [3]

A second structure, Annex B, may be recovered north of Annex A. A second wall has been uncovered that extends east from the synagogue for at least 4.20 m. It is parallel to the north wall of Annex A, and is of the same character. [3]

8. Ornamentation.

The moldings of the two surviving portals appear to be derived from classical models (see: Kefar Bar'am A, B:1, I-2). [6]

CENTRAL PORTAL

The fasciae of the monolithic doorposts continues around the door's lintel, which extends beyond the jambs. The lintel and cornice are not decorated.

WEST PORTAL
Moldings are similar to the central portal, but the lintel does not extend beyond the jambs.

9. <u>Coins, ceramics, and other artifacts found within the building complex</u>.
The material sealed in the fill of Annex A include Middle and Late Roman pottery and coins; the latest coin belongs to Probus, 282 C.E. [4] Other identified coins are: Hasmonean (one), Jewish (Agrippa I ?), Vespasian (one), Tyrian, dated to the first-second centuries (two), Roman colonial, Tyre, early third century (one), and Roman Imperial, fourth century (four).

10. <u>Inscriptions</u>.
Evidence of an inscription comes from a letter written by the Jewish pilgrim Samuel <u>bar</u> (son of) Simson, dated ca. 1211. Allegedly inscribed on a lintel over one of the synagogue's doors, in Hebrew/Aramaic, it reads:

> Scholom son of Levi erected [made ?]
> [this lintel.] [6]

It has been suggested the inscription may actually belong to Kefar Bar'am B (B:1, II-6), but was assigned to this site in error. [9]

11. <u>Donors or patrons</u>.
It is uncertain whether Scholom donated or actually fabricated the lintel.
Similar wording is found in inscriptions at Kefar Bar'am B (B:1, II-6), and 'Alma (B:1, II-1).

12. <u>Date</u>.
The synagogue has been dated ca. 300 C.E. on the basis of stratified pottery and coins. [3] It may not have been completed at the time of the 306 earthquake that destroyed the synagogue at Khirbet Shema' (B:1, I-2). The coins and finds uncovered at Meron I suggest that Meron was abandoned during the reign of Constantius II (360 C.E.). [3]

13. <u>Bibliography</u>.

1. Meyers, Carol L., Eric Meyers, J. Strange. "Excavations at Meiron in Upper Galilee, 1971, 1972: A Preliminary Report." <u>BASOR</u>, 214 (April 1975), 2-24.

2. Idem. "Meiron, 1975." <u>ASOR Newsletter</u> 3-4 (Oct.-Nov. 1975), 4-5.

3. Meyers, Carol, Eric Meyers, J. Strange. "Excavations at Meiron in Upper Galilee, 1974, 1975: Second Preliminary Report." <u>AASOR</u>, 43 (1978), 73-98.

4. Hanson, Richard S. "Meiron Coins: 1974-1975." AASOR, 43
    (1978), 99-103.

5. Wilson, Charles. "Notes on Jewish Synagogues in Galilee."
    PEFQS, I (1869), 37 ff.

6. Kohl, Watzinger, pp. 80-88.

7. Frey, J. B. CIJ, #978.

8. Goodenough, E. R. Jewish Symbols. Vol. I. (1953),
    pp. 200-201; Vol. III, fig. 543.

9. Hüttenmeister, F. Antiken Synagogen. Vol. I, pp. 311-314.

10. Meyers, Eric M., James F. Strange, Carol L. Meyers. Exca-
    vations at Ancient Meron. Cambridge, Ma., 1981.

NABRATEIN A

B:1, I-5

1. Name of site and map reference.

    Nabratein, Nebratein, Kefar Niburaya, Nabaraya, en-Nabratein,
    Nayoraya.

    1978.2678 (2.114)

    Plan 5

2. Survey of site.

    The isolated ruins of the village are located about 4 km.
    north of modern Safed. On the plain west of Lake Huleh is a
    deep ravine, Wadi el-'Ammuka, with a gradually descending hill
    on its south. The synagogue ruins are located on a small
    terrace of this hill. E. Renan visited the ruins in 1864, and
    published an inscription that he found on a lintel.[5] In
    1905, Kohl and Watzinger cleared the synagogue and published
    the results in 1916.[3] The site was thoroughly excavated in
    1980 and 1981 under the direction of Eric M. Meyers.[1,2]
    Information regarding the history of the village is scarce.

3. Character and sections of the building as suggested by extant
    and identifiable remains.

    The remains of three buildings were uncovered; all were built
    of local limestone.[2]

    Building One:

    PLAN

    A broadhouse with its interior divided by two rows of columns.
    It was uncovered three to four meters below Building Three.[2]

    ENTRANCES

    Southern wall, probable.

    Northwest, certain.

    PAVEMENT

    Plaster.

Building Two, phase A:[2]

PLAN

The broadhouse was elongated to a basilica form. The interior
was divided into a central nave and flanking aisles by two
longitudinal rows of columns (three per row).

ENTRANCES

A single entrance is located in the center of the facade
(south) and an auxiliary entrance on the east.

Building Two, phase B:[2]

The building required repair following extensive damage by
an earthquake.

PLAN

Essentially unchanged, except the two platforms (see no. 6)
and pavement were raised.

Building Three:[1]

NARTHEX

A narthex may adjoin the building's southern wall.

PLAN

The main hall is divided by two longitudinal rows of columns
(four per row) into a central nave flanked by aisles. Unfluted
columns, with Attic-type bases, rest on pedestals set
directly on the pavement.

ENTRANCES

A single entrance was in the center of the facade (south) wall,
and a second entrance on the west. The latter opened onto an
adjoining room.

BENCHES

Double tiered benches are along the east and west walls; a
single tier on the north wall.[3]

PAVEMENT

The pavement is constructed of limestone flags.

4. Measurements.

Building Three:
Main hall: 16.9 x 11.65 m.[3]
            20.4 x 17 m.[4]
Nave: 4.25 m. wide.[3]
East and west aisles: 2.20 m. wide.[3]

5. Orientation.
Building One:[2]
The broad wall with double bema (see no. 6) is on the south
facing Jerusalem.
Building Two and Three:[1,2]
Facade and bemas on narrow south wall facing Jerusalem.

6. Character and form: apse, niche, Torah Shrine, bema, chancel.
Building One: [2]
A long platform, possibly a single or double bema, was built
against the hall's broad southern wall. A depression in the
exact center of the hall may indicate the position of a
reader's platform.
Building Two, phase A: [2]
The uppermost portion of an elaborate aedicula (Torah Shrine)
was uncovered in the southwest corner of the hall. It was
decorated with two rampant lions, carved in high relief,
flanking a central scallop shell with a carved
double hole to hold the ner ha tamid (perpetual light). Over
the shell is a pointed gable.
In addition, fragments of the aedicula's double pilasters
were uncovered. One bema was located in the southeast corner,
and a longer one (6 x 30 cm.) was situated under the Torah
Shrine (aedicula).
Building Two, phase B: [2]
The synagogue underwent extensive repairs following its
damage by an earthquake. The large fragment of the phase A
aedicula was incorporated into the synagogue's raised bema
where it served as the topmost step of that bema.
The second bema, in the southeast corner, was also raised.

7. Auxiliary rooms/structures.
Building Three: A room is indicated adjoining the synagogue's
west wall. South of the synagogue is a Byzantine house of
the sixth-seventh century. On the western slope of the hill
is an earlier house dated to the first and second century
C.E. [1]

8. Ornamentation.
Building Two, phase A: [2]
Fragments of numerous animals were found in the debris,
including the two rampant lions decorating the elaborate
aedicula (see no. 6).
Kohl and Watzinger reported the moldings of the portals of the
building they uncovered were similar to ones at Kefar Bar'am
(B:1, I-2). [3] The fasciae of the south portal extends around
the lintel, which is decorated with a relief of a wreath, tied
with a Hercules knot, enclosing a menorah. Above the lintel
is a pulvinated frieze decorated with bay or laurel leaves. [9]
The lintel of the side door is decorated with a rich grapevine
issuing from an amphora.

A column pedestal is decorated with a figure of a running
hare carved on the front, and a defaced head, possibly a
lion's, on the back. A lion, carved in deep relief, has been
suggested to be one of a pair that flanked an amphora, part
of the decoration of lintel over a window.[9]

9. <u>Coins, ceramics and other artifacts found within the building</u>
<u>complex</u>.
Building Two, phase A:[2]
Coins and ceramics were reported found in the ruins; they were
used to establish the building's date (see no. 12).
Building Three:[1]
Underneath the latest pavement, 23 coins were uncovered dated
to the period between 650-700 C.E.[1] A gold coin dated to
Justinian I was found in the fill just below the synagogue's
threshold.[1]
A sixth century black ceramic bowl was decorated with a
depiction of a Torah Shrine.

10. <u>Inscription</u>.
A Hebrew inscription is carved on the south lintel in a single
line on the third fascia flanking the menorah. The crude
carving technique combines the use of relief and incised
lettering. It has been suggested the inscription may be a
later addition to the lintel.[1,11] The inscription, known
for over a century, remained undecipherable until 1960.[11]

> [According] to the number four hundred and
> ninety four years after the destruction
> [of the Temple], the house was built during
> the office of Hanina son of Lezer and
> Luliana son of Yudan.

The date is equivalent to 564 C.E. The only known dated
inscription found in a synagogue in Tetracomia, it does not
follow the standard formula of Palestinian synagogue inscriptions, but is similar in form to inscriptions in the synagogue
at Dura Europos: a date and commemoration of the building of
"the house" under the leadership and supervision of synagogue
officials.[11] This formula is also popular in pagan and
Christian inscriptions found in Syria.[11]

12. <u>Date</u>.[2]
Building One: Early second century C.E.
Building Two, phase A: 250-306.
Building Two, phase B: 306-350/363.
Building Three: 564-700.

13. Bibliography.

1. Meyers, Eric. "Excavations at En-Nabratein, Upper
      Galilee: The 1980 Season." ASOR Newsletter, 2
      (September, 1980), 3-11.

2. Idem. Private communication with author. August 6, 1981.

3. Kohl, Watzinger, pp. 101-106.

4. Conder, SWP, p. 243.

5. Renan, E. Mission, pp. 777 f.

6. Wilson, C. PEFQS, I (1869), 37 ff.

7. Klein, Samuel. Corpus Inscr., pp. 81 f.

8. Frey, J. B. CIJ, #977.

9. Goodenough, E. R. Jewish Symbols. Vol. I (1953),
      pp. 203-204, Vol. III, illus. 516-518, 523.

10. Avi-Yonah, Michael. Oriental Art in Roman Palestine.
      Rome: Centro di Studi Semitica, 1961, p. 35.

11. Avigad, N. "A Dated Lintel Inscription from the Ancient
      Synagogue of Nabratein." Rabinowitz Bulletin.
      Vol. III. (1960), pp. 49-56.

12. Avi-Yonah, Michael. "Kefar Neburaya." EJ. 1972 ed.

13. Hüttenmeister, F. Antiken Synagogen. Vol. I, pp. 343-346.

14. Meyers, E. M., J. F. Strange, C. L. Meyers. "The Ark from
      Nabratein--A First Glance." BA. (Sept., 1981), 237-
      243.

'ALMA
B:1, II-1

1. Name of site and map reference.
   'Alma.
   1962.2735 (2.7)

2. Survey of site.
   The site is located 9.5 km. north of modern Safed. In 1880,
   V. Guérin reported finding several architectural fragments in
   the village, which he suggested were from a synagogue.[1] A
   fragment of a lintel inscribed with a Hebrew inscription,
   found in 1914,[2] by 1921 was in secondary use as a bench.[3]

3. Character and sections of the building as suggested by extant
   and identifiable remains.
   A surveyor for the British Mandatory Government reported
   finding the ruins of an ancient building, "probably a

synagogue," near the village's modern mosque. The ruins
included two granite columns, fragments of limestone columns,
and bases of columns resting on pedestals of unequal size.[3]

8. Ornamentation.

The inscribed lintel is decorated with three rows of ornamental leaves. A second stone, reused in a gate, is decorated
with a six-petaled rosette.

10. Inscriptions.

A second fragment of the 1914 lintel was found in 1957,
reused in a dwelling about 100 m. from the first find. The
two stones form part of a large single bilingual lintel. The
one-line Hebrew inscription was found in 1914.[2,4]

> May there be peace upon this Place
> and upon all the Places of His People
> Israel. . . .[2,4]

The second part, found in 1957, is in Aramaic.

> . . . Amen, Selah, I Jose the son of
> Levi the Levite the craftsman who
> made. . . .[6]

The name "Jose the Levite" appears in an inscription found
at Kefar Bar'am B (B:1, II-6), as does the term "place" to
refer to a synagogue. The term "craftsman" is unique in
Palestinian synagogue inscriptions.[6] On fragments of a
second lintel, discovered in 1949, is inscribed portions of
a two-line Aramaic inscription.

Line 1: donor's name ending in "nh," from Tiberias.
Line 2: the making (or donating ?) of the lintel, followed
by: "May the King of the World. . . ."[5]

11. Donors or patrons.

It has been suggested that Jose the Levite was an itinerant
craftsman who worked on several synagogues in Galilee.[6]
The donor of the lintel came from Tiberias, south of 'Alma.[5]

12. Date.

All the inscriptions have been dated to the third century.[5,6]

13. Bibliography.

1. Guérin, V. DGHA. Vol. VIII. (1880), p. 455.

2. Dalman, G. PJB, X. (1914), 47.

3. British Mandatory Government of Palestine. Archives.
       Jerusalem: Rockefeller Museum.

4. Frey, J. B. CIJ, #973.

5. Amiran, Ruth. _Rabinowitz Bulletin._ Vol. III. (1960), p. 68.

6. Hestrin, Ruth. _Rabinowitz Bulletin._ Vol. III. (1960), pp. 65-67.

7. Hüttenmeister, F. _Antiken Synagogen._ Vol. I, pp. 9-11.

BEERSHEBA

B:1, II-2

1. Name of site and map reference.

Beersheba, Beerscheva, Khirbet Abû-esh Sheba, Bersabe.

189.259

2. Survey of site.

Josephus (BJ III:39) states that the village of Beersheba (Bersabe) marks the southern limit of Upper Galilee. The village is located at the eastern extreme of the Valley of Beth ha-Cerem. In 1905, L. H. Vincent discovered and copied an Aramaic inscription on a screen pillar reused in a modern dwelling.[1]

10. Inscriptions.

The Aramaic inscription is only partially legible.

1. Line ends with name "Joshua."

2. Line ends with "upon his soul."

3. Contains the name "Tanhum" and ends with "his soul."

It has been suggested that three different individuals worked on the inscription.[1]

11. Donors or patrons.

Joshua and Tanhum perhaps either donated the pillar, or are the commemorated deceased.[1]

12. Date.

The unusual spelling of the suffix of the third person singular masculine in lines 2 and 3 suggests a "late" date for the inscription, about the sixth century.[1]

13. Bibliography.

1. Sukenik, E. L. _The Ancient Synagogue of El-Hammeh._ Jerusalem: Rubin Mass, 1935, pp. 67-68.

2. Goodenough, E. R. _Jewish Symbols._ Vol. I. 1953, p. 223.

3. Frey, J. B. _CIJ_, #1196.

DALTON

B:1, II-3

1. Name of site and map reference.
    Dalton, Kafr Dallāta.
    1970.2698 (2.38)

2. Survey of site.
    The village is located six km. south of Safed. In his 1933
    survey, Braslavsky reported the discovery of two doorposts,
    remnants of a wall, and a number of pillars, which he postu-
    lated were from a synagogue.[1] In the early 1950s, the
    Israel Department of Antiquities surveyed the village and
    reported the discovery of the remains of an ancient synagogue
    under the town's modern mosque. A column with a heart-shaped
    cross-section, a capital, and a threshold were found in
    secondary use in modern buildings.[3] When the village was
    surveyed again in 1974, the ruins had badly deteriorated and
    nearly disappeared.[4]

10. Inscriptions.
    Braslavsky has published an inscription discovered in the
    course of the 1950s survey. The stone is inscribed with 16
    lines in Hebrew on the obverse, and 5 illegible lines on the
    reverse.[3] All that has been translated on the obverse are
    portions of five lines.
    Line 4: "Mercy"
    Line 7: "Seat"
    Line 8: "His memory for good"
    Line 11: "His memory for good"
    Line 16: "Blessing, amen, selah [shalom ?]"[3]

12. Date.
    Hüttenmeister dates the architectural remains found in the
    village to the third to fourth centuries on the basis of
    their similarity to other Galilean-type synagogues.[4] The
    inscription has been dated to the "early" Medieval period.[3]

13. Bibliography.

    1. Braslavsky, J. BJPES, 2 (1934/1935), 14 ff.

    2. Idem. BJPES, 5 (1938), 124 ff.

    3. Idem. Studies in our Country, Its Past and Remains.
            Tel Aviv, 1954, pp. 274 ff.

    4. Hüttenmeister, F. Antiken Synagogen, Vol. I, pp. 96-98.

ER-RAMAH
B:1, II-4

1. <u>Name of site and map reference</u>.
   Er-Ramah, ar-Rāma.
   184.260 (2.127)
2. <u>Survey of site</u>.
   Located at the foot of Mount Ha-ari near the ancient border of
   Tetracomia and Sepphoris, it is about 12.5 km. west-southwest
   of modern Safed.
   A decorated lintel inscribed with an Aramaic inscription was
   found near the village on the 'Akko (Ptolemais)-Safed road.[1]
8. <u>Ornamentation</u>.
   Below the first line of inscription, and flanking the second,
   are two winged genii holding aloft a wreath. They are similar
   to genii at Kefar Bar'am A and B (B:1, I-2, B:1, II-6).
10. <u>Inscriptions</u>.
    An inscription in Aramaic reads:
    Line 1: "In grateful memory of Rabbi Eliezer, son of Teodor,
    who built this house as a guest house."
    Line 2: ". . . is dead [or buried] in front of the gate."[1]
    S. Klein, on reexamining the inscription, read the first two
    words of line 2 as "wreath" not "dead" or "buried."[2]   It
    would be against Jewish <u>halakah</u> to have a grave located so
    near a synagogue (see Khirbet Shema' B:1, I-3). Klein
    suggests the inscription refers to a memorial represented by
    the wreath.[2]   The use of the term "gate" to refer to a
    synagogue occurs as well at 'Ammudim (B:1, I-1), Daburah
    (G:2, II-4), and I'billin (B:2, II-4).
12. <u>Date</u>.
    The inscription has been considered to be contemporary with
    the two synagogues at Kefar Bar'am (B:1, I-2, B:1, II-6).[2]
13. <u>Bibliography</u>.

   1. Ben-Zvi, I. <u>Monatsschrift für Geschichte und Wissenschaft
      des Judentums</u>, 76 (1932), 554-556.

   2. Klein, S. <u>JPOS</u>, 13 (1933), 94-96.

   3. Avi-Yonah, M. <u>QDAP</u>, X (1942), 131.

   4. Sukenik, E. <u>The Ancient Synagogue at El-Hammeh</u>, p. 25.

   5. Idem. <u>Ancient Synagogues</u>, p. 77.

   6. Frey, J. B. <u>CIJ</u>, #979.

   7. Hüttenmeister, F. <u>Antiken Synagogen</u>. Vol. I, pp. 367-369.

JASSUD-HAMMA'LE
B:1, II-5

1. **Name of site and map reference.**
   Jassud-Hamma'le, Yesud ha-Ma'ala, at-Tulēl, Thella.
   2077.2739 (2.164)

2. **Survey of site.**
   The site is located near the eastern boundary of Tetracomia,
   on the west shore of former Lake Huleh. In 1913, J. Goldhar
   published a fragment of an Aramaic inscription from a column
   found in the village; it is now lost.[1] In July, 1974, the
   ruins of a building identified as the synagogue of ancient
   Jassud-Hamma'le were uncovered by N. Tflinsky. He assumed
   the 1913 inscription came from this ruin.[4]

3. **Character and sections of the building as suggested by extant
   and identifiable remains.**
   The building, constructed of local basalt, has not been
   cleared, but an inscribed column (see no. 10) may belong to
   it.[A]

   PLAN
   Two rows of columns (four per row) divide the interior into a
   central nave flanked by aisles. The northwest column is out
   of position, possibly owing to a later renovation of the
   building. A water basin, 90 x 100 cm., was found in the
   hall's northwest corner.[4,5]

4. **Measurements.**
   Main hall: 15.3 x 11 m.[5]
   Nave: 5.5 m.[4]
                6.0 m.[6]
   Distance between columns: 2.5 m.[4]

5. **Orientation.**
   The long axis of the building is north-south; the facade is
   unknown.[4,5]

8. **Ornamentation.**
   A single capital was found in the ruins; no description is
   available.[4]

10. **Inscriptions.**
    A column, now lost, contained this inscription:

             Remember be for good Rabbi Mathia, son
             of . . . that made [?] this column . . .
             [third line missing] . . . Amen.[2]

11. Donors or patrons.

Rabbi Mathia was probably the donor, not the fabricator of the column. [2]

12. Date.

The capital, on the basis of its "style," has been dated to the fourth century. [4,5]

13. Bibliography.

1. Goldhar, J. Admat Qodes, (1913), p. 258.

2. Klein, S. ZDPV, 51 (1928), 136 f.

3. Frey, J. B. CIJ, #971.

4. Tflinsky, N. HA, 48/49 (1974), 28.

5. Idem. HA, 51/52 (1974), 6 f.

6. Hüttenmeister, F. Antiken Synagogen, Vol. I, pp. 514-515.

KEFAR BAR'AM B

B:1, II-6

1. Name of site and map reference.

Kefar Bar'am, Kafr Bir'im, Kefr-Berein.

1891.2724 (2.17)

2. Survey of site.

See Kefar Bar'am A (B:1, I-2). Kefar Bar'am B had been completely dismantled sometime before 1905. [1] The following information is based on nineteenth-century drawings, photos, and reports. [A]

3. Character and sections of the building as suggested by extant and identifiable remains.

The building was constructed of local limestone ashlars set without mortar. [2]

PLAN

Early surveyors described two rows of columns dividing the interior into a central nave flanked by aisles. [2,3] An 1866 photograph [1] shows a heart-shaped base inside the hall, indicating the probable existence of a transverse colonnade. [A] A fragment of a heart-shaped column found in 1960 300 meters north of Kefar Bar'am A was judged to have come from the smaller synagogue. [10] In 1869, Wilson reported finding two pedestals in situ and the remains of columns and capitals strewn throughout the building's interior. [2]

ENTRANCES

South: Photographs and survey reports indicate a single monumental entry in the center of the facade wall. [1]

4. Measurements.

Main hall: 19.85 x 14.78 m. [2]

5. Orientation.

The long axis of the basilica is north-south; the facade was on the south, facing Jerusalem.

8. Ornamentation.

The monolithic doorposts were decorated with finely carved moldings, including a twisted ropelike torus that continued around the T-shaped lintel. The lintel was decorated with a pair of genii holding a wreath framing a large rosette. The photograph indicates that the cornice was decorated with an interlace pattern with a boss between each ogee curve. [1]

10. Inscriptions.

A Hebrew inscription was carved on the lower portion of the door lintel.

> May there peace in this Place and all
> the Places of Israel. Jose the Levite,
> the son of Levi, made this lintel. May
> blessing come upon his deeds. Peace. [7]

The term "place," and the name, "Jose the Levite," also appear in an inscription at 'Alma (B:1, II-1).

11. Donors or patrons.

Jose the Levite may have been an itinerant craftsman who worked on several synagogues in Galilee. See 'Alma (B:1, II-1).

12. Date.

Its letter form suggests that the inscription may be dated to the second to the third centuries. [4] This date also is supported by the style of the building's architectural form and decoration, which was considered similar to other "early" Galilean synagogues. [1] (For problems associated with early dates see Kefar Bar'am A, B:1, I-2.)

13. Bibliography.

1. Kohl, Watzinger. Pp. 89-91.

2. Wilson, Charles. PEFQS, I (1869), 37 ff.

3. Robinson, Edw. ZDMG, 7 (1853), 42.

4. Lidzbarski, Mark. Handbuch der Nordsemitischen Epigraphik nebst Ausgewählten Inskriften. Weimer, 1898, p. 485. (Rpt. Hildesheim, 1962).

5. Dussaud, Rene. Les Monuments Palestiniens et Judaiques. Paris, 1910, no. 116.

6. Klein, S. Corpus Inscr., pp. 78 f.

7. Sukenik, E. Ancient Synagogues, pp. 70 f.

8. Frey, J. B. CIJ, #974.

9. Goodenough, E. R. Jewish Symbols. Vol. I, p. 201.

10. Hüttenmeister, F. Antiken Synagogen. Vol. I, pp. 35-38.

PEQI'IN

B:1, II-7

1. Name of site and map reference.

   Peqi'in, Peki'in, Baca, Baqa, al-Buqē'a.

   181.264 (2.117)

2. Survey of site.

   The village is located west of Meron in a small valley on the slopes of Mount Ha-ari, 15 km. west of modern Safed.

8. Ornamentation.

   Several decorated stones believed to have come from an ancient synagogue were reused in the village's modern buildings. Two were incorporated into a synagogue built in the village in 1873; a third was reused in a house.[1,2]

   1. Found under a layer of plaster in the modern synagogue was a stone block decorated with a seven-branched menorah flanked on the left by a lulab and ethrog, and on the right by a shofar and "casket" or "incense shovel."[4]

   2. The second stone reused in the synagogue measures 55 cm. long by 40 cm. wide by 30 cm. thick. It displays finer workmanship than the first stone and is decorated with a Torah Shrine with closed doors. The wings of the doors are divided into three narrow rectangles. Above the doors is a shell and arcuated lintel surmounted by a gabled roof.[4]

   3. The third stone, a fragment, is decorated with a relief of a grapevine.

12. Date.

    The reliefs have been dated to the end of the second century or the beginning of the third.[2,5]

13. Bibliography.

1. Ben-Zvi, I. <u>PEFQS</u> (1930), pp. 210-14.

2. Sukenik, E. <u>PEFQS</u> (1931), pp. 22-25.

3. Idem. <u>The Ancient Synagogue of Beth Alpha</u>. London: Oxford Univ. Press, 1932, pp. 24, 28-29.

4. Goodenough, E. R. <u>Jewish Symbols</u>. Vol. I. (1953), p. 218. Vol. III, figs. 572, 573.

5. Hüttenmeister, F. <u>Antiken Synagogen</u>. Vol. I, pp. 350-353.

GUSH HALAV B

B:1, IIIA-1

1. Site name and map reference.
   Gush Halav, Giscala, el-Jîsh, al-Ğis.
   1920.2701 (2.60b)

2. Survey of site.
   See Gush Halav A (B:1, I-1).
   Synagogue B was built in the village; a Maronite church now stands on what may have been its site, although excavations beneath the church have revealed meager evidence of the earlier building.[1]

3. Character and sections of the building as suggested by extant and identifiable remains.
   In 1974, a corner pillar, heart-shaped in cross-section, was uncovered under the church.[5] Pedestals, moldings, and other architectural fragments reused in the church have been considered similar to those found at synagogue B;[1] and a lintel, reused over the church entrance, may have come from the earlier synagogue.[1]

12. Date.
   Architectural fragments have been dated from the late second to early fourth centuries.[1] (For problems associated with early dates see Kefar Bar'am A, B:1, I-2.)

13. Bibliography.

1. Kohl, Watzinger. Pp. 107-111.

2. Wilson, Charles, <u>PEFQS</u>, I (1869), 37 ff.

3. Kitchener, H. <u>PEFQS</u> (1877), p. 124.

4. Goodenough, E. R. <u>Jewish Symbols</u>. Vol. I. (1953), p. 205.

5. Hüttenmeister, F. <u>Antiken Synagogen</u>. Vol. I, pp. 146-147.

KEFAR HANANYAH

B:1, IIIA-2

1. Name of site and map reference.

Kefar Hananyāh, Hananya, Kafr 'Inān.

1897.2588 (4.89)

2. Survey of site.

In 1933, the Palestine Exploration Society reported the discovery of the remains of a rock-cut building in the village. [1]

3. Character and sections of the building as suggested by extant and identifiable remains.

The building is constructed on a terrace on the southwestern incline of a hill. Its foundations could be traced by the rock cutting. Large portions of the north and east walls were extant. [2]

PLAN

Two longitudinal rows of columns divided the building's interior into a central nave and two aisles. The column bases of one row were reported in situ. The columns and high square pedestals are considered similar to those at Meron (B:1, I-4). [2]

4. Measurements.

Main hall: 12.25 x 11.5 m. [6]

5. Orientation.

SSW 160°. [6]

9. Coins, ceramics, and other artifacts found within the building complex.

A bronze polycandelon was found at el-Mekr (1633.2598), 5 km. east of Ptolemais; it was inscribed with the name Kefar Hananyah. The polycandelon was in the form of a ring carrying twelve lamps, with an additional lamp hanging from a hook at the center of the circle. Assumed to have decorated the synagogue at Kefar Hananyah, possibly the building described above (no. 3), the polycandelon is now in the Musée Mariemont, Belgium. [1]

10. Inscriptions.

An inscription, cut on the bottom of the ring, is in a difficult form of Hebrew/Aramaic, [4] making its precise translation problematic. The inscription is interrupted in two places by a seven-branched menorah flanked by a lulab and ethrog:

> This polycandelon . . . for the sacred
> place at Kefar Hananiya [Hananyah].
> Blessed be their memory. Amen, Selah,
> Peace. [5]

The second word also has been translated as either "circle"
or "crown." [4]   The term "place" to refer to a synagogue
occurs at Kefar Bar'am B (B:1, II-6) and 'Alma (B:1, II-1).

12. Date.
The ruins have been dated to the third century. [2]   The lamp,
on the basis of the inscription's letter forms, has been
dated to the fifth or sixth centuries. [3,6]

13. Bibliography.

1. Braslavsky, J. BJPES I, 2 (1933), 20 f.

2. British Mandatory Government. Archives. Jerusalem:
   Rockefeller Museum.

3. Frey, J. B. CIJ, #980.

4. Goodenough, E. R. Jewish Symbols. Vol. VIII. (1958),
   pp. 168-169. Vol. X. (1964), pp. 34-35.

5. Kahane, P. P. The Bible in Archaeology. Jerusalem:
   Israel Museum Catalogue 6, 1965, no. 17.

6. Hüttenmeister, F. Antiken Synagogen, Vol. I, pp. 256-258,
   526-527.

AL-MAGHAR

B:1, IIIB-1

1. Name of site and map reference.
   Al-Maghar, el-Mŭghâr, Mughr el-Kheit.
   2008.2660 (2.77)

2. Survey of site.
   The site is located 4.5 km. north-northeast of modern Safed.
   In 1881, Conder and Kitchener reported finding two columns,
   a column base, and a building foundation, which they suggested
   belonged to a synagogue. [1]   Additional doorposts were found
   in 1964. [2]
   The available evidence is insufficient to establish the
   identity of the ruin. [A]

13. Bibliography.

1. Conder, C., Kitchener, H. SWP I, (1881-1883), p. 254.

2. Hüttenmeister, F. Antiken Synagogen. Vol. I, p. 187.

'AQBARA

B:1, IIIB-2

1. Name of site and map reference.

   'Aqbara, 'Akbara, 'Akbare, Khirbet al-'Uqeiba.

   197.260 (2.4)

2. Survey of site.

   The cliff of 'Aqbara (Khirbet al-'Uqeiba) is located more
   than 3 km. south of modern Safed; the modern village of
   'Akbara is at its foot. Josephus reported that he fortified
   "the rock called Acchabaron" (Vit. 37; BJII:573-574).
   In 1880, V. Guérin reported the ruins of a building with an
   eastern orientation, which he identified as a church.[1] The
   archives of the British Mandatory Government list extensive
   ruins and foundations in the locale of 'Aqbara.[2] J.
   Braslavy and G. Foerster reported finding the ruins of a
   building situated by a spring at 'Aqbara, which they have
   identified as a synagogue.[3,4] E. Meyers surveyed the site
   for evidence of Josephus' fortifications and identified the
   ruins above the cliff as a square, medieval caravansary and
   road.[7] A survey of the entire triangular area west and
   south of Khirbet al-'Uqeiba appeared to be devoid of any sign
   of permanent, ancient occupation. No mention is made of a
   "possible" synagogue ruin.[7]

12. Date.

   Foerster considered the ruins contemporary with the "early
   Galilean type" synagogue, and included this site in his
   study on the relationship of the synagogue to Hellenistic and
   Roman art and architecture.[4,5]

13. Bibliography.

   1. Guérin, V. DGHA (1880), 351 f.

   2. British Mandatory Government of Palestine. Archives.
      Jerusalem: Rockefeller Museum.

   3. Braslavy, J. in All the Land of Naphtali (1967), 113.

   4. Foerster, G. QAD 5 (1972), 38.

   5. Idem. "Galilean Synagogues and Their Relationship to
      Hellenistic and Roman Art and Architecture"
      (Jerusalem, Hebrew Univ.), dissertation, 1972.

   6. Hüttenmeister, Antiken Synagogen, Vol. I, p. 507.

   7. Meyers, Eric M., James F. Strange, Dennis E. Groh, "The
      Meiron Excavation Project: Archaeological Survey in
      Galilee and Golan, 1976," BASOR 230 (April, 1978), 3.

AYYALET HA-ŠAHAR
B:1, IIIB-3

1. Name of site and map reference.
   Ayyelet ha-Šahar.
   2050.2696 (2.14)

2. Survey of site.
   The site is located one km. northeast of Tell Hazor. Two
   rows of columns were reported to be standing in a north to
   south direction. A capital was found 100 m. east of the ruins.
   The ruins have been identified as those of a possible synagogue.[1] The evidence is too inconclusive to make an
   attribution.[A]

13. Bibliography.

    1. Hüttenmeister, F. Antiken Synagogen, Vol. I, pp. 29-30.

KHIRBET NATOR
B:1, IIIB-4

1. Name of site and map reference.
   Khirbet Nator, Horvat Nator, Khirbet al-Muntar.
   2054.2649 (2.111)

2. Survey of site.
   The site is located 9 km. east of modern Safed.

3. Character and sections of the building as suggested by extant
   and identifiable remains.
   Only a single column and base remain of a rectangular building
   reported found at this site.[1]
   PAVEMENT
   The pavement is a mosaic; no further description is
   available.[1]

4. Measurements.
   Main hall: 40 x 20 m.[2]

5. Orientation.
   The building is reported to have been positioned north-
   south.[2]

9. Coins, ceramics, and other artifacts found within building
   complex.
   A lamp was found in the debris.[1]

12. Date.
    The lamp has been dated to the fourth or fifth centuries.[1]

13. Bibliography.

   1. Yeivin, S. <u>A Decade of Archaeology</u>. (1960), p. 42.

   2. Hüttenmeister, F. <u>Antiken Synagogen</u>, Vol. I, pp. 334-335.

KHIRBET SHURA

B:1, IIIB-5

1. <u>Name of site and map reference</u>.
   Khirbet Shura, Khirbet Shora, Horvat Šura.
   2041.2641 (2.148)

2. <u>Survey of site</u>.
   The site is located 7 km. east of modern Safed.

3. <u>Character and sections of the building as suggested by extant</u>
   <u>and identifiable remains</u>.
   In 1926, the remains of a "public building" were reported
   found here. They include basalt foundations, walls, dressed
   stones, a reservoir, and a lintel.[1] In 1957, additional
   architectural fragments were uncovered southwest of Khirbet
   Shura. These fragments include columns and bases. It has
   been presumed that they are from a ruined synagogue,[2]
   although this attribution is by no means certain.[3,A]

5. <u>Orientation</u>.
   The ruins, found in 1957, are positioned northeast to
   southwest.[2]

8. <u>Ornamentation</u>.
   The lintel, found in 1926, measures 1.35 long by .45 high by
   .35 m. thick.[1] It is decorated with three square panels:
   The middle panel has been effaced, the right panel contains
   a wreath enclosing a rosette, and the left is carved with
   different patterns running horizontal with the lintel in
   parallel lines. (The lintel is now in Rosh Pinna.)

10. <u>Inscriptions</u>.
   An architectural fragment found in 1942 near Khirbet Shura
   carries a fragmentary commemorative inscription; the stone
   is now reported to be missing. The inscription may have
   expressed the gratitude of the donors.[2]

12. <u>Date</u>.
   The ruined building reported found in 1957 has been dated to
   the Roman or Byzantine periods.[2]

13. Bibliography.

   1. British Mandatory Government. Archives. Jerusalem:
         Rockefeller Museum.

   2. Israel Department of Antiquities and Museums. Archives.
         Jerusalem: Israel Museum.

   3. Hüttenmeister, F. Antiken Synagogen, Vol. I, pp. 421-422.

KHIRBET TIEBA
B:1, IIIB-6

1. Name of site and map reference.
   Khirbet Tieba, Horvat Tieba, Horvat Tuba.
   2072.2629 (2.156)

2. Survey of site.
   The site is located near the border of Tiberias and
   Gaulanitis, by the Jordan River.

8. Ornamentation.
   Two basalt lintels were found near this site.[1] One lintel
   consists of a pediment and niche. The second has its pediment
   decorated with plant motifs flanked by birds (eagles ?). The
   lintels have been compared stylistically to others found at
   synagogue sites in Galilee,[2] but the evidence is too inconclusive to establish the identity of the building.[3,A]

12. Date.
   The lintels are considered similar to ones found at other
   so-called "early" type Galilean synagogues; therefore they
   have been dated ca. third century.[2] This date must be
   considered doubtful in light of current excavations at
   Capernaum (B:3, I-1), and elsewhere in Galilee.[A]

13. Bibliography.

   1. Israel Department of Antiquities and Museums. Archives.
         Jerusalem: Israel Museum.

   2. Foerster, G. "Galilean Synagogues and their Relationship
         to Hellenistic and Roman Art and Architecture."
         Diss. Hebrew Univ., 1972.

   3. Hüttenmeister, F. Antiken Synagogen, Vol. I, pp. 464.

KHIRBET TIRIYA
B:1, IIIB-7

1. Name of site and map reference.
   Khirbet Tiriya, Horvat Tīrīya, Khirbet Tīrīha.
   180.265 (2.154)

2. Survey of site.
   The site is located 16 km. west of modern Safed. It has been
   suggested that the stone, decorated with a Torah Shrine, that
   is now in the modern synagogue at Peqi'in (B:1, II-7) may have
   originally been part of a no longer extant synagogue at this
   site. [1]

13. Bibliography.

   1. Braslavsky, I. Hayada'ta et ha'Eretz. Vol. VI. (1964),
      p. 269.

   2. Hüttenmeister, F. Antiken Synagogen Vol. I, p. 462.

NABRATEIN B
B:1, IIIB-8

1. Name of site and map reference.
   Nabratein, Nebratein, Kefar Neburaya, Nabaraya, en-Nabraten.
   1978.2675 (2.115)

2. Survey of site.
   The isolated ruins of the village are located on the side of
   a hill 4 km. north of modern Safed. A validated synagogue
   (B:1, I-5) has been uncovered on a terrace on the south slope
   of the hill. Additional architectural fragments have been
   found about 250 m. south of this ruin. [1] Guérin suggested
   these were part of a second synagogue located in the village
   and reported finding a column base and capital similar to
   those used in other Galilean synagogues. [1] All other evidence of the building has since disappeared. [2] The evidence
   is too inconclusive to make an attribution. [A]

13. Bibliography.

   1. Guérin, V. DGHA. Vol. VII, p. 441.

   2. Hüttenmeister, F. Antiken Synagogen, Vol. I, p. 347.

QAZYON
B:1, IIIB-9

1. Name of site and map reference.
   Qazyon, Qasyūn, Kasyoun, Qisyon, Qision, Khirbet Qasyūn.
   1997.2720 (2.123)

2. Survey of site.
   The site is located 9 km. north-northwest of modern Safed.
   In 1864, E. Renan reported the discovery of the ruin of a
   "sacred" building.[1]   He, followed by Guérin, believed it to
   be a synagogue;[1,2]   Kohl and Watzinger suggested it was a
   pagan temple, similar in plan to the Tychaion at Is-Sanamên.[3]

3. Character and sections of building as suggested by extant
   and identifiable remains.
   The building apparently was surrounded by a colonnade that
   may have enclosed a birkeh (reservoir) similar to the one at
   Is-Sanamên.[3]

5. Orientation.
   The building is aligned 180 degrees to the south, toward
   Jerusalem.[3,7]

10. Inscriptions.
    A six-line Greek inscription inscribed on a stone was found
    inside the building; lines five and six are unclear. An
    additional line was added on the left, and a laurel leaf
    medallion, enclosing a disputed inscription, was placed to
    the right.

> For the salvation of the Roman Caesars,
> L[ucius] Sept[imius] Severus Pius
> Pert[inax] Aug[ustus], and M[arcus]
> Aur[elius] A[nton]inus [[and L[ucius]
> Sept[imius] G]]eta, their sons, by a
> vow of the Jews.[4]

The additional line on the left reads "and Julia Domna
Augusta." Within the medallion on right (conjectured) is
inscribed "and the legions."[4]

11. Donors or patrons.
    It has been suggested that the inscription was part of "a
    votive offering" made by Galilean Jews for the well-being of
    the emperors during the campaign against the Parthians; in the
    first century B.C.E. Julius Caesar had granted the Jews exemp-
    tion from participation in the imperial cult, but sacrifices
    daily in the Jerusalem Temple for the emperor's well-being.[8]
    Inscriptions have been uncovered in Egypt recording dedications

by Jews of <u>Proseuchae</u>, prayers on behalf of the Ptolemaic ruler,[5,7] but there is no evidence of Jewish participation in a pagan temple cult. It may be that this inscription is no more than a commendation to the royal family unrelated to an actual "votive offering" in a pagan temple.[A]

12. <u>Date</u>.

The inscription is dated between the spring of 196 C.E. and the end of January, 198 C.E., the dates when Caracalla was Caesar but not yet Augustus.[5,7]

13. <u>Bibliography</u>.

1. Renan, E. <u>Mission</u>, pp. 774-776.

2. Guérin, V. <u>DGHA</u>. Vol. VII. (1880), pp. 447-449.

3. Kohl, Watzinger, pp. 209-210.

4. Frey, J. B. <u>CIJ</u>, #972.

5. Ibid., #1432, 1440-1444.

6. Goodenough, E. R. <u>Jewish Symbols</u>. Vol. II. (1953), p. 140.

7. Lewis, David. "The Jewish Inscriptions in Egypt," in <u>Corpus Papyrorum Judaicarum</u>. Vol. III. eds. V. A. Tcherikover, A. Fuks, M. Stern. Cambridge: Harvard Univ. Press, 1964, pp. 141-143.

8. Smallwood, <u>Jews</u>, pp. 134-135, 147-148, 496-497.

9. Hüttenmeister, F. <u>Antiken Synagogen</u>, Vol. I, pp. 359-362.

SAFED
B:1, IIIB-10

1. <u>Name of site and map reference</u>.
Safed, Zefat, Safat, Safad.
1964.2636 (2.138)

2. <u>Survey of site</u>.
Located on a mountain 850 m. above sea level, the site is 40 km. north of Tiberias.

8. <u>Ornamentation</u>.
A lintel decorated with an eagle was found near Safed and identified as being part of a no longer extant synagogue in Safed.[1] The evidence is too inconclusive to make an attribution.[2,A]

12. Date.
    The lintel has been dated to the "Talmudic" period,[1] and to
    the third century.[2]

13. Bibliography.

    1. Avigad, N. EI. VII (1964), 18 ff.

    2. Hüttenmeister, F. Antiken Synagogen. Vol. I, pp. 386-387.

SAFSĀF
B:1, IIIB-11

1. Name of site and map reference.
   Safsāf, Sifsufa, Sufsaf, Safsafa, Sŭfsâf.
   1919.2684 (2.141)

2. Survey of site.
   The site is located 7 km. northwest of modern Safed.

8. Ornamentation.
   A lintel surmounted by a niche, was found in secondary use
   in the village mosque.[1] It measures 1.50 m. in length and
   is decorated with a wreath tied with a Hercules knot and
   flanked by bucranium. The entire composition is placed
   within a highly stylized grape vine showing ogee type curves.
   The niche above the lintel is enclosed within decorated
   voussoirs that do not, however, fit the niche. Its original
   voussoirs are now built into a wall on the left of the
   entrance into the mosque.[2] The shell within the niche is
   hinged at the bottom.[2]
   The evidence is too inconclusive to make an attribution.[A]

12. Date.
    The lintel has been dated to the third to fourth centuries.[3]

13. Bibliography.

    1. Kitchener, H. PEFQS, (1878), pp. 138 f.

    2. Goodenough, E. R. Jewish Symbols. Vol. I. (1953),
           p. 211. Vol. III, fig. 548.

    3. Hüttenmeister, F. Antiken Synagogen, Vol. I, pp. 392-393.

SASA

B:1, IIIB-12

1. Name of site and map reference.

   Sasa, Sa'sa.

   1872.2704 (2.136)

2. Survey of site.

   The site is located 850 m. above sea-level, 11.5 km. northwest of modern Safed, near the ancient border with Tyre. The
   tombs of the Talmudic Rabbis Sissi, Levi ben Sisi, and Yose
   ben Sisi are traditionally located in the village's ancient
   necropolis.[1]

3. Character and sections of the building as suggested by extant
   and identifiable remains.

   Several carved stones found in secondary use in the village
   mosque are attributed to an ancient building. These remnants
   include a hewn stone threshold, parts of a mud floor, a row
   of well-chiseled stones, and a stylobate. It has been
   suggested the building was broadhouse in form, and was a
   synagogue,[2,3] but the evidence is too inconclusive to make
   an attribution.[1,A]

5. Orientation.

   The building faced west.

8. Ornamentation.

   Two lintels were found, one decorated with an egg and dart
   molding, the other with a "leaf" motif.

12. Date.

   The ruins have been dated to the third to fourth centuries.[2,3]

13. Bibliography.

   1. Goodenough, E. R. Jewish Symbols. Vol. I. (1953), p. 263.

   2. Foerster, G. HA, 28/29 (1969), 4.

   3. Hüttenmeister, F. Antiken Synagogen. Vol. I, p. 383-384.

The Hasmonean king Alexander Janneaus (103-76 B.C.E.), named Sepphoris as the administrative capital of Lower Galilee. The Romans subsequently divided the region into two districts: Tiberias in the east, and Sepphoris in the west. This division remained in effect until the Byzantine period, when two smaller city-territories were formed from parts of Sepphoris: Helenopolis and Exaloth-Nain. These formed independent administrative units, but geographically and culturally they were closely associated with Sepphoris; therefore, they are included within this survey.

Fifteen ruins within Sepphoris' borders have been identified as ancient synagogues, but only three can be verified: 'Ammudim, Beth She'arim, and Japhia. Although these three buildings appear to share several architectural details with synagogues uncovered in Tetracomia, they also differ from them in many respects.

Architectural fragments bearing Jewish inscriptions or motifs have been found at six other sites; five sites are in the disputed category. Kafr Kanna and Nazareth have perplexing evidence that suggests Jewish and Christian coexistence; however, the study of Jewish and Christian relationships during the Roman and Byzantine periods has not progressed to the point that any firm conclusions can be drawn regarding the attribution of the architectural finds from these two towns.

'AMMUDIM
B:2, I-1

1. Name of site and map reference.
   H. 'Ammudim, Umm al-'Amad, Khirbet Umm al-'Amed.
   1887.2467 (4.8)
   Plan no. 6

2. Survey of site.
   Located 12.5 km. west-northwest of Tiberias, the site is near an ancient route that passed along the east end of the Netopha Valley. In Biblical times 'Ammudim may have been the site of Bezer, a city of refuge for the people of Reuben (Deut. 4:43). Today, the village is on the very edge of an area of cultivated land.

In 1869, Charles Wilson reported the ruin,[2] and it was one of the synagogues surveyed and partially excavated by the German expedition headed by Kohl and Watzinger in 1905-1906.[1] In 1930, a stone with an inscription engraved on it was found.[3]

3. Character and sections of the building as suggested by extant and identifiable remains.

The synagogue is built of local limestone ashlars set without mortar. The exterior faces of the walls were finished; the interior was left rough, probably to be plastered.[2]

PLAN

Two rows of longitudinal columns (seven per row) and a north transverse colonnade (two columns) divide the main hall into a central nave surrounded on three sides by aisles. The columns and bases rest on pedestals set on a stylobate. The inner angles of the two corner pedestals are cut away, forming two half pedestals; the bases and column shafts are heart-shaped in cross-section.

ENTRANCES

South: A large central portal is flanked by two smaller ones.

East: An auxiliary entrance, in the center of the wall, opens onto a side aisle.

BENCHES

Two tiers of benches are placed along the eastern and western walls.

PAVEMENT

Flagstone, overlaid at a later date with mosaic, forms the pavement.[1]

4. Measurements.[1]

Main hall:	18.75 x 14.10 m. (internal measurements)
West aisle:	ca. 3.15 m. wide
East aisle:	ca. 3.15-3.20 m. wide
North aisle:	ca. 3.15 m. wide
Nave:	6.21 m. wide
Inscribed stone:	0.39 m. high; present length: 0.46 m.[6]

5. Orientation.

The long axis of the synagogue is north-south; its facade, on the south, faces Jerusalem.

6. Character and form: apse, niche, Torah Shrine, bema, chancel.

A foundation, uncovered on the interior of the building in front of the central portal, is attributed to a later addition to the building dated to the period following the building's abandonment as a synagogue.[1] Goodenough, however, suggests it was the foundation of a Torah Shrine that blocked the large central portal.[4]

8. Ornamentation.

Two lintels were discovered broken and reused in nearby buildings;[1] the figurative motifs were effaced.

1. The lintel of the central entrance bore two lions, with their paws resting on a calf's head, facing a two-handled vase.[1]

2. The lintel of the east entrance was divided into three panels, a wreath in the central panel flanked by floral rosettes.[1]

Also found in the ruins were fragments of a frieze decorated with floral ornaments,[1] and capitals, described variously as "Ionic,"[1] or of a "peculiar Jewish type."[2] The mosaic pavement is described as "plain."[3]

9. Coins, ceramics, and other artifacts found within building complex.

Surface finds include pottery bowls with inverted lips and carination, similar to ones found at Gush Halav A (B:1, I-1) and Kefar Hananyah (B:1, IIIA-2); they are dated to the third century C.E.[7] Also found were shallow "Galilean bowls" with flat or shallow conical bases or convex bases, sometimes with carination between rib and base, similar to ones found throughout Galilee; they are dated to the third to fourth centuries (See Khirbet Shema', B:1, I-3).[7]

10. Inscriptions.

Five lines of Aramaic inscribed on a stone built into one of the synagogue's walls read:

> Yo'ezer the hazan/ and Shimeon/ his
> brother made/ this Gate of the Lord/
> of Heaven.[6]

The word "gate," possibly in reference to a synagogue, is found on the lintels of three synagogues: I'billin (B:2, II-4), Daburah (G:2, II-4), and Er-Ramah (B:1, II-4). At 'Ammudim the term "gate" may refer to the synagogue as a whole, not just its door's lintel.[5,6] The expression "Gate of the Lord of Heaven" is unusual for synagogue inscriptions.[6]

11. Donors and patrons.

Hazan is a synagogue functionary; the term also appears in a synagogue inscription at Apheca (G:4, II-1). If the word "gate" is accepted as a synonym for "synagogue," then

Yo'ezer and his brother Shimeon were either in charge of the building of the synagogue or major donors to its construction.[A]

12. Date.

The synagogue was originally dated to the end of the second or early third century.[1] (See Kefar Bar'am A [B:1, I-2].) The epigraphy is considered similar to inscriptions found at other Galilean synagogues and has been assigned to the third to fourth centuries.[6] Recent discoveries at Capernaum (B:3, I-1), however, suggest that these early dates must be reconsidered.[A]

13. Bibliography.

1. Kohl, Watzinger, pp. 71-79.

2. Wilson, Charles, PEFQS, I (1869), 37 ff.

3. Sukenik, E. Ancient Synagogues, p. 27.

4. Goodenough, E. R. Jewish Symbols. Vol. I (1953), pp. 199-200.

5. Sonne, I. "Appellations of Synagogues." Tarbiz, 27 (1958), 557 ff.

6. Avigad, N. "An Aramaic Inscription from the Synagogue at Umm el-Amed in Galilee." Rabinowitz Bulletin. Vol. III. (1960), pp. 62-64.

7. Meyers, Eric. Shema', pp. 18, 170, 185.

8. Hüttenmeister, F. Antiken Synagogen. Vol. I, pp. 12-15.

9. Hüttenmeister, F. "The Aramaic Inscription from the Synagogue at H. 'Ammudim." IEJ, 28, 1-2 (1978), 109-112.

BETH SHE'ARIM

B:2, I-2

1. Name of site and map reference.
   Beth She'arim, Sheikh Ibreiq, Besara.
   1625.2343 (3.29)
   Plan 7.

2. Survey of site.
   Located 18 km. southeast of modern Haifa, Beth She'arim once was part of the estate of Berenice, daughter of Agrippa I and sister of Agrippa II. The town experienced a large influx of displaced Judaean Jews following the second Jewish revolt. Patriarch Judah ha-Nasi, the redactor of Mishnah, settled in

Beth She'arim and made it the seat of the Sanhedrin. After
his death, in ca. 220 C.E., and burial in the town's famed
necropolis, Beth She'arim became the central burial place for
Jews.[1,3]

Originally the city was believed to have been surrounded by
a wall;[1] it now appears that buildings built closely
together acted as a defense perimeter.[3]

Archaeological evidence suggests that the town was destroyed
by fire in the middle of the fourth century, possibly during
a Jewish uprising against Emperor Gallus in 352.[1,3]

During an investigation of the traditional tomb of Sheikh
Ibreiq, a Moslem holy man, B. Maisler (Mazar) and I. Ben-Zvi
identified the site as ancient Beth She'arim,[1] and the site
was excavated from 1936 to 1940 and in the 1950s.[3,7] The
necropolis is spread in a semicircle on the northeast, north,
and west slopes of the hill of Beth She'arim, and on the
slopes of neighboring hills to the north and west. Catacomb
14, one of the earliest tomb caves, dates to the end of the
second century C.E.[3] The cave was first cut, and then its
elaborate triple arched facade was added later. It is similar
to the facades of several Galilean synagogues, for example,
Meron. The interior of several catacombs are decorated with
simply executed reliefs, grafitti, and drawings in a variety
of religious, secular, and pagan motifs. Over 250 epitaphs
were found, the majority in Greek.[1,3] The synagogue was
built on a slope of the hill about 130 m. above sealevel and
about 7 m. below the hill's summit. Southwest of the synagogue is a large two-storied basilica, Building B.[1]

Five building periods have been assigned to the history of
the site; the synagogue was built during period IIIA and
renovated during period IIIB (see below, no. 12).[1]

3. <u>Character and sections of the building as suggested by extant
and identifiable remains</u>.

STAGE I

The synagogue was constructed of large ashlars, without
bosses, well cut and laid in straight courses. There is also
evidence of reused material in its construction.[1]

TERRACE

Southeast: The terrace was reached by four broad stairs
ascending from street level; it is paved with large well-
dressed flagstone.

COURT
Southeast: It has been described as an inner court[1,5] or a "shrine."[6] The court was entered from the terrace through three broad doors in its south wall; two threshholds are in situ. Two conduits carried rainwater from the synagogue's roof to two rock-cut cisterns under the court's mosaic pavement. The "shrine" and two cisterns have been proposed as having some ritualistic function,[6] but there is no evidence to support this theory.[1] More likely the court simply provided communication between the terrace and main hall of the synagogue.

PLAN
A rectangular hall was divided by two longitudinal rows of columns (eight per row) into a central nave flanked by aisles.

ENTRANCES
On the southeast are three entrances, one large portal flanked by two smaller ones. On the southwest, a small door opens onto the side aisle.

PAVEMENT
The pavement is laid with marble slabs.

STAGE II:
This building was essentially the same, except that the central facade entrance is walled up (see no. 6).[1]

4. Measurements.[1,5,7]
Court and main hall: 35 x 15 m.
Main hall: 28 m. long.
Nave: 6.30 m. wide.
Bema: 5 m. long x 6.30 m. wide.
Terrace: 27 x 2.80 m.

5. Orientation.
The building's long axis is northwest-southeast. The facade is on the southeast facing Jerusalem.

6. Character and form: apse, niche, Torah Shrine, bema, chancel.
STAGE I
A raised platform (bema ?) was built against the northwest wall, the width of the nave and enclosed between walls that incorporated the two northernmost columns of the two colonnades. The platform is paved with flagstone.[5]
STAGE II
The central entrance (southeast) was walled in and a niche added in its place.[1]

7. <u>Auxiliary rooms/structures</u>.

The synagogue was built within a complex of buildings and courts.

Building B: A basilica (40 x 15 m.), built of large well-cut ashlars, had a paved court, cisterns and anteroom. It was divided into a central nave and two side aisles by two longitudinal rows of columns (five per row), and decorated with plastered and painted walls, marble revetments, and a mosaic pavement. The basilica has been dated to the second or third century.[1,4,5,8] By the first half of the fourth century, the basilica apparently was used as a large private dwelling, although its original function may have been to house the Beth-din, a rabbinical court.[8]

Southeast of the synagogue is a large room with benches along three of its walls; its rock-cut cellar passed below the synagogue's terrace. North of the synagogue is a large oven and reservoir; either part of a bath house or a glass factory.[1,4]

8. <u>Ornamentation</u>.

STAGE I

Fragments of an architrave were found that resemble those of catacomb 14.[7] Also uncovered were capitals and bases similar to those used for arched openings of catacomb 11 and 14.[7]

STAGE II

The interior walls of the synagogue were painted. Marble fragments with inscriptions and decorations were affixed to the walls, including part of a relief showing two trees, an unidentified animal, and a fish. A second fragment may be part of a zodiac.[5]

9. <u>Coins, ceramics, and other artifacts found within building complex</u>.

Nearly 100 lamps and lamp fragments, many Roman coins, pots and sherds, bronze and iron objects were reported found in the debris.[8]

STAGE I

Imitation <u>terra sigillata</u> ware was uncovered that was considered typical of pottery dated to the second half of the third century C.E.[8]

STAGE II

Fourth century lamps were found, as well as a coin hoard of close to 1200 copper coins, discovered in a burnt layer in

the basement of Building B. All the coins have been dated
to the period of Constantine I (306-337) and his son
Constantinius (337-361).[8]

10. Inscriptions.

Sixteen Greek and one Hebrew inscription were found in the
synagogue and in its adjoining buildings,[2] most in fragmentary condition. The following three Greek inscriptions
were carved on marble slabs found in a small room adjoining
the synagogue on the northwest side.

> Rabbi Samuel who arranged [the limbs of
> the dead] and of Judah who lays out the
> corpse.[2]

> Jacob from Caesarea, the head of the
> synagogue, of Pamphylia. Shalom.[2]

> . . . gos, son of Gaius dedicated
> [this] . . .[2]

11. Donors and patrons.

The synagogue apparently received support not only from local
Jews, but also from nonresidents who sought burial in the
town's famed necropolis (see inscription, no. 2).[A]

12. Date.

Two periods of the synagogue are postulated.[1,7]

STAGE I

Period IIIA comprehends the first half of third century to
the beginning of the fourth.

STAGE II

Period IIIB is the first half of the fourth century, ending
abruptly with the town's destruction in 352.

13. Bibliography.

1. Mazar (Maisler), Benjamin. Beth She'arim: Report on the
    Excavations during 1936-1940. "Catacombs 1-4."
    Vol. I. New Brunswick: Rutgers Univ. Press, 1973.

2. Schwabe, M., B. Lifshitz. Beth She'arim: The Greek
    Inscriptions. Vol. II. New Brunswick: Rutgers
    Univ. Press, 1974, pp. 189-198.

3. Avigad, Nahman. Beth She'arim: Catacombs 12-23. Vol. III.
    New Brunswick, Rutgers Univ. Press, 1976.

4. (Maisler). QDAP, 9 (1942), pp. 196-198.

5. (Maisler). QDAP, 10 (1944), pp. 212-215.

6. Goodenough, E. R. Jewish Symbols. Vol. I (1953),
    pp. 208-211.

7. Avigad, N. "Excavations at Beth She'arim." IEJ (1954),
    pp. 100 ff.

8. Mazar. IEJ, 6 (1956), p. 261.

9. Hüttenmeister, F. Antiken Synagogen. Vol. I, pp. 68-71.

JAPHIA

B:2, I-3

1. Name of site and map reference.
    Japhia, Yafia, Yāfā.
    1761.2327 (3.161)
    Plan 8.

2. Survey of site.
    The town lies on two ridges of a hill, about 3 km. southwest
    of Nazareth. Japhia's defenses were strengthened by Josephus
    to safeguard the important southern routes into Galilee; but
    the town was captured by Titus, after a fierce battle that
    saw many of the townfolk perish (Josephus, BJ II:573, III:
    289-306). Following the revolt, the town was rebuilt,
    regaining a sizeable Jewish community that remained until the
    fourth century.
    The synagogue, built on a hill north of town, had its founda-
    tion on a rock terrace that shows evidence of earlier quarrying.

3. Character and sections of the building as suggested by extant
    and identifiable remains.
    The eastern and western portions of the building have been
    destroyed; only a part of the southern wall is extant. It
    was built of dressed ashlar masonry, set on a bedding of
    rubble 15 cm. high. [1]
    PLAN
    A row of four column pedestals, aligned west to east, are
    2.90 m. north of the south wall. Evidence remains of a
    fifth pedestal east of pedestal four. Seven meters north of
    pedestal two are four large stones, embedded in a rock-cut
    trench running parallel to the southern row of pedestals,
    which the excavators assume are the foundations for the
    northern colonnade. [1]
    Two cisterns and a cavity found beneath the hall's pavement
    may be left from earlier quarrying; however, the opening of
    one cistern (between pedestals four and five) is above the
    pavement's level and is fairly well preserved.

4. Measurements.[1]

    Main hall: 15.70 m. wide; length unknown.

    Nave: 6.90 m. wide

    South aisle: 2.90 m. wide

5. Orientation.

Basing their opinion on the alignment of the pedestals and on the mosaic pavement (see below, no. 8), the excavators judge that the building faced east.[1] This placement is unusual for synagogues in this territory (see Beth She'arim B:2, I-2, and 'Ammudim B:2, I-1).[A] It has been postulated that the reasons for Japhia's unusual orientation was its location near the sea west of Jerusalem; therefore, the synagogue's east facade suggests the direction of Jerusalem although the city is actually southeast.[1] A second theory is that the synagogue was a broadhouse, with its broad southern wall the focal point (see: Khirbet Shema' B:1, I-3, and Husifah C:2, I-2).[7]

8. Ornamentation.

Two lintels found in secondary use in the village may have come from the synagogue:[1,2]

Lintel one is divided into three equal panels by a guilloche molding; the central panel contains a wreath tied with large fillets. The two flanking panels each contain an eagle with a small wreath held in its beak; the bodies are frontal, heads in profile and wings outspread.

Lintel two is decorated with a menorah flanked by rosettes. A Corinthian style capital has a carved lion's head projecting from one side of its abacaus; traces of effaced figures are on the other three sides.[6]

Mosaic pavement: Only a few fragments are preserved in the south aisle and the nave.[1]

South aisle: Squares, rectangles, and simple geometric patterns are surrounded by guilloche bands.[1,6]

Nave: A large panel, 4.10 m. square, is inscribed with a circle, 3.80 m. in diameter, within which is a second circle, 1.90 m. in diameter. In the space between the two circles were 12 small intersecting circles (no. 478); only two survive. One contains an image of an ox, the other the head of a horned animal, possibly a "buffalo."[1] Beside the image of the buffalo is set a fragmentary legend in Hebrew, "[Eph]raim," but the symbol of the tribe Ephraim is an ox; the buffalo is the symbol of the tribe of Manasseh. The circles either

contained symbols of the twelve tribes of Israel,[1] or a
zodiac similar to ones uncovered at Beth Alpha (B:4, I-1),
Hammat Tiberias B (B:3, I-4), Husifah (C:2, I-2), and Na'aran
(F:4, I-2).[4]

Between the 12 circles and the panel's frame are intertwined
acanthus leaves enclosing various animals. Dolphins are
shown between the interlaced circles and larger circle, in
triangular spaces. In a corner, usually reserved for the
seasons in the zodiac panels, is the image of a tiger. A
rectangular panel in the southwest corner of the nave contains
an image of an eagle with widespread wings, perched on two
pairs of volutes flanking the head of "Helios"[1] or
"Medusa."[4]

12. Date.

The pavement has been dated, because of its style, to the
late third or early fourth century.[1,8] The architectural
fragments found reused in the village are considered contemporary to those of the "early" Galilean synagogues.[6]
The joint use of sculpture and mosaic is unusual in synagogues; a second example occurs at Eshtemoa (E:4, I-2).
(See Table 11.)

13. Bibliography.

1. Sukenik, E. "The Ancient Synagogue at Yafa, near
       Nazareth." Rabinowitz Bulletin. Vol. II. (June,
       1951), pp. 6-24.

2. Vincent, L. H. "Ancient Synagogue at Yafa." RB, XXX
       (1921), 434-438.

3. Fitzgerald, G. M. "Remains of an Ancient Synagogue at
       Yafa in Galilee." PEFQS (1921), pp. 182-183.

4. Goodenough, E. R. Jewish Symbols. Vol. I. (1953),
       pp. 216-218. Vol. III, figs. 989-994.

5. Avi-Yonah, M. "Places of Worship in the Roman and
       Byzantine Periods." Antiquity and Survival, II
       (1957), 262-272.

6. Foerster, G. "On the Mosaic of the Japhia Synagogue."
       Yed., XXXI, 1-4 (1967), 218-224.

7. Idem. "The Synagogues at Masada and Herodion." JJA,
       3/4 (1977), 11.

8. Hüttenmeister, F. Antiken Synagogen. Vol. I, pp. 479-482.

GVAT HIRBET JEBATA
B:2, II-1

1. Name of site and map reference.
   Gvat Hirbet Jebata, Gabatha, Găbatā.
   1705.2311 (3.56)

2. Survey of site.
   The site is situated on a hill nine kilometers west-southwest
   of Nazareth. About 49 meters from the stone remains of a
   building, rock graves were found.[1] One of the building's
   stones appears to have been decorated with a five-branched
   menorah flanked by two objects, possibly a lulab and ethrog.
   A debased Ionic capital also was found in the debris.
   In the summer of 1974, Adam Druks of the Israel Department of
   Antiquities made a cut into the hill and discovered the outer
   wall of a public building. The wall measured 15 meters long
   with remains up to three meters high. The building has not
   been excavated.[3]
   It is unclear whether the stone remains reported earlier[1]
   belong to the public building Druks uncovered.[A] The evidence is too inconclusive to make an attribution.

12. Date.
    Schumacher dated the ruins to the Medieval period,[1] but the
    later discovery was dated to the period of Mishnah.[3]

13. Bibliography.

    1. Schumacher, G. "Felsengräber in Dshebāta." ZDPV, VIII
       (1885), pl. III, fig. 3, pp. 63 ff.

    2. Goodenough, E. Jewish Symbols, Vol. I, p. 222. Vol. III,
       fig. 582.

    3. HA 53 (January, 1975), p. 39.

    4. Hüttenmeister, F. Antiken Synagogen. Vol. I, pp. 137-138.

HORVAT AL-ISHĀQĪYA
B:2, II-2

1. Name of site and map reference.
   Horvat (Khirbet) al-Ishāqīya, H. as-Seh-Ishāq.
   1622.2326 (3.76)

2. Survey of site.
   At a site situated between Beth She'arim and Yoqna'am, the
   1881 Survey of Western Palestine reported the discovery of
   rows of columns, running east to west.[2]

10. Inscriptions.

In 1961, a column fragment carved with an incomplete Aramaic inscription was reported found.

> Judan bar Serida made this column
> with help . . . .[1]

12. Date.

The inscription has been dated to the third to fourth century.[1]

13. Bibliography.

1. Avigad, N. BIES, 31 (1967), pp. 211-213.

2. Conder, C., Kitchener, H. SWP I, p. 307.

3. HA 6 (1961), p. 1.

4. Hüttenmeister, F. Antiken Synagogen. Vol. I, p. 186.

HORVAT QOSHET
B:2, II-3

1. Name of site and map reference.

Horvat Qoshet, Khirbet Qoshet, Horvat Qasta.

1887.2373 (4.122)

2. Survey of site.

The site is located 14 km. southwest of Tiberias. A notice dated December 1921 in the Rockefeller archives reports that fragments of white mosaic pavement were accidentally uncovered at this site during the plowing of a field.[2] In 1969, fragments of a marble screen were found nearby,[1] but it is not known whether the screen came from the building with the mosaic pavement.[A]

8. Ornamentation.

The marble fragments are decorated with a menorah carved in high relief set against a background of inhabited acanthus scrolls in low relief. The menorah's base is considered to be somewhat similar to the bases of menorot depicted on the Arch of Titus, Dura-Europos synagogue frescoes, and mosaics in the Na'aran synagogue (F:4, I-2).[1] According to the proposed reconstruction, the menorah measures 60 cm. high by 75 cm. wide.[1] The fragments may be part of a chancel screen placed in front of the Torah Shrine.[1]

12. Date.

The screen has been dated to the fifth-sixth centuries.[1,3]

13. Bibliography.

1. Foerster, G. "Some Menorah Reliefs from Galilee." IEJ, XXIV, 3-4 (1974), 191 ff.

2. British Mandatory Government. Archives. Jerusalem: Rockefeller Museum.

3. Hüttenmeister, F. Antiken Synagogen, Vol. I, pp. 358-359.

I'BILLĪN
B:2, II-4

1. Name of site and map reference.
   I'billīn, 'Abellin, Ăvelim.
   168.247 (3.13)

2. Survey of site.
   I'billīn is the name of a valley and village in Galilee about 12 km. northwest of the city of Sepphoris. The ancient caravan route leading from Egypt to Damascus passed near the village, as did the Roman road connecting Ptolemais and Sepphoris.[3]

8. Ornamentation.
   In 1934, two lintels were discovered in secondary use in the village of I'billīn; they are conjectured to be part of a synagogue or Jewish tomb.[1] One lintel, now used as a step for the southern door into the village's Greek Orthodox Church, measures 65 cm. long by 55 cm. wide, and is decorated with a five-branched menorah and various geometrical patterns.

10. Inscriptions.
    The second lintel measures 1.15 cm. long by 40 cm. wide by 25 cm. thick and is broken in two places. An Aramaic inscription, set within a rectangular frame (26 x 18 cm.), is flanked by a six-pointed star (a hexagram) set within a circle. The inscription has been badly defaced, making translation difficult:

> Remembered be for good . . . / [son
> of . . .]/ who gained merit [by making
> (i.e., contributing)]/ this gate./ Amen.
> Shalom.[2]

The term "gate" may refer to the object donated, that is, the lintel.[4] This term is also found on synagogue lintels at Daburah (G:2, II-4) and er-Ramah (B:1, II-4), and on a plaque at 'Ammudim (B:2, I-1).[A]

11. Donors and patrons.
   The lintel apparently was donated by a synagogue member; similar donations were made at Daburah and er-Ramah, but not at 'Ammudim. (A)

12. Date.
   The date is unknown.

13. Bibliography.

1. British Mandatory Government. Archives. Jerusalem: Rockefeller Museum.

2. Braslawski, Y. "A Synagogue Inscription at 'Abellin." BJPES 2, 3-4 (1935), 10-13 (Heb.).

3. Klein, S. Galilee, Geography and History of Galilee from the Return from Babylonia to the Conclusion of the Talmud (Jerusalem, 1967), p. 59.

4. Hüttenmeister, F. "The Aramaic Inscription from the Synagogue at H. 'Ammudim." IEJ 28, 1-2 (1978), pp. 109-112.

5. Idem. Antiken Synagogen, Vol. I, pp. 27-29.

KAFR KANNĀ
B:2, II-5

1. Name of site and map reference.
   Kafr Kannā, Kefr Kenna, Kafr Cana.
   1822.2394 (4.82)

2. Survey of site.
   Kafr Kannā, located 6.5 km. northeast of Nazareth, is considered to be the traditional site of Jesus' first miracle (John 2:1-11); however, Khirbet Qana, further to the north, may be the more likely locale. (9) A mosaic pavement was uncovered under the town's modern Franciscan church. (8) Two lintels, now lost, were reported to have come from an earlier building on the site, conjectured to be a synagogue. (5,6) Additional ruins were discovered near Kafr Kannā at a site called Karm ar-Rās (1813.2397). Some of the architectural fragments are described as similar to the synagogue at Capernaum (B:3, I-1). (5)

10. Inscriptions.
   The Aramaic inscription set in the mosaic pavement under the Franciscan church originally contained at least two columns of text separated by a vertical line. Each column had four lines; only the right column is intact.

> Honored be the memory of Jose, son of
> Tanhum son of Bitah, and his sons, who
> made this mosaic; may it be a blessing
> for them. Amen.[3]

A fragmentary inscription is on the left:

> . . . this . . . blessing . . .[1]

The name "Yudan, son of Tanhum" is known from an Aramaic
inscription found at Sepphoris (B:2, II-6). "Yudan" may be
related (a brother ?) to "Jose" named in this inscription.[3]
Teblah has been translated either as "mosaic"[3] or as
derived from the Semitic root "Tebel," "to plunge into the
water, to bathe."[1] The latter translation suggests the
dedication refers to a baptistry connected to a synagogue,[3]
a questionable interpretation.[A]

11. Donors and patrons.

The pavement was a memorial for a father.[3] It has been
suggested it was associated with a "synagogue" built and used
by "Jewish-Christians."[5,7] See Nazareth (B:2, IIIB-2) and
David's Tomb (E:1, IIIA-1). This attribution has yet to be
proved.[A]

12. Date.

The inscription has been dated on the basis of epigraphic
evidence to the third to fourth centuries.[2]

13. Bibliography.

1. Clermont-Ganneau, C. "The Hebrew Mosaic of Kefr Kenna."
   PEFQS (1901), pp. 375-389.

2. Lidzbarski, M. Ephemeris für semitische Epigraphik.
   Vol. I. (1902), pp. 313-315.

3. Avi-Yonah, M. "Mosaic Pavements in Palestine." QDAP,
   II, (1932), 178-179.

4. Frey, J. B. CIJ, 987.

5. Bagatti, B. "Antichita de Khirbet Qana e Kefr Kenna."
   LA, XV, (1964-1965), 251-292.

6. Loffreda, S. "Scavi a Kafr Kanna." LA, XIX, (1969),
   329-348.

7. Ovadiah, A. Corpus, #92.

8. Hüttenmeister, F. Antiken Synagogen. Vol. I, pp. 246-249.

9. Meyers, Eric, James Strange, Dennis Groh. "The Meiron
   Excavation Project: Archaeological Survey in
   Galilee." BASOR (April 1978), 5.

SEPPHORIS

B:2, II-6

1. Name of site and map reference.
   Sepphoris, Saffūrīya, Sippori, Diocaesarea.
   1761.2399 (3.145)

2. Survey of site.
   The site is located 5 km. north-northwest of Nazareth. In
   the Roman and Byzantine periods, the city was the capital
   and administrative center for the territory of Sepphoris/
   Diocaesarea; until the middle of the fourth century, it was
   a center of Jewish law and life, the home of the Sanhedrin.

10. Inscriptions.
    A fragment of mosaic pavement was uncovered north of the
    exterior wall of the medieval church of St. Anne. The
    fragment bore a four-line Aramaic inscription (incomplete):[1]

> Honored be the memory of Rabbi Yudan,[2]
> the son of Tanhum, the son of . . . .

The name "Jose, son of Tanhum," occurs at Kafr Kannā (B:2,
II-5).

A carelessly executed four-line Greek inscription was carved
on a lintel in secondary use in the church of St. Anne:

> By Gelasios the scholastikos, the most
> illustrious comes, the son of Aetios
> the comes, by Judah the archisynagogos,
> by Sidonios the archisynagogos--these
> enclosures to the well-being [or in
> honor] of Janes [John] Aphros [or
> Aphrodisias] the archisynagogos of Tyre
> [or the Tyrian], the most illustrious.[3]

11. Donors and patrons.
    Yudan and Tanhum mentioned in the mosaic pavement and Judah
    carved on the lintel are common Hebrew names. The other names
    and titles (except rabbi) are Greek. Comes appears at Hammat
    Gadara (G:8, I-2) and Ramat Aviv (C:3, IIIA-1). Archisyna-
    gogos is inscribed on a stone found in Jerusalem (E:1, II-1).

12. Date.
    The Aramaic inscription has been dated to the fourth century,
    before 352 (the date of the uprising against Gallus).[1,2]
    The Greek inscription has been dated to the first half of the
    fourth century[5] or the first half of the fifth century.[3]

13. Bibliography.

1. Clermont-Ganneau, C. Répertoire d'Épigraphie Sémitique.
   Vol. 2. (1910), no. 862.

2. Avi-Yonah, M. JPOS, 15 (1934), 39 f.

3. Schwabe, M. In Festschrift für David Yellin. (1935),
    pp. 100-112.

4. Sukenik, E. The Ancient Synagogue of El-Hammeh. (1935),
    pp. 43 f.

5. Lifshitz, B. Donateurs, #74.

6. Hüttenmeister, F. Antiken Synagogen. Vol. I, pp. 400-418.

HORVAT OFRAT

B:2, IIIB-1

1. Name of site and map reference.
    Horvat (Khirbet) Ofrat, H. Tayyiba, Taiyebe, Khirbet et-
    Tayyibe.
    1690.2433 (3.116)

2. Survey of site.
    Situated 3.5 km. southeast of Safar'am, the site is on the
    road from Safar'am to Nazareth. H. Kitchener reported
    finding architectural remains that he considered similar to
    others found at sites of Galilean synagogues, including
    heart-shaped columns, but he excluded the site from his list
    of possible synagogues. [1,2]
    The site was visited in the summer of 1974, and additional
    column fragments and the foundation of a wall near a spring
    were found. [3] Presently no evidence indicates that the site
    was a synagogue, although the column fragments are reported
    to be like those found in other Galilean synagogues. [3]

12. Date.
    The ruins are dated to the third century. [3]

13. Bibliography.

    1. Kitchener, H. PEFQS. (1878), p. 124.

    2. Kitchener, H. and C. Conder. SWP I (1881), p. 321.

    3. Hüttenmeister, F. Antiken Synagogen. Vol. I, p. 348.

NAZARETH

B:2, IIIB-2

1. Name of site and map reference.
    Nazareth.
    178.234 (3.113)

2. Survey of site.

Nazareth lies on the steep slope of a hill on or near several important ancient trade routes. The caravan road from Damascus to Egypt crossed the Plain of Jezreel some 9.6 km. south of Nazareth, and a branch road to 'Akko (Ptolemais) passed about the same distance north of the village. A third route led south from Nazareth through Endor, and by way of Jericho to Jerusalem. According to the New Testament (Luke 2:51), the village is the traditional site of the Annunciation, and was Jesus' home until his expulsion.[4]

The town receives mention in the list of Priestly Courses uncovered at Caesarea (C:2, I-1). Constantine may have included Nazareth in the territory of Helenopolis, a city-territory he founded in honor of his mother.

3. Character and sections of the building as suggested by extant and identifiable remains.

B. Bagatti conducted excavations in Nazareth on behalf of the Franciscan Custody of the Holy Land; in his opinion, two synagogues existed in the town.[1]

1. "Synagogue of the Jewish-Christians": The remains of a "pre-Byzantine" building were reported under the modern Church of the Annunciation. Bagatti described the earlier building as having a "synagogal" form. Several of its architectural elements are considered similar to those found at the synagogue at Caesarea, particularly the capitals.[1]

2. "Synagogue of the Jews": Bagatti suggests that this synagogue was located northwest of the Franciscan monastery (1783.2343). Its existence is predicated on the discovery of several architectural elements preserved in the garden of the monastery.

11. Donors and patrons.

Bagatti has accepted as fact that the people of Nazareth were "Judeo-Christians," and that the two buildings he describes belonged to them.[1,4] At the present time, there is no scholarly consensus regarding the existence of Judeo-Christians, nor is there any accepted definition as to who these people were. For this reason, as well as the lack of Jewish motifs or inscriptions, these ruins are placed in the unaccepted category.[A]

12. Date.

The "Synagogue of Jewish-Christians" is dated to the third-fourth centuries;[1] the "Synagogue of the Jews" is dated to the second-third centuries.[1]

13. Bibliography.

1. Bagatti, B. Excavations in Nazareth I (1969), 114-116; 140-146; 169; 233 f.

2. Kopp, Clemens, "Beitrage zur Geschichte Nazareths." JPOS XVII (1938), 38 f.

3. Idem. JPOS XX (1946), 29-42.

4. Finegan, Jack. The Archaeology of the New Testament. Princeton, 1969, pp. 27-33.

5. Hüttenmeister, F. Antiken Synagogen. Vol. I, pp. 339-342.

SA'AV
B:2, IIIB-3

1. Name of site and map reference.
Ša'av, 'Sa'ab, Ša'ib, Cha'ab, Shaib, Saab.
173.255 (3.131)

2. Survey of site.
The site is sixteen km. east-southeast of 'Acre (Ptolemais). Architectural fragments, including a column pedestal and capital, were discovered reused in the modern mosque in the village; it was assumed they originally came from a synagogue in the vicinity;[1] but the evidence is too inconclusive to make an attribution.

13. Bibliography.

1. Guérin, V. DGHA. Vol. VI. (1880), 454 f.

2. Hüttenmeister, F. Antiken Synagogen. Vol. I, p. 379.

SIKNIN
B:2, IIIB-4

1. Name of site and map reference.
Siknin, Sahnīn, Sukhnîn.
177.252 (3.142)

2. Survey of site.
The site is 22 km. east-southeast of Ptolemais. The foundations of an ancient building including column bases found in

the village, were considered to have belonged to a synagogue. [1] Although literary evidence does refer to a synagogue in this village, the physical evidence is too scanty
to allow an attribution. [3,A]

13. Bibliography.

1. Guérin, V. DGHA. Vol. VI. (1880), pp. 469-471.

2. Hüttenmeister, F. Antiken Synagogen. Vol. I, pp. 393-396.

USHA
B:2, IIIB-5

1. Name of site and map reference.
    Usha, Hŭša, Ūša.
    1638.2444 (3.158)

2. Survey of site.
    Located 12 km. east of modern Haifa, the site is on the border
    with Ptolemais. The Sanhedrin, reestablished in Usha in 140
    C.E., were responsible for a set of regulations that became
    known as the "Enactments of Usha." Because of the Sanhedrin,
    a number of well-known talmudic sages resided in the vil-
    lage. [2] The ruins of a building found in the village,
    including several column bases and capitals were assumed to
    come from an ancient synagogue. [1]
    A recent survey of the area uncovered additional architectural
    fragments "that appear to have come from a synagogue." [3]
    Although literary evidence attests to the presence of the
    Sanhedrin in the city, and possibly to three synagogues, [4]
    the physical evidence is too inconclusive to make possible an
    attribution for the architectural fragments. [A]

13. Bibliography.

1. Guérin, V. DGHA. Vol. VI. (1880), pp. 415 f.

2. Mantel, H. Studies in the History of the Sanhedrin.
       Cambridge: Harvard Univ. Press, 1961, pp. 140-174.

3. HA, 21 (1967), 26.

4. Hüttenmeister, F. Antiken Synagogen. Vol. I, pp. 469-475.

Herod Antipas became the Tetrarch of Galilee and Peraea
following the death of his father, Herod the Great, in 4 B.C.E.
He founded the city of Tiberias in 18 C.E. and named it in honor
of Emperor Tiberius, who had just celebrated his sixtieth birth-
day and the twentieth anniversary of his holding the Tribunica
Potestas (Avi-Yonah, "The Foundation of Tiberias," IEJ, I, 3
(1950-1951), 167-169). Tiberias became the first city in Jewish
history to be endowed with the municipal framework of a Greek
polis (Ibid., 161). Following the first Jewish revolt (ended
70 C.E.), Galilee was divided into two regions: Tiberias in the
east, and Sepphoris in the west. Tiberias soon became the principal city on the Sea of Galilee, a status it has always main-
tained, as well as the religious center for Palestinian Jewry.

Four ruins in this city-territory have been validated as
synagogues--two are in the ancient city of Tiberias and two north
of the Sea of Galilee, at Capernaum and Chorozin. Arbela, 6 km.
northwest of the city of Tiberias, is similar in appearance to
Capernaum and Chorozin, but its archaeological evidence is too
inconclusive to make an attribution. Architectural fragments
bearing Jewish inscriptions and/or motifs have been found at three
other locations. One additional site, Migdal, has evidence of a
first century ruin tentatively identified as a synagogue.

The synagogues in Tiberias represent a typological spectrum
from the so-called "early" Galilean to the latest "Byzantine,"
and illustrate not only the stylistic variations, but the dating
difficulties associated with the study of Palestinian synagogue
art and architecture.

CAPERNAUM
B:3, I-1

1. Name of site and map reference.
   Capernaum, Kefar Nahum, Kapernaum, Kapharnaum, Tel Hum.
   2041.2541 (4.91)
   Plan 9
2. Survey of site.
   The ancient village of Capernaum is in the fertile Ginnesar
   Valley, on the northwest shore of the Sea of Galilee 5 km.

from the estuary of the Jordan River. During the Roman and
Byzantine periods, the town's economy was based on agriculture,
fisheries, and related industries. A prosperous hub of trade
and commerce, it was located on an important crossroad linking,
Galilee with Gaulanitis and Damascus.

The village receives prominent mention in the New Testament
as the center for Jesus' activities in the Galilee and as the
home of St. Peter.

The Capernaum Jews did not take an active role in the first
revolt, but did grant Josephus refuge to recover from wounds
suffered during a battle against the forces of Agrippa II
(Josephus, Vit. 403). The extent of their participation in
the second revolt is not known, although it has been suggested
that the town did suffer damages.[12] Capernaum was destroyed
in the seventh century and never rebuilt.[12]

Most of the houses in the city were built with native basalt.
The synagogue, and Byzantine octagon church, dedicated to
St. Peter, were the only structures made of beautifully dressed
white limestone ashlars. The site was surveyed by E.
Robinson in 1857, and partially cleared by C. Wilson in
1866;[7] in 1894, it became the property of the Franciscan
Custody of the Holy Land, who granted permission to Kohl and
Watzinger to clear the synagogue.[1] Additional excavations
were undertaken by the Franciscans, but were interrupted by
World War I and did not resume until 1921.[8] New excavations were begun in 1968 and are still in progress.[2-6] The
synagogue stood on a high artificial platform built on top of
walls, floors, and water channels dated to the Late Hellenistic
period (Franciscan chronology: 200-63 B.C.E.).[2,12]

3. Character and sections of the building as suggested by extant
    and identifiable remains.

The synagogue was constructed of white limestone ashlars set
without mortar. The exterior walls were finished, the interior
left rough to receive plaster.[7] The building's foundation
was built of basalt.[2]

TERRACE

Lateral stairways on the southeast and southwest corners of
the synagogue ascend from street level to a terrace that runs
the full length of the facade and adjoining court. The
terrace was in the form of a narrow open porch paved with
smooth slabs of stone. A rough strip along the outer edge
may have been for a railing.

COURT

A trapezoidal court adjoins the synagogue's east wall.

Court entrances:

On the south was a large central door, with a smaller one to its west. The east side held three evenly spaced doors. On the north were three unevenly spaced doors, and on the west, a single door opens onto the synagogue's west aisle.

Colonnades along the north, east, and south of the court form a covered portico. The unfluted columns, with Attic-type bases, rest on pedestals placed on stylobates. The southwest column (and possibly the northwest) abut the synagogue wall. The southeast and northeast pedestals had the inner angles of their bodies cut away to form two half pedestals; the bases and column shafts have heart-shaped cross-sections.

PAVEMENT

The floor is constructed of flagstone.

PLAN

Two longitudinal rows of columns (seven columns each) and a north transverse colonnade (two columns) divide the main hall into a central nave surrounded on three sides by aisles. The unfluted columns, with Attic-type bases, rest on pedestals placed on stylobates. The northeast and northwest corner pedestals, bases, and columns are similar to some in the courtyard.

ENTRANCES

On the south, a large central door is flanked by two smaller ones. A single door opens on the east from the aisle into the courtyard. The northwest side has a door in the north wall of the west aisle that opens onto an adjoining annex (see no. 7).

BENCHES

Two tiers of benches are coterminous with the east and west walls of the main hall. A rounded fragment of an upper bench found in situ in the southwest corner of the hall is decorated with a relief of a head with disheveled hair. It may be the "Chair of Moses" used by the synagogue elder[11] (see Chorozin [B:3, I-2]).

WINDOWS

A large arched window over the central entrance had a smaller double window above it. Small windows were above the facade's side entrances.

ROOF

Fragments of flat terracotta tiles and semi-cylindrical riders were found in the debris. [2,12]

PAVEMENT

The pavement was made of flagstone.

GALLERY

The existence of a gallery has been postulated on the basis of small columns, capitals, and other architectural fragments found in the interior. [1,9,12] The synagogue's foundations, however, appear too weak to support an upper floor. [2,3]

4. Measurements.
Main hall: 24.4 x 18.65 m. [9,12]
East and west aisles: 3.56 m. wide. [9]
North aisle: 2.27 m. wide. [9]
Nave: 8.38 m. wide. [9]
Terrace: 18.65 x 3.30 m. [9,12]
Court: North: 13.34 m. wide; south: 11.26 m. wide; 20.4 m. long. [9]
Annex: 5.45 x 5.45 m. sq. [12]

5. Orientation.
The long axis of the building is north-south, the facade is on the south facing Jerusalem.

6. Character and form: apse, niche, Torah Shrine, bema, chancel.
Fragments of painted stucco, found inside the hall's main entrance, were thought to be part of a screen (theba) that blocked the central door. [1,8] Additional fragments of painted stucco were found in the street south of the synagogue's southwest corner. [3] Two platforms were recently uncovered on the interior, flanking the central door. The basalt foundation of the west platform forms a roughly 2.7 m. square installation; the east foundation has been disturbed. The date of the platforms' installation is unknown, but may antedate the synagogue pavement. [3] They may have supported aediculae similar to the one proposed for Meron (B:1, I-4). [18]

7. Auxiliary rooms/structures.
The northwest annex contains an adjoining room built of basalt on a layer of fill; it can be entered either through the door at the end of the north aisle or by way of an external double staircase built against its west and east walls. [12]

8. Ornamentation.
The synagogue was decorated with numerous reliefs carved with sharply cut surfaces that produce a lively, coloristic

effect. The figurative motifs show evidence of defacement.
Facade: [11]

1. The lower story is divided by four pilasters into a wide
   middle and two narrower lateral fields. The pilasters
   were united by a simple entablature, and a large arched
   window rose from the two medial pilasters. The keystone
   of the window arch is decorated with an acanthus wreath
   tied with a Hercules knot and encloses a scallop shell.
   The lower frieze has traces of two eagles holding a
   Hercules knot in their beaks.

2. On the upper story, the windows were framed by double
   twisted columns capped with Corinthian style capitals
   supporting an arcuated lintel and a pediment decorated
   with a scallop shell. A frieze above the windows echoed
   the arch over the large central window; it is decorated
   with acanthus leaves and lions, now defaced. The cornice
   has egg and dart moldings and dentils.

3. Entrances: The well-cut moldings of the doors are
   derived from classical models (see Kefar Bar'am A, B:1,
   I-2). The lintel of the central door is decorated with
   a mutilated relief of an eagle with outspread wings. The
   frieze above is carved from the same stone and is
   decorated with six genii, now defaced, carrying aloft
   five garlands above an eagle, also defaced. Above the
   frieze was a cyma supported on two consoles; the fronts
   of the consoles are decorated with date palms. [1]
   The side doors are framed by pilasters resting on Attic-
   type bases and surmounted by decorated lintels. Both
   lintels are badly mutilated.

4. The walls are divided into fields by pilasters, with
   Attic-type bases standing on plinths and crowned with
   simple capitals, joined by an undecorated entablature.
Interior: [1]

1. Columns: The unfluted columns have Attic-type bases and
   are crowned with Corinthian style capitals. They stand
   on high pedestals.

2. The walls are divided into fields by pilasters with Attic-
   type bases and Corinthian style capitals. A frieze ran
   above the pilasters; only the north wall contained
   figurative motifs.

3. The north frieze [1,11] consists of two eagles, their backs
   to one another and the tips of their tails almost touching,

hold two ends of a garland in their beaks. To their right is a harnessed "sea-goat" (Capricorn ?). A wheeled carriage, possibly a portable Torah Shrine, is shown in perspective;[1,11] on its front are double-winged doors surmounted by a scallop shell gable. The side of the carriage is similar to a pentastyle Ionic temple with a grooved convex roof. Only two of the four carriage wheels are shown.

A stone decorated with a five-branched menorah crowned with a shell was found west of the synagogue.[11] Its position in the building is uncertain. The menorah originally may have had seven branches; the outermost ones were possibly destroyed when the stone was cut for reuse.

COURT

1. Entrance: The lintel of the south door is decorated with a pedimented Torah Shrine; its double-winged doors are divided into three panels.[1,11]

2. Capitals: One capital differs from the others:[1] its acanthus leaves are carved only superficially and lack any connection with their stalks and in place of the standard middle caliculi is a six-pointed star. A second capital has a different symbol on each of its four faces: olive branch, pomegranate, wreath, and seven-branched menorah flanked by a shofar and incense shovel.[11]

3. Lions:[12] The hindquarters of two three-dimensional lions were found outside the synagogue. They may have been used either as acroteria on the building's roof[9] or may have flanked a Torah Shrine or screen.[1]

9. <u>Coins, ceramics, and other artifacts found within building complex.</u>

Three limestone lavers were discovered that are in the form of hollow, inverted frustums measuring about 70 cm. high, 66 and 33 cm. top and bottom, respectively, with a capacity of 60 liters.[12]

In the northwest annex, glass and ceramic jars and fragments littered the interior. The coin, glass and ceramic evidence has not yet been fully published; the last report was dated 1970.[2] Thousands of copper coins dated to the fourth and fifth centuries were uncovered in the levels of artificial fill of the platforms, sealed by thick layers of mortar.

Coins were also reported found under the court's pavement and
the hall's stylobates. Beneath this stratum were coins and
ceramics dated from the Hellenistic period to the Middle
Roman period (Franciscan chronology: 135-254 C.E.). (See
no. 12 for implications of numismatic evidence on the synagogue's dating.)

10. Inscriptions.

A Greek inscription carved on a column reads:

> Herod, son of Mo[ni]/ mos and Justos/
> his son, together with their/ children
> --erec--/ ted/ this column.[9]

An Aramaic inscription was carved on a second column:

> Halphai, son of Zebedee, son of Johanan/
> made this column/ May blessing be his.[9]

11. Donors or patrons.

The terms "erected" and "made" are interpreted to refer to
donations, not the fabrication of the column.[9,11] The
wording of the Greek inscription may indicate that the
building was financed wholly or partly by public subscrip-
tion.[12] The Aramaic inscription is poorly done, suggesting
it dates to a later period, when the Jewish community may
have suffered a financial reversal.[12]

12. Date.

The early dates proposed by Kohl and Watzinger[1] were
initially accepted by many scholars,[9,11,12,13,14,16] but
the reported discovery of thousands of coins in the synagogue's
fill and mortar, particularly directly beneath the stylobates,
has resulted in the proposal of a new, controversial
chronology.[2,3,13,15,16,17] The following three chronologies
have been proposed:

Kohl and Watzinger:[1]

    Built: late second century.

    Destroyed: by the early fourth century.

Foerster:[13]

    Built: second or third century.

    Repaired or renovated: fourth century.

    Destroyed: not stated.

Corbo and Loffreda:[2,3,15]

    200-63 B.C.E.: walls, floors, and water channels
                constructed.

    300-450 C.E.: artificial platform erected over the
                above installations.

350-400 C.E.:   construction of synagogue begins.

450 C.E.:   synagogue completed.

638-750 C.E.:   synagogue destroyed.

The available evidence confirms Corbo and Loffreda's chronology,[18,A] but it has been rightfully suggested that the basalt-stone structures under the synagogue must be excavated to prove that these structures date to the fourth century before sceptics will be convinced of the synagogue's late date.[19]

13. Bibliography.

1. Kohl, Watzinger, pp. 14-21.

2. Corbo, V., S. Loffreda, A. Spijkerman. La sinagoga di Cafarnao'dopo gli scavi del 1969. Collectio Minor n. 9. Jerusalem: Franciscan Press, 1970.

3. Corbo, Virgilio. Cafarnao I: Gli Edifici della Citta. Jerusalem: Franciscan Press, 1975.

4. Loffreda, Stanislao. Cafarnao II: La Ceramica. Jerusalem: Franciscan Press, 1974.

5. Spijkerman, Augusto. Cafarnao III: Catalogo delle Monete della Citta. Jerusalem: Franciscan Press, 1975.

6. Testa, Emmanuele. Cafarnao IV: Graffiti della Casa de S. Pietro. Jerusalem: Franciscan Press, 1972.

7. Wilson, C. W. PEFQS, I (1869), 37-41.

8. Orfali, G. Capharnaum et ses Ruins, 1905-1921. Paris: August Picard, 1922.

9. Sukenik, E. Ancient Synagogues, pp. 7-21, 52 f.

10. Frey, J. B. CIJ. #982-983.

11. Goodenough, E. R. Jewish Symbols. Vol. I. (1953), pp. 189-192; Vol. III, figs. 452, 458-479.

12. Sapir, D., D. Ne'eman. Caparnaum. Tel Aviv: Historical Sites Library, 1967.

13. Foerster, G. "Notes on Recent Excavations at Capernaum." IEJ, 21 (1971), 207 ff.

14. Idem. "Galilean Synagogues and Their Relationship to Hellenistic and Roman Art and Architecture." Diss. Hebrew University, 1972, ch. III.

15. Loffreda, S. "The Late Chronology of the Synagogue at Capernaum." IEJ, 23 (1973), 37-42.

16. Avi-Yonah, M. "Editor's Note." IEJ, 23 (1973), 43-35.

17. Loffreda, S. "A Reply to the Editor." IEJ, 23 (1973), 184.

18. Strange, J. F. "The Capernaum and Herodium Publications."
    BASOR, 225 (April, 1977), 65-75.

19. Hüttenmeister, F. Antiken Synagogen. Vol. I, pp. 260-269.

CHOROZIN

B:3, I-2

1. Name of site and map reference.
   Chorozin, Chorozain, Korazin, H. Karaza, Khirbet Karazeh.
   2031.2575 (4.96)
   Plan 10

2. Survey of site.
   Chorozain is in a mountainous area 4 km. north of Capernaum.
   The village was built on the north, south, and east slopes of
   a low hill, about 46-61 m. above sea level. To the north of
   the village is the ancient road that crossed the Jordan River
   near its entry into the Sea of Galilee. Chorozain, Bethsaida,
   and Capernaum receive mention in the New Testament (Matt.
   11:21; Luke 10:13) as villages reprimanded by Jesus for
   failing to accept his teachings. The Talmud mentions the
   village in regard to the 'Omer offering and Shavuot pilgrimages
   to Jerusalem (BT Men. 85a, 85b). Eusebius describes the
   village as being in ruins (Onom. 174:23).[11]
   Charles Wilson visited the ruins in 1869,[7] and reported the
   discovery of a synagogue. The synagogue was partially cleared
   by Kohl and Watzinger in 1905,[1] and completely cleared in
   1926 by N. Makhouly and J. Ory,[2] who, in addition, reported
   finding the ruins of a second colonnaded building about 200 m.
   west of the synagogue; the building is no longer extant. Its
   disposition was described in their report as similar to that
   of the synagogue: Two longitudinal rows of columns (three
   columns per row) were joined on the north by a third colonnade
   of one column, to divide the hall into a central nave surrounded on three sides by aisles; the main entrance was on the
   east. The interior of the building had up to five tiers of
   benches along three of its walls.[2] It has been suggested
   recently that the building may have been a first-century
   synagogue,[15] but this is disputed.[20] The Israel Department of Antiquities and Museums carried out further excavations
   of the village under the direction of Z. Yeivin;[3,4,5] his
   report postulates that the village was built after the second
   Jewish revolt and expanded further in the late second and

third centuries. It may have been partially destroyed during
riots following the death of Julian the Apostate (363 C.E.),
but city life resumed in the fifth century and continued until
the seventh or eighth century, when the village was abandoned
(see no. 12).

Chorozain was built on a series of terraces, the most important
buildings on the top most level,[3] including the synagogue,
which was built 61 m. above sea level, and surrounded by a
block of buildings. The town's main north-south street passed
along the synagogue's east wall, and a second street along its
north.

3. Character and sections of the building as suggested by extant
and identifiable remains.

The synagogue was mainly built with local basalt ashlars set
without mortar, but the western wall was built of roughly cut
stones laid in mortar. The interior walls bear traces of
plaster.[7]

TERRACE

A stairway on the synagogue's south, and a possible one on
the east, ascend from street level to a terrace that runs the
full length of the building's facade.

COURT

Adjoining the synagogue's west wall was a court, almost
rectangular in shape, that narrows toward the south. A small
room at the north end of the court can be entered only from
the synagogue (see no. 7).

PLAN

Two longitudinal rows of columns (five per row) and a north
transverse colonnade of two columns, divide the main hall into
a central nave surrounded on three sides by aisles. Monolithic columns, with Attic-type bases, rest on square pedestals
set on stylobates. The column base and pedestal are cut from
one stone block. The corner pedestals had the inner angles of
their bodies cut away to form two half pedestals, and the
bases and column shafts have heart-shaped cross-sections.

ENTRANCES

The south side has a large central portal flanked by two
smaller ones. On the northwest, a door leads into an annex
(see no. 7).

BENCHES

Two tiered benches are coterminous with the north, east, and
west walls. A large boulder interrupts the bench in the

northwest corner. A "Chair of Moses"[10] was found about 3 m. north of the southeast corner of the hall (see no. 8).

WINDOWS

A large arched window has been postulated over the central entrance; additional windows are possible over the side entrances.

PAVEMENT

The pavement is constructed of basalt slabs.

4. Measurements.

Main hall: 22.71 x 14.94 m. [7]
            20.00 x 13.00 m. [8]
            22.80 x 16.70 m. [5]

Nave: 6.60 m. wide [5]

East and west aisles: 3.20 m. wide [8]

North aisle: 3.50 m. wide [8]
             3.07 m. wide [1]

Terrace: Up to 9.5 m. wide [5]

Court: Widest point on north: 5 m. [5]

5. Orientation.

The long axis of the building is north-south; the facade is on the south facing Jerusalem.

7. Auxiliary rooms/structures.

The northwest annex is entered only through the hall. Several steps were preserved between the annex and the courtyard wall; they may have formed part of a staircase that led to a gallery. [5] A large building east of the synagogue had a series of rooms adjoining the synagogue's wall. [5]

A second building bordered the northern portion of the square in front of the synagogue and consisted of a series of rooms and three underground chambers, one of which may have been a miqvah. [5]

8. Ornamentation.

The synagogue was decorated with relief carvings executed by several different artisans. The style is cruder than that of the decorations at nearby Capernaum (B:3, I-1). [10] There is some evidence of defacement of figurative motifs.

Facade: [10]

1. On the lower story, the three doors were framed by pilasters; two additional pilasters were at the building's corners.

2. On the upper story, three elaborately carved conches may have decorated windows located above the three facade entrances.

3. The cornice of the pediment had two horizontal platforms on which three-dimensional lions may have stood. Below the cornice is a frieze of lions amid acanthus leaves. The pediment is crowned with an eagle, now defaced.

4. Entrances: The lintel of the large central door is plain; its cornice was supported by two consoles. One side door's lintel is decorated with an inhabited vine scroll.

Interior: [10]

1. The northern columns are diapered in a pattern of rosettes, lozenges, and circles. The capitals are described as "quasi-Ionic." [2]

2. The walls were divided into fields by pilasters with Attic-type bases and Corinthian style capitals. A frieze that ran along a part of a wall appears to have been decorated with four vintage scenes, possibly Dionysiac: [10]

> A man, holding a staff in right hand, grasps a cluster of grapes in his left hand.
> A man, with a woman to his right, holds a bunch of grapes; other grapes hang between them.
> Two men tread grapes in a wine press.
> A man reaches for a bunch of grapes hanging between him and a seated woman to his right.

Additional fragments were decorated with various motifs: a "Medusa" (Helios ?) head, and an acanthus wreath with an Ionic aedicula (Torah Shrine ?) in the center. [10] Other fragments of the frieze contain images of a galloping centaur, a lion attacking a centaur, a "lioness"? suckling her young, a lion devouring its prey, and fragments of a menorah. [10] Another fragment of stone is carved with what appears to be branches of a menorah.

3. A "Chair of Moses," carved from a single block of basalt, [10] measures 56 cm. high by 73 cm. broad, and a maximum thickness of 56.5 cm. in the seat. The support is ornamented with a rosette.

4. A headless three-dimensional lion, and a pair of paws of a second, were found in the southern part of the hall. [10]

9. <u>Coins, ceramics, and other artifacts found within building complex.</u>

Four groups of pottery have been identified: [5]

> 1. Early: Lamps of late third century B.C.E.
> 2. 4th-5th C.: "Byzantine types."
> 3. 7th-8th C.: "Early Arab ware."
> 4. Middle Ages: Glazed ware.

Over one thousand coins were found in two hoards.[6] The
first group was uncovered across the street and northeast of
the synagogue (locus 52 on plan). The earliest coin is
Hadrian, struck in 134 C.E.; the latest, Dowager Empress
Helene, was struck in ca. 340 C.E. Over 90% of the coins are
dated between 290 and 340 C.E. The majority are from
Sepphoris, Hippos, Caesarea, and Tyre. The second group are
found under the synagogue's threshold. The majority date
from ca. 390 C.E. through the fifth century.

10. Inscriptions.

A four-line Aramaic inscription is carved on the front of the
"Chair of Moses" (no. 8). The translation is uncertain.

> Remembered be for good Judan b. Ishmael/
> who made this stoa [?]/ and its steps.
> For his work/ may he have a share with
> the righteous.[8]

"Stoa" may refer to the entire synagogue.[8] Lines 2 and 3
are disputed: " . . . made this stoa and its staircase from
his property. . . ."[18]
Another translation reads: " . . . made this portico and its
staircase. . . ." Portico refers to the synagogue's
terrace.[16]

11. Donors or patrons.

Judan b. Ishmael, a major donor to the synagogue, was honored
by having his generous contribution recorded on the synagogue's seat of honor. It has been suggested he was the first
"elder" given the privilege to sit in the coveted "Chair of
Moses."[8]

12. Date.

Eusebius, writing in the mid-fourth century, describes the
city in ruins; this has led to the suggestion that the synagogue was built after his visit.[13] This theory has been
disputed, however, and the following chronology proposed:[3]

> 2nd-4th C.: Building and first occupation of synagogue.
> 5th-6th C.: Synagogue rebuilt following its partial
> destruction in the mid-fourth C.

The early dates conform to Kohl and Watzinger's chronology of
Galilean synagogues[1] (Kefar Bar'am A, B:1, I-2), but recent
excavations at Capernaum (B:3, I-1) and elsewhere in Galilee
have placed these dates in doubt.[A]

13. Bibliography.

1. Kohl, Watzinger, pp. 41-53.

2. British Mandatory Government. Archives. Jerusalem:
   Rockefeller Museum.

3. Yeivin, Ze'ev. "The Synagogue at Chorazain." In All the
   Land of Naphtali. Jerusalem: Israel Exploration
   Society, 1967, pp. 135-138.

4. Idem. "Carved Menorahs at Chorazin." Qad., II (1969),
   98 ff.

5. Idem. "Excavations at Khorazin." EI, XI (1973), 158-162.

6. Meshorer, Y. "Coins from the Excavation at Khorazin,"
   EI, XI (1973), 158-162.

7. Wilson, C. PEFQS, (1869), pp. 37 ff.

8. Sukenik, E. Ancient Synagogues, pp. 21-24, 60.

9. Frey, J. B. CIJ. #981.

10. Goodenough, E. R. Jewish Symbols. Vol. I. 1953,
    pp. 193-199; Vol. III, figs. 486-502, 544.

11. Avi-Yonah, M. Oriental Art in Roman Palestine, pp. 34-36.

12. Finegan, Jack. The Archaeology of the New Testament.
    Princeton: Princeton Univ. Press, 1969, pp. 56-58.

13. Loffreda, S. "The Late Chronology of the Synagogue of
    Capernaum." IEJ, XXIII (1973), 37.

14. Kloetzli, Godfrey. "Coins from Chorazin." LA, 24 (1974)
    359-369.

15. Yeivin, Ze'ev. Personal interview. July, 1975; May, 1977.

16. Avigad, Nahum. EAEh. 1975 ed.

17. Foerster, G. "The Synagogues at Masada and Herodion."
    JJA, 3/4 (1977), 8-9.

18. Naveh, Joseph. Personal interview. May, 1977.

19. Hüttenmeister, F. Antiken Synagogen. Vol. I., pp. 275-281.

20. Chiat, Marilyn. "First Century Synagogues: Methodological
    problems." Ancient Synagogues: Current Stage of
    Research. Ed. by Joseph Gutmann. Brown Judaic
    Studies 22. Chico: Scholars Press, 1981, pp. 49-60.

HAMMAT TIBERIAS A

B:3, I-3

1. Name of site and map reference.
   Hammat Tiberias, al-Hamma, el-Hammeh, el-Hammam.
   2015.2418 (4.65)
   Plan 11

2. Survey of site.
   The ancient site of Tiberias lies less than a meter above the
   level of the Sea of Galilee, ca. 210 m. below sea level. It
   was built on a terrace of alluvial soil, lake sediment, and
   layers of basalt; the last-named was used for construction.[1]
   According to the Talmudim, Tiberias had thirteen synagogues,
   including those of the Babylonians and Tarsians, and a special
   one for the city's boule (Avi-Yonah, IEJ 1 (1951), 160 ff.).
   Tombs traditionally assigned to Talmudic sages Johanan ben
   Zakkai, Meir Ba'al ha-Nes, Akiba, Ammi, and Assi are in the
   cemetery north of the city.
   Synagogue A is located on the shore of the Sea of Galilee,
   about 500 m. north of the city's ancient wall. It was
   excavated in 1921 by N. Slouschz on behalf of the Palestine
   Exploration Society.[1]

3. Character and sections of the building as suggested by extant
   and identifiable remains.
   Evidence indicates the synagogue underwent three distinct
   building stages.[4,6]
   STAGE I
   PLAN
   A nearly square basilica was divided into a central nave and
   flanking aisles by two longitudinal rows of columns (five
   columns each). The basalt columns are not directly opposite
   one another; they are on pedestals that rest on a stylobate;
   the western stylobate is narrower than its eastern counterpart.
   ENTRANCES
   Possibly in the southern wall, their number is unknown.[4,6]
   PAVEMENT
   The pavement is made of basalt flagstone.
   STAGE II
   PLAN
   The interior arrangement remains essentially unchanged. A
   forecourt and narthex adjacent to the east wall may have been
   added at this time.[4,6]

ENTRANCES

The southern (?) doors were closed and two[1,2] or three[6] entrances opened in the north wall. An additional entrance in the southern corner of the east wall opened onto the narthex.

BENCHES

A step or bench ran the entire length down the center of the west aisle.

PAVEMENT

The pavement is mosaic.[3]

STAGE III

PLAN

The northern entrances were blocked and new ones opened in the west wall.[4]

PAVEMENT

Two successive layers of marble slabs, removed from an earlier structure in the vicinity of the synagogue, were used as pavement.

4. Measurements.[1,8]

Main hall: 12 x 12 m.

East court: ca. 12 x 8 m. wide.

5. Orientation.

The building is aligned north-south. Initially the facade (south) was toward Jerusalem; when the southern doors were closed, niches were added in their place making them the focal point.[1,2,4]

6. Character and form: apse, niche, Torah Shrine, bema, chancel.

STAGE II

The southern entrances were converted into "niches" or "recesses." The largest, the central niche, was almost as wide as the nave. A transverse colonnade of four small columns separated the niche from the nave. Fragments of a marble chancel screen were uncovered in this area. Two other niches were cut in the south end of the east aisle; a "Chair of Moses" was in situ in the larger of the two (see no. 8).[1,2]

7. Auxiliary rooms/structures.

STAGE II

A narthex and court were added adjacent to the hall's east wall.[6] A water canal runs along the exterior of the building and enters into the west aisle.[1,2] The water system may be related to baths initially planned for the site.[8]

8. Ornamentation.
   STAGE III
   1. A small Corinthian style capital possibly crowned one of the transverse colonnade's columns.[1] It is decorated with a seven-branched menorah on three of its faces.[12]
   2. A capital with a cross in place of the menorah was found near one of the entrances. (Vincent dates this capital to the fourth-fifth centuries.)[9]
   3. Fragments of a marble chancel screen include a small marble column crowned by a lotus capital,[12] a small square pillar with a "crown-shaped" capital, an oblong slab decorated with a superficially incised seven-branched menorah flanked by a shofar,[12] a marble slab decorated with a vine scroll issuing from an amphora,[12] and a marble fragment decorated with a rich floral scroll bearing pomegranates and grapes.[12]
   4. A stone seven-branched menorah found near an entrance.[12] It is carved from a single block of limestone measuring 60 cm. wide by 46 cm. high by 13 cm. thick. On its top are seven hollowed out grooves, probably to hold earthen oil lamps. The menorah may have been attached to a wall, as its reverse side is unfinished.
   5. A "Chair of Moses" measures 94 cm. high by 60 cm. broad. It is carved out of a single block of white limestone; its back is rounded.[12]

9. Coins, ceramics, and other artifacts found within building complex.
   A series of trial pits dug through the narthex pavement and under the west side of the basilica revealed numismatic and ceramic material that has been used to date the building sequences. Much of this material has not yet been reported in publications.[4,5,6]

12. Date.[1-6]
    Stage I: Synagogue built ca. 250 C.E.
    Stage II: Main period of occupation 4th-5th centuries.
    Stage III: Building in use (as a synagogue ?) until the 10-11th centuries.

13. Bibliography.

   1. Slouschz, N. "Concerning the Excavations and/or the Synagogue at Hamat-Tiberias." JJPES, I (1921), 5-36.

   2. Idem. "Synagogue at Hamat-Tiberias." JJPES, I, 2 (1925), 49-51.

3. Avi-Yonah, Michael. "Mosaic Pavements in Palestine."
    QDAP, 2 (1933) 158, #85.

4. Oren, Eliezer D. "Early Islamic Material from Ganei-
    Hamat (Tiberias)." Archaeology, 24 (June, 1971),
    274-277.

5. Idem. "Ganei-Hamat (Tibériade)." RB 3 (July, 1971),
    435-437.

6. Idem. "Tiberias." IEJ, 21 (1971), 235.

7. Mann, Jacob. The Jews in Egypt and in Palestine under
    the Fatamid Caliphs. 2 vols. London: Oxford Uni-
    versity Press, 1920.

8. Vincent, L. "Hamat-Tiberias." RB, XXX (1921), 438-441.

9. Idem. "Les Fouilles Juives d'el-Hammat, A Tibériade."
    RB, XXXI (1922) 415-422.

10. Sukenik, E. The Ancient Synagogue of el-Hammeh, pp. 60-61.

11. Idem. Ancient Synagogues, pp. 58-59.

12. Goodenough, E. R. Jewish Symbols. Vol. I, 1952,
    pp. 214-216; Vol. III, figs. 562-568.

13. Hüttenmeister, F. Antiken Synagogen. Vol. I, pp. 159-163.

HAMMAT TIBERIAS B
B:3, I-4

1. Name of site and map reference.
    Hammat Tiberias, al-Hamma, el-Hammeh, el-Hammam.
    2018.2414 (4.66)
    Plan 12.

2. Survey of site.
    The synagogue, located about 1.5 km. south of modern Tiberias,
    is adjacent to the southern wall surrounding the ancient city.
    It is situated on a terrace above the famed hot springs and
    baths near the shore of the Sea of Galilee.
    The synagogue was discovered and excavated in 1961 and 1962
    by M. Dothan, on behalf of the Israel Department of Anti-
    quities and Museums. No final report has been published.

3. Character and sections of the building as suggested by extant
    and identifiable remains.
    The building underwent four stages of construction.[6]
    STAGE I
    The ruins suggest a public building with rooms around a
    central court.

STAGE II

This stage has not been cleared.

STAGE III

Stage III consists of two phases.

PLAN

In the first phase, a basilica, possibly a broadhouse, was separated by colonnades of three columns each, into a nave flanked on the east by two aisles and on the west by one.

ENTRANCES

The main entrance is unknown; a door led into the basilica from a narrow hall to the southeast.

PAVEMENT

It is possibly paved with mosaics.[1]

During the second phase, the main hall retained essentially the same form, but the narrow hall to the southeast was closed and divided into compartments (see no. 6).

PAVEMENT

The pavement was mosaic (see no. 3).

STAGE IV

A much larger synagogue was built above older one; it may have undergone two to three phases of development.[1]

COURT

An inner court was added adjacent to the west wall; part of it may have been roofed. It was paved with basalt slabs.

PLAN

The main hall was divided by two longitudinal rows of columns, joined on the north by a transverse colonnade, into a central nave surrounded on three sides by aisles. Only the stylobates of the colonnades survive.

ENTRANCES

On the west, three entrances opened from the court. On the northeast a door opens into a "hall" along the basilica's north wall. Several other doors open into the main hall from adjacent chambers.

PAVEMENT

The pavement consists of several layers of mosaic (see no. 8).

4. Measurements.

STAGE II and III

13 x 14 m. [7]

14.5 m. wide. [1,9]

STAGE IV

19 m. x 15 m. [1]

5. Orientation.

STAGE II AND III

The "compartments" on the south have a slight deviation to the east (130 degrees south). [11]

STAGE IV

The apse faces true south, toward Jerusalem (145 degrees south). [11]

6. Character and form: apse, niche, Torah Shrine, bema, chancel.

STAGE III, PHASE II

The narrow hall south of the basilica was divided into compartments. One, an aedicula directly in front of the nave, is raised one step above the nave's pavement, and has a rectangular niche cut into its back wall.

STAGE IV

A semicircular apse, the width of the nave, projected slightly beyond the south wall. Three broad steps ascend from the nave pavement to the apse and benches line its rear wall. It may have had a wooden floor. [1] A paved cellar, 2 m. deep, was uncovered below the apse. The apse is flanked by rooms possibly used for storage. [1]

7. Auxiliary rooms/structures.

STAGE II and III

A large public building, dated to the first century, was adjacent to the synagogue's east wall. [6]

STAGE IV

Storage rooms flanked the apse; several were plastered cisterns; a large inner court was added on the west. Various other buildings were west, south, and north of the synagogue.

8. Ornamentation.

STAGE II, PHASE II

A beautiful and elaborate mosaic pavement has survived almost intact. The nave pavement is divided into three panels. [5,9] Panel 1, directly before the aedicula, is enclosed within a wide guilloche border (#199). In the center of the panel is an image of a Torah Shrine flanked by two seven-branched menorot. The flames erupting from the menorot's branches turn inward, in accordance with Jewish tradition. [9] The Torah Shrine is similar in several respects to ones depicted at other synagogue sites (Beth Alpha, B:4, I-1, Beth She'an A, B:4, I-2, Khirbet Susīya, E:4, I-4 and Jericho, F:4, I-1).

Here the shrine is in the form of a rectangular cabinet surmounted by a gabled roof that has a pediment enclosing a
conch shell. A curtain, clasped in the middle, hangs before
the shrine's two closed doors (see: Beth She'an A, B:4, I-2).
The shrine is flanked by other Jewish ritual objects: the
lulab, ethrog, shofar, and incense shovel.

Panel 2[5,9] depicts a zodiac arranged in a radial form framed
by a narrow black border. The twelve signs, each within a
segment of the circle, go counterclockwise (see Beth Alpha,
B:4, I-1). In a smaller inner circle is Helios and his
quadriga; the four seasons are in the corners. The zodiac
signs are those derived from Greco-Roman mythology. The nude
figure of Libra is unusual, as he is shown uncircumcised; this
has led some scholars to suggest that the artist was not
Jewish.[9]

In Panel 3,[5,9] a lengthy Greek inscription (see no. 10)
is flanked by two lions, possibly meant to represent the
Lions of Judah, possibly counterparts to the three-dimensional
lions found at Capernaum (B:3, I-1), Chorozin (B:3, I-2), and
Kefar Bar'am A (B:1, I-2). The aisles are decorated with
beautifully executed geometric motifs, including a fish scale
pattern (#448) and quatrefoils (#109).

STAGE IV

Several layers of crudely executed mosaic pavements were
uncovered; they were in unimaginative geometric patterns
interspersed with plant motifs.

9. Coins, ceramics, and other artifacts found within building
   complex.

   These are not documented. Lamps, metal, glass, pottery
   vessels, and coins have been reported found in the storage
   rooms flanking the apse.[1]

10. Inscriptions.

    STAGE III, PHASE II

    1. A Greek inscription, divided into nine squares, is set
       into Panel 3. Five of the squares are to be read
       facing south; four face north. The names are of donors
       to the synagogue; two squares are devoted to one major
       contributor.

            Severus, the pupil of the most illustrious
            Patriarchs, has made this blessing. Amen.[7]

    2. A Greek and an Aramaic inscription are placed together
       within a single tabula ansata between the columns of the

east colonnade. The Greek inscription commemorates and
blesses the donor Severus and a synagogue official named
Iullus. The three-line Aramaic inscription reads:

> May Peace be unto all those who donated
> in this Holy Place and who in the future
> will donate. Let their lives be blessed.
> Amen. Amen. Selah. And again Amen.(7)

3. A five-line Greek inscription, set in the eastern aisle,
commemorates the donor Profuturos who " . . . made one
of the halls for this Holy Place."[7] The inscription
ends with the word shalom (peace) in Hebrew characters.

11. Donors or patrons.

STAGE III, PHASE II

The synagogue has been identified as the "Synagogue, of
Severus" because of several occurences of this name in the
inscriptions.[1]

12. Date. [1-4]

Stage I: First century, public building.

Stage II: Third century, synagogue.

Stage III, phase I: Early fourth century.

Stage III, phase II: Second half of fourth century.

Stage IV: Fifth-sixth centuries; building destroyed in the
eighth century.

13. Bibliography.

1. Dothan, M. "Hammat-Tiberias." IEJ, XII (1962), 153-154.

2. Idem. RB, 70 (1963), 588-590.

3. Idem. "The Aramaic Inscription from the Synagogue of
Severus at Hamat Tiberias." EI, VIII (1967), 183-185.

4. Idem. Qad., I (1968), 116-123.

5. Kitzinger, E. Israeli Mosaics of the Byzantine Period,
pp. 13 f.

6. Avi-Yonah, M. "Hammath." EJ. 1972 ed.

7. Lifshitz, B. "L'Ancienne Synagogue de Tibériade,
Mosaïque et ses Inscriptions." Journal for the
Study of Judaism, IV (July 1973), 43-55.

8. Idem. Donateurs, #76.

9. Avi-Yonah, M. Ancient Mosaics. London: Cassel, 1975,
p. 52.

10. Hachlili, Rachel. "The Zodiac in Ancient Jewish Art:
Representation and Significance." BASOR, 228 (Dec.,
1977), 61-77.

11. Hüttenmeister, F. Antiken Synagogen. Vol. I, pp. 163-172.

KOKHAV HA-YARDEN
B:3, II-1

1. Name of site and map reference.
   Kokhav ha-Yarden, Kaubab el-Hawa, Belvoir, Agrippina ?
   1994.2218 (4.95)

2. Survey of site.
   Situated 22 km. south of Tiberias, this site may be the location of the ancient city of Agrippina, capital of one of the two
   toparchies in Galilee during the reign of Herod the Great.

3. Character and sections of the building as suggested by extant
   and identifiable remains.
   The ruins of an ancient building are on a low terrace near a
   spring, about 700 meters southeast of the Crusader fortress.
   The fragments include basalt columns and a platform aligned
   north-south attributed to an ancient synagogue. [1,2]

8. Ornamentation.
   Several stones were found in secondary use in the Crusader
   fortress. A basalt lintel is decorated with a seven-branched
   menorah flanked by a shofar, lulab and ethrog. On one side
   is a pedimented Torah Shrine. Above the molding is a tabula
   ansata, without an inscription. An inscription (see
   no. 10) is inscribed on the bottom of the lintel's right-
   hand side. A stone is decorated with a double meander pattern
   that encloses animals and plants (see Kefar Bar'am A, B:1, I-2).
   Several smaller fragments are decorated with vines, rosettes
   and geometric patterns.

10. Inscriptions.
    The first two lines of the six-line Aramaic inscription on
    the basalt lintel are missing.

> [Blessed be the memory of . . ./ and
> his . . ./] who have donated (?)/
> this lintel (?)/ (line five is unclear)/
> the forgiver [gave] their work (?)/
> Amen, Amen, Selah. [1]

A Greek inscription engraved on a second stone has not been
published.

12. Date.
    The ruins and inscriptions are dated to the third to fourth
    centuries, on the basis of similarities to the "early"
    Galilean type synagogue. [1,2]

13. Bibliography.

    1. Ben-Dov, Meir. "Kockav ha Yarden." Qad. II (1969), 27.

    2. Hüttenmeister, F. Antiken Synagogen. Vol. I, pp. 272-274.

SARONA

B:3, II-2

1. Name of site and map reference.
   Sarona, H. Sāruna.
   1949.2355 (4.135)

2. Survey of site.
   The site is 10 km. southwest of the city of Tiberias.

8. Ornamentation.
   A lintel, found near Sarona, is decorated with two birds
   flanking a menorah. This motif (birds and menorah) is rare
   in Palestinian synagogue decoration; only one other example
   is known: a marble chancel screen found in Tiberias (B:3,
   II-3). A similar motif was found on an architectural fragment
   uncovered at Priene in Asia Minor; on a tomb in one of the
   Jewish catacombs of Monteverde, Rome; and on an ossuary in
   Spain.[1]

12. Date.
   The lintel has been dated to the second to third century.[1,2]

13. Bibliography.

    1. Foerster, G. "Some Menorah Reliefs from Galilee." IEJ.
       24, 3-4 (1974), 196.

    2. Hüttenmeister, F. Antiken Synagogen. Vol. I, p. 382.

TIBERIAS

B:3, II-3

1. Name of site and map reference.
   Tiberias.
   201.243 (4.153)

2. Survey of site.
   Marble columns, various architectural and decorative fragments,
   and inscriptions are all that remain of one or more synagogues built within the ancient walls of Tiberias. The
   location of the building(s) is not known.[1]

8. Ornamentation.

Several basalt stones are decorated with menorot, others with conch shells and garlands of grape vines. A marble chancel screen, carved in a lattice work pattern with circles emphasizing the intersecting points, has a crudely carved seven-branched menorah in the center of the upper border of its frame. The menorah is flanked by two schematized birds; their heads are effaced. The motif of heraldic birds flanking a menorah is rare; it occurs only one other time in Palestine, at nearby Sarona (B:3, II-2).[2]

10. Inscriptions.

Two inscriptions were inscribed on stones uncovered in the Roman baths in Tiberias.[3]

1. An Aramaic inscription is inscribed on a broken stone tablet:

> [Remem]bered for good and bless[ed] . . .
> Tor[ah]. Amen.[3]

2. A Greek inscription is on the bottom part of an abacus. A rosette separated the two lines.

> May the Lord's goodness be on Abraham
> the marble worker.[3]

3. Another Greek inscription probably came from a Jewish tomb. It mentions the name Leontina, daughter of Samuel the Gerusiarch, and the wife of Thaumasios the head of the synagogue of Antioch.[3]

12. Date.

The chancel screen fragments have been dated to the second-third centuries, on the basis of their style.[2]

13. Bibliography.

1. Ben-Dor, Meir. "Tiberias." Qad. IX, 2-3 (1976), 79.

2. Foerster, G. "Some Menorah Reliefs from Galilee." IEJ. XXIV, 3-4 (1974), 196.

3. Schwabe, M. BIES, 18 (1954), 160-163.

4. Hüttenmeister, F. Antiken Synagogen, Vol. I, pp. 436-461.

ARBELA
B:3, IIIA-1

1. Name of site and map reference.
   Arbela, Irbid, Arbel.
   1955.2468 (4.9)
   Plan 13

2. Survey of site.
   The ruined village of Arbela is located 6 km. northwest of
   Tiberias, halfway between that city and Capernaum. It is at
   the strategic point of entry into the Arbela Valley. Remains
   of caves fortified by Josephus (Vit. 188) have been found
   nearby. Explorers who visited the site in the nineteenth
   century reported on the condition of the ruins;[2] the site
   was partially surveyed and cleared by Kohl and Watzinger in
   1905.[1]

   The ruins, identified as a synagogue, are located in the lower
   part of the village, some distance down the north slope of a
   hill. The building's southern wall abuts a cliff; a portion
   of bedrock was cut away to provide room for its facade, but
   not an entrance.

3. Character and sections of the building as suggested by extant
   and identifiable remains.
   PLAN
   Two longitudinal rows of columns (five per row), joined on
   the north by a transverse colonnade of two columns, divide
   the main hall into a central nave surrounded on three sides
   by aisles. The columns' pedestals stand directly on the
   building's basalt foundations. The northeast and northwest
   pedestals have the inner angles of their bodies cut away to
   form half pedestals; their bases and column shafts have
   heart-shaped cross-sections.
   ENTRANCES
   The main entrance is in the northern one-third of the east
   wall. An additional door is possible in the middle of the
   north wall.[1]
   BENCHES
   The building's pavement is three steps below ground level, and
   two of the steps continue around the north end of the hall,
   forming a double-tiered bench. Multiple-tier benches are
   coterminous with the east and west walls. There are no benches
   along the south wall.

PAVEMENT
The pavement is flagstone.

4. <u>Measurements</u>.
Main hall: 17.18 x 15.9 m. [2]
                     18.2 x 16.7 m. [1]
                     18.20 x 18.65 m. [8]

5. <u>Orientation</u>.
The existence of a northern colonnade, the lack of benches along the southern wall, and the effort to place the facade on the south would all appear to indicate the building's orientation is toward the south, and Jerusalem.

6. <u>Character and form: apse, niche, Torah Shrine, bema, chancel</u>.
A niche uncovered in the south wall is believed to have been added later, when the building was converted into a mosque, [1] but this conclusion has been questioned. [4,5,7,9] It may have been added during a renovation of the synagogue in the fifth or sixth century. [6]

8. <u>Ornamentation</u>.
A portion of the building's eastern portal is extant. [1] The threshold, jambs, and lintel appear to have been carved from a single block of stone. The lintel, broader than the door's aperture, is decorated with a pulvinated frieze (vine scroll ?). Two debased Corinthian capitals were found near the east and north colonnades. They both bear evidence of holes meant to receive pegs. [1] A third debased Corinthian capital, found near the north wall, differs from the others in style; it is possibly part of a later renovation. Fragments of a debased Ionic capital consist of two flat spirals flanking a volute; poorly modeled egg and dart molding separates it from the abacus.
The lower portion of a pair of half columns found near the north colonnade may have formed part of a window decoration. [1]

10. <u>Inscriptions</u>.
The archives of the British Mandatory Government report that an inscription was carved on a corner of a heart-shaped column near the east entrance into the building; no further information is available. [3]

12. <u>Date</u>.
The building has been dated to the end of the second century to the early fourth, on the basis of its similarity to "early" Galilean synagogues. [1] See Kefar Bar'am A (B:1, I-2), and Capernaum (B:3, I-1) for problems associated with early dates for Galilean synagogues.

13. Bibliography.

1. Kohl, Watzinger, pp. 59-70.

2. Wilson, C. PEFQS, I (1869), 37 ff.

3. British Mandatory Government. Archives. Jerusalem: Rockefeller Museum.

4. Sukenik, E. The Synagogue at el-Hamman, p. 75.

5. Goodenough, E. R. Jewish Symbols. Vol. I, (1953), p. 199, Vol. III, fig. 503.

6. Avigad, N. In All the Land of Naphtali (1967), pp. 98-100.

7. Hachlili, Rachel. "The Niche and the Ark in Ancient Synagogues." BASOR, 223 (Oct. 1976), 43-54.

8. Hüttenmeister, F. Antiken Synagogen. Vol. I, pp. 15-17.

9. Avi-Yonah, M. "Synagogues." EAEh. 1978 ed.

MIGDAL

B:3, IIIA-2

1. Name of site and map reference.
Migdal, Magdal, Magdala, Majda, Taricheia.
1987.2481 (4.106)
Plan 14

2. Survey of site.
The ruins of the ancient town of Migdal are on the western shore of the Sea of Galilee, 5 km. north-northwest of Tiberias. During the first Jewish revolt, Migdal was a zealot stronghold until it fell to the Romans (Josephus, Vit. 463-504). It receives mention in the Gospels as the home of Mary Magdalene (Matt. 15:39, Mark 15:40).
V. Corbo and S. Loffreda began excavating the site in 1975; they reported discovering the remains of a first-century "synagogue" that had been destroyed during the first revolt, and later rebuilt as some form of water reservoir, possibly a nymphaeum. The building (B-1) is in a block of seven "rooms" (block D) located in the town's northern sector. Its identity as a synagogue has been questioned. [5]

3. Character and sections of the building as suggested by extant and identifiable remains.
The building was constructed of finely hewn basalt blocks laid on a foundation of roughly hewn rocks. The interstices are filled with mortar and chips of stone. [1]

Two building stages are postulated. [1]

STAGE I

PLAN

Two longitudinal rows of columns (three per row), joined on the south by a single column to form a transverse colonnade, divide the main hall into a central nave surrounded on three sides by aisles. The basalt columns stood on pedestals that rest directly on the pavement. The southeast and southwest bases and columns have heart-shaped cross-sections.

ENTRANCES

They are unknown, but the main entrance may have been in the east wall. [1]

BENCHES

A five-tiered bench was coterminous with the north wall.

PAVEMENT

The pavement is of basalt flagstone.

STAGE II

PLAN

The pavement level of the main hall was raised to the second step of benches; under the raised pavement was a collection channel for water.

4. Measurements. [1]

Main hall: 8.16 x 7.25 m. (external)

Room D-2: 2.84 x 3.75 m.

5. Orientation.

The building is aligned north-south; the focal point may have been opposite the benches, that is, the southern wall facing Jerusalem. [1]

7. Auxiliary rooms/structures.

Building D-2 adjoins the building's east wall; its south wall is a continuation of the "synagogue's." A single entrance is located in the western corner of the south wall. A water channel, located below the room's pavement, carried water to a small pool to its east. Adjacent to the northern portion of the building's east wall is an open court paved with large basalt stones, furrowed on the three sides to collect water that flowed along a channel into the "synagogue/reservoir." [1,2]

8. Ornamentation.

The pedestals and one surviving capital have been described as "beautifully austere." [1]

9. Coins, ceramics, and other artifacts found within building
    complex.
    Pottery and coins indicate two clear and distinct building
    stages. [1]

    STAGE I
    Pottery is dated to the end of the Hellenistic period to the
    first Roman period (63 B.C.E. - 70 C.E.).

    STAGE II
    Pottery is dated to the end of the second revolt (135 C.E.)
    and coins are dated to the first revolt (66-70 C.E.). Four
    coins date to the third century and the latest coin, found in
    the top layer, dates to Constantine the Great.

12. Date. [1]

    Stage I: "Synagogue," destroyed in 70 C.E.

    Stage II: Reservoir, in use until the second century, when
               it was replaced by a water tower.

13. Bibliography.

    1. Loffredo, S., V. Corbo. "La Citta' Romana di Magdala."
           Studi Archeologici I, Studii Biblici Franciscani
           Collectio Maior N. 22. Jerusalem: Franciscan
           Printing Press, 1976, pp. 355 ff.

    2. Idem. HA, 57/58 (April, 1976), 9.

    3. Foerster, Gideon. "The Synagogues at Masada and
           Herodion." JJA, 3/4 (1977), 6-11.

    4. Hüttenmeister, F. Antiken Synagogen. Vol. I, pp. 316-318.

    5. Chiat, Marilyn. "First Century Synagogues: Methodological
           Problems." Ancient Synagogues: Current Stage of
           Research. Ed. by Joseph Gutmann. Brown Judaic
           Studies 22. Chico: Scholars Press, 1981, pp. 49-60.

HORVAT WERADIM
B:3, IIIB-1

1. Name of site and map reference.
    Horvat Weradim, Khirbet el-Werdat, H. al-Wuredat, H. Wadi
    al-Hammam.
    Site A: 1962.2483 (4.159)
    Site B: 1963.2484 (4.160)

2. Survey of site.
    Located 6.5 km. northwest of Tiberias, the site is in the
    valley of Wadi al-Hammam.

3. Character and sections of the building as suggested by extant
    and identifiable remains.

    Site A: In 1925, J. Braslavsky reported finding fragments of
    pillars and a heart-shaped pedestal purporting to resemble
    those of "early" Galilean synagogues.[1] In 1974, the Israel
    Department of Antiquities reported the discovery of additional
    pedestals, bases, capitals, doorposts, and a lintel, the
    last-named decorated with an eagle.[2]

    Site B: Fragments of a wall, large doorposts, and other
    architectural fragments were found 500 m. northwest of Site A.
    It is possible this material may have been swept down the
    Wadi al-Hammām from a site to the north.[3] The evidence is
    too inconclusive, however, to make an attribution.[2,3,A]

13. Bibliography.

    1. Site A: Braslavsky, J. BJPES, I, 2-4 (1925), 139 f.

    2. Site A: Hüttenmeister, F. Antiken Synagogen. Vol. I,
        p. 477.

    3. Site B: Idem., p. 478.

Scythopolis, one of the cities of the Roman Decapolis, was founded by Egyptianized Greeks settled in the area by the Ptolemaic heirs of Alexander the Great. These people included soldiers of Scythian origin or natives of the Greek cities of the Bosphorous Kingdom, which may account for the city's unusual name (Avi-Yonah, "Scythopolis," IEJ 12, 2 (1962), p. 128). In Talmudic literature, the city is known as Beth She'an (Beit Se'an) or Bêshun.

The six verified synagogues uncovered in Scythopolis are evidence of the complexity involved in the study of ancient synagogues in Palestine. They are: Beth Alpha, Beth She'an A, Beth She'an B, Tel Menora (Kefar Qarnaim), Ma'oz Hayyim, and Rehov. All the synagogues are contemporary in date, showing several similar architectural and decorative features. Four synagogues have mosaic pavements decorated with figurative motifs, Beth Alpha, Beth She'an B, Tel Menora, and Ma'oz Hayyim. Only Tel Menora shows evidence of deliberate mutilation. Beth She'an A and Rehov have nonfigurative pavements. All six synagogues are decorated with menorot, and four also bear inscriptions.

Four synagogues, Beth Alpha, Beth She'an A, Ma'oz Hayyim, and Rehov, are in the form of basilicas with two longitudinal rows of columns; Beth She'an B and Tel Menora appear to have been "prayer rooms." All the basilicas save one (Rehov) have apses; three show evidence of a later wall intended to close off the chancel area from the nave. In addition, the southern ends of Rehov's two aisles are closed off by later walls.

A basalt lintel decorated with a menorah, found at Kafr Danna, may be all that remains of a synagogue located at that site.

BETH ALPHA
B:4, I-1

1. Name of site and map reference.
   Beth Alpha, Beit Ilfā, Bet Alfa.
   1903.2139 (6.23)
   Plan 15
2. Survey of site.
   The synagogue was built at the foot of the north slope of

Mount Gilboa in the eastern part of the Jezreel Valley. The
abundance of water and rich soil make this region particularly
well-suited for agriculture. Beth Alpha is not mentioned in
ancient sources; the synagogue is named after the adjacent
ruins of Khirbet Beit Ilfā. There is no evidence of occupation of the site earlier than the end of the Roman Period.
The foundations and mosaic pavement of the synagogue were
uncovered accidentally in December, 1928, in the course of
digging a water channel for a nearby settlement, and the
synagogue was excavated in 1929 under the direction of
E. L. Sukenik on behalf of Hebrew University, Jerusalem.[1]

3. Character and sections of the building as suggested by extant
   and identifiable remains.

The synagogue is located on a narrow street surrounded by
dwellings. It is built of untrimmed local limestone; the
foundation stones are larger and more carefully shaped than
those of the walls. The pillars are of basalt imported from
a distance of at least 3 1/2 km.[1] The building bears
evidence of several structural changes, particularly to its
facade.[1]

STAGE I

COURT

Walls enclosed the court's east, west, and north sides; there
are columns on the south side. The entrance is in the middle
of the west wall.

NARTHEX

The court's columns formed the north side of the narthex.
Possibly six columns stood between two antae supporting an
arched entablature. The narthex pavement is one step lower
than the court's.

PLAN

The main hall is divided by two rows of pillars (5 each) into
a broad central nave and flanking aisles. The endmost pillars
abut the north wall. The pillars, coated with plaster, rest
directly on pavement; they may have supported an arched
entablature.[1]

ENTRANCES

On the north, one large central portal is flanked by two
smaller doors. On the west, a side door leads into the
annex (see no. 7).

BENCHES

Benches of untrimmed stone blocks coated with plaster are built along the south, east and west walls. The widest, ca. 1 meter, are built against the south wall, flanking the apse.

PAVEMENT

The pavement is mosaic.[3]

STAGE II

COURT

The south columns were replaced by a wall pierced with two doors opening onto the narthex. Foundations for a water vessel were uncovered in the center of courtyard. The court was paved with crude mosaic.

NARTHEX

Column drums from Stage I were used in the construction of a new wall; one base was uncovered in situ.

PLAN

The main hall remained unchanged.

BENCHES

Benches were added along the north wall on either side of the central door, and between the two southernmost pillars of the east colonnade.

PAVEMENT

The pavement was mosaic. (See no. 8.)

GALLERY

Fragments of columns, half-columns and capitals, uncovered near the north end of the hall, were conjectured to have come from an upper gallery that may have extended over the two aisles and narthex.[1] The stairs ascending to the gallery are postulated to have been in the western annex.[1]

ROOF

The building may have had a sloping roof, as evidenced by some flat and convex tile fragments uncovered in the debris. No remains of an architrave have been found, suggesting that the roof beams may have been supported on arches of untrimmed stone.[1]

4. Measurements.[1]

Court, Narthex, and Basilica: 27.70 x 14.20 m.

Court: 9.65 x 11.9 m.

Narthex: 2.57 m. wide.

Main hall: 10.75 x 12.40 m. wide.

Nave: 5.40 m. wide.

West aisle: 2.75 m. wide.

East aisle: 3.10 m. wide.

Bema: 1.55 m. long x 0.90 m. wide x 0.45 m. high.

Apse: 2.40 x 3.80 m. wide; projects 2.40 m. beyond external
wall.

5. Orientation.

The apse faces south, toward Jerusalem.

6. Character and form: apse, niche, Torah Shrine, bema, chancel.

STAGE I

Three narrow steps ascend to a semicircular external apse.

The apse has two levels:

Level I is 1/2 m. above the hall pavement (two steps). Two
perpendicular rounded hollows, 16 cm. deep and 20 cm. wide,
are cut 2.22 m. apart into its surface; they may have been
cut for posts supporting a curtain (paroketh) closing off the
Torah Shrine.

Level II is .25 cm. higher. A small cavity cut into the apse
pavement was coated with plaster and covered with flagstones
(one in situ); it was possibly used as a genizah.

STAGE II

BEMA

A bema was added one step above the basilica's pavement. It
is built atop the Stage II mosaic pavement, against the
second pillar from the south in the east colonnade.

7. Auxiliary rooms and/or structures.

STAGE I and II

A narthex and a courtyard are on the north. An annex adjoins
the hall on the west; its floor is three steps above basilica's
pavement. The south wall and portions of the west wall of
the annex are intact; its northern limit is unknown.

8. Ornamentation.

STAGE I

Fragments of an earlier mosaic pavement were uncovered 15 cm.
below the present floor. They are decorated with a guilloche,
a snake (?), and simple geometric patterns. [3]

STAGE II

The entire building complex was now paved with mosaic; the
courtyard and narthex pavements were badly damaged. The hall
pavement was uncovered in perfect condition. There is no
sign of iconoclastic mutilation (see no. 12).

NAVE [1]

The nave pavement is divided into three panels (the middle is
the largest) surrounded by a 60-90 cm. wide border.

The south border is divided into squares from right to left that enclose a bird with long red legs, a hen with her chicks, and a pomegranate tree. Below, in trapezoids, are a cluster of grapes and a fish.

The east border depicts two intertwining vine branches enclosing images of various animals, including a fox eating grapes, a hare, and three "goblets."

The southern end is covered by the later bema and benches. On the north border, two inscriptions are flanked by two large animals, a lion on the east, and an ox ("buffalo" ?) on the west.[1]

The west border is filled with squares framing baskets of fruit, especially bunches of grapes.

The north panel[1] shows the Binding of Isaac (Akedah). The scene is portrayed in a narrative form intended to be read from left to right: Two servants are shown holding Abraham's donkey, next, a ram is tethered to a tree, followed by Abraham, Isaac, and the flaming altar. Evidence that the artist was copying from a pagan source can be noted in Abraham's dress (chiton) and pose; the "airborne" Isaac is similar in several respects to popular images of the god Mithra, i.e., his Phrygian cap and flowing cape.[A]

The middle panel[1] depicts a zodiac circle. A double zodiac wheel formed by two concentric circles is surrounded by a guilloche band (#194); the pagan god Helios with his quadriga is placed in the inner circle (1.20 m. diameter). Personifications of the seasons are in the four corners, but they do not correspond to their neighboring months. The reason for this is unknown; it also occurs at Husifah (C:2, I-2). The twelve signs of the zodiac are in the outer circle; as at Hammat Tiberias B (B:3, I-4) they run counterclockwise. Unlike the pavement in the nearby Byzantine Monastery of Kyria Mary, where the months are personified according to the later Byzantine tradition of labors, the zodiac symbols here are generally in the earlier Greco-Roman tradition, Leo as a Lion, Cancer as a Crab, etc. Several are unusual: Saggitarius is a human archer, not a centaur, and Aquarius is a figure drawing water from a well, rather than pouring water out of an amphora. It is uncertain why the artist chose these particular symbols.[10]

The south panel[1] shows a Torah Shrine flanked by two large menorot, lions, and other objects associated with Jewish

ritual. Drapes (<u>paroketh</u>) frame the sides of the panel. The
Torah Shrine rests on a wide, three-legged base; its two doors
are closed. On its lintel are three amphorae; horns extend
from its ends. A large gabled roof crowns the Shrine; in the
center of its pediment is a conch shell. A lantern suspended
from the apex of the roof may represent the <u>Ner ha-Tamid</u>, the
perpetual light. On the Shrine's roof are two peculiar birds,
possibly representing the Cherubim of the Temple. Other
ritual objects, a shofar, lulab, and ethrog, and incense
shovels are strewn about the panel.

The west aisle is decorated with patterned panels that may be
based upon textile designs.[7]

The walls were plastered with a thick coating of lime and
painted with simple designs of red flowers.

9. <u>Coins, ceramics, and other artifacts found within building
complex</u>.

Thirty-six bronze coins were found in the genizah (not sealed).
Seven are identifiable; the earliest dates to Constantine the
Great (306-337), the latest to Justin I (518-527).[1]

Potsherds, used to secure plaster to the hall's interior wall,
have been dated to the late Roman and Early Byzantine
periods.[1]

10. <u>Inscriptions</u>.

Two inscriptions in the north border are placed within tabula
ansatae. They are intended to be read facing the south
(apse).

An Aramaic inscription consists of seven lines; the entire
right side is destroyed; it was executed in a poor Aramaic
script. The inscription refers to the donations of members
of the congregation "in kind" (wheat etc.) to the construction
of the synagogue. The first two lines provide a date in the
"reign of Justin," either I (518-527) or II (565-578).[1]

Of the Greek inscription, all five lines are complete:

> May the craftsmen who carried out this
> work, Marianos and his son Hanina, be
> held in remembrance.[1]

These two Jewish artisans are also responsible for one of the
annex pavements at Beth She'an A (B:4, I-2).

11. <u>Patrons and donors</u>.

From the Aramaic inscription, it would appear many members of
the community contributed something to finance the synagogue's
construction.[A]

12. Date.

The synagogue's two stages have been dated as follows:[1]

STAGE I

This stage dates to the fifth century, on the basis of numismatic evidence: the synagogue was built before the reform of the coinage system by Anastatius I in 498, which withdrew all earlier coins from circulation.

STAGE II

A sixth-century date is based on the inscription naming Emperor Justin. The synagogue was destroyed by an earthquake sometime in the sixth century.

13. Bibliography.

1. Sukenik, E. L. The Ancient Synagogue of Beth Alpha. London: Oxford Univ. Press, 1932.

2. Idem. Ancient Synagogues, pp. 6, 31 ff, 48, 58 ff, 65, 76 f, 85 f.

3. Idem. "A New Discovery at Beth Alpha." Rabinowitz Bulletin. Vol. II, (June, 1951), p. 26.

4. Frey, J. B. CIJ. #1162-1166.

5. Goodenough, E. R. Jewish Symbols. Vol. I. (1953), pp. 241-253, Vol. III, figs. 632-635, 638-641.

6. Hiram, Asher. "Die Entwicklung der Antiken Synagogen und altchristlichen Kirchenbauten in Heiligen Lande." Wiener Jahrbuch für Kunstgeschichte, 19 (1962), 12.

7. Goldman, Bernard. The Sacred Portal. Detroit: Wayne State Univ. Press, 1966.

8. Kitzinger, Ernst. Israeli Mosaics of the Byzantine Period. New York, 1965, pp. 13-15, 20.

9. Lifshitz, B. Donateurs, #77.

10. Hachlili, Rachel. "The Zodiac in Ancient Jewish Art: Representation and Significance." BASOR 228 (Dec. 1977), 61-77.

11. Hüttenmeister, F. Antiken Synagogen. Vol. I, pp. 44-50.

12. Chiat, M. J. "Synagogue and Church Architecture in Byzantine Beit She'an." JJA 8 (1980), 6-24.

BETH SHE'AN A
B:4, I-2

1. Name of site and map reference.
   Beth She'an, Beit Se'an, Beisan, Bēsān, Bêshun, Scythopolis.
   1975.2131 (6.1008)
   Plan 16

2. Survey of site.
   During the Hellenistic and Roman periods, the main part of the
   town of Scythopolis moved down from Tell el-Husn into the
   neighboring valleys. In 1950, the area at the foot of Tell
   el-Husn was investigated by N. Tsori, on behalf of the Israel
   Department of Antiquities. A synagogue was uncovered on Tel
   Mastaba (Istaba), about 280 meters north of the sixth-century
   city wall. Tel Mastaba is the westernmost of the two hills
   north of Scythopolis. Its summit is crowned by the Monastery
   of Kyria Mary. The synagogue (A) is located about 500 m.
   north-northwest of the monastery. Excavations have revealed
   three building stages.

3. Character and sections of the building as suggested by extant
   and identifiable remains.
   The synagogue was built of thick (90-95 cm.) basalt blocks;
   its limestone columns and thresholds may come from an earlier
   building in the vicinity.[1] Only the north wall of the
   synagogue survives above its foundation. Three stages of
   development are proposed:[1]

   STAGE I

   PLAN
   The main hall is divided into a central nave and flanking
   aisles by two longitudinal rows of columns (four columns per
   row). Four limestone bases of the northern colonnade, in situ,
   rest on a basalt stylobate 60 cm. wide. The pavement of the
   aisles is higher than the nave; the northern aisle is 16-23 cm.
   higher.

   ENTRANCES
   The facade has three entrances, a large central portal flanked
   by two smaller doors. On the north, a door opened onto an
   adjoining room. "Openings" were located next to apse, and
   near the east end of the north wall; their function is not
   given.

   PAVEMENT
   The pavement is mosaic.

STAGE II

NARTHEX

A narthex was added along the full length of synagogue's facade; it may have had a basalt bench along its north wall. Its pavement was limestone, set 31 cm. lower than the level of the north aisle.

PLAN

The north wall of the synagogue was extended along the narthex. (See no. 7.)

ENTRANCES

"Openings" in the main hall were closed. Four stone steps were added in front of the closed opening next to the apse.

PAVEMENT

The pavement is mosaic.

STAGE III

BENCHES

Benches were added along the north wall of the main hall.

PAVEMENT

The pavement is mosaic.

4. <u>Measurements</u>.[1]

Main hall: 17.00 x 14.20 m.

Narthex: 3.00 x 14.20 m.

Apse: 5 m. long x 3.40 m. wide.

Room 4:   4.90 x 2.30 m.

Room 7:   5.70 x 5.40 m.

Room 8:   3.00 x 2.20 m.

5. <u>Orientation</u>.

The apse faces 280 degrees northwest, away from Jerusalem (see no. 11).[1,4]

6. <u>Character and form: apse, niche, Torah Shrine, bema, chancel</u>.

STAGE I

An external semicircular apse, raised 50 cm. above nave pavement, was built on a stone foundation 40 cm. thick.

STAGE II

The apse was paved with mosaic. In the middle of the pavement is a section of plaster 100 cm. long x 23 cm. wide; it may have supported a Torah Shrine.[1]

STAGE III

A low wall built in front of the apse separates it from the nave. Cut into the nave's pavement on both sides of the apse are four hollows, into which posts (15 cm. square) of a chancel screen were fitted. Fragments of the posts were <u>in situ</u>.

7. Auxiliary rooms and/or structures.

STAGE I

Room 4 was added, and adjoined the north aisle.

STAGE II

Room 4 was paved with mosaics. The narthex and room 7 were added, and room 7 was paved with mosaic. Of room 9, added south of 7, only the northwest corner is intact; it was paved with mosaic.

STAGE III

The north door into room 7 was closed and a bench placed in front of it. A Greek inscription is set into the room's new mosaic pavement (see no. 10). Room 8 was added; a Samaritan inscription is set into its mosaic pavement (see no. 10). Rooms 6, 10, 11 were added adjoining the synagogue's north wall. Room 10 opens onto the synagogue's north aisle. The entire synagogue was now surrounded by a complex of rooms and annexes.

8. Ornamentation.

STAGE I

Little remains of the original mosaic pavement; its pattern is unknown.

STAGE II

A new mosaic pavement was laid; it remained intact through Stages II and III. Five panels are enclosed within a wave pattern (#190) and guilloche (#199) border.[1]

Panel 1, nearest the main entrances into the synagogue hall, shows clusters of grapes and a Greek inscription set within a tabula ansata. In Panel 2, intersecting circles (#438) frame various fruits. Panel 3 depicts squares and lozenges framing different fruits and vegetables arranged around a central octagon (#583). Panel 4 shows a triple circle, with a star motif in the center, set within a rectangle. Panel 5 is directly in front of the apse.[1] A central Torah Shrine is shown flanked by seven-branched menorot, shoforot, and incense shovels. Diamond shaped "stars" flank the menorot. Above the Torah Shrine is a stylized vine scroll, badly mutilated, but it apparently held grapes within its tendrils. The Torah Shrine differs from the ones depicted at Beth Alpha (B:4, I-1), Khirbet Sūsīya (E:4, I-4), and Jericho (F:4, I-1), in that a drapery is shown hanging between two smaller columns, rather than the usual double doors. See Hammat Tiberias B (B:3, I-4) for a gathered drapery in front of the doors.

The apse had a mosaic pavement set in an interlace pattern
(#481) laid atop a smooth plaster floor.

In room 7, large tesserae were laid in a simple geometric
pattern (#344). A large square in the center contains nine
octagons (three to a row); the center octagon encloses a
circle containing the Greek inscription. (See no. 10.)

Room 8 was paved in a simple lozenge pattern (#311), surrounded
by an ivy-leaf border. In the center is a circle framing a
Samaritan inscription. (See no. 10.) Fragments of a marble
screen decorated with a menorah were found in the ruins.

9. Coins, ceramics, and other artifacts found within building
complex.

Byzantine glass flasks, bowls, bottles, and chalices, flat
and bell shaped covers, and a bronze chain were all found in
rooms adjoining the synagogue.[1] Additional finds include a
bronze menorah, probably part of an oil lamp, and fragments
of stemmed glass lamps intended to fit into a polycandelon.[1]

In rooms 6, 10, and 11 was found pottery, dated to the sixth-
seventh centuries and a bronze censer with a pyramidal
cover.[1]

10. Inscriptions.

Three Greek inscriptions and one Samaritan were found:

1. In the nave by the main entrance, only three words
    survive: "Year . . .; month January . . ."[1]

2. In the north aisle, four lines are visible, too badly
    damaged to read.[1]

3. Room 7 contains five lines: "The work of Marianos and
    his son Hanina,"[1] the same Jewish craftsmen who laid
    the mosaic pavement at Beth Alpha (B:4, I-1).

4. The Samaritan inscription, in Room 8 reads:

        God help Afray, Sahay, 'Anan.[5]

11. Donors or patrons.

The unusual orientation of the building to the northwest and
the Samaritan inscription in Room 8 have led some scholars
to believe that the synagogue was Samaritan.[4] N. Tsori,
the synagogue's excavator, discounts this theory.[1,2] He
contends that no motif connected with the Samaritan tradition
has been found in the building or in its mosaics. He suggests

that the Samaritan inscription was added at a time when there
was cooperation between the Samaritan and Jewish communities
against common enemies; the building may have been used by
members of both faiths as a common assembly hall. Tsori
explains the orientation by the disputed ruling in T. Meg.
4:22, which states that synagogue entrances are to be made
in the east like the Temple and Tabernacle. The synagogue's
entrances, however, are in the southeast; Jerusalem and Mount
Gerazim are both to the southwest. No adequate explanation
has been forthcoming regarding this building's unusual orientation, or its attribution. [A]

12. Date.

Stage I: End of the fourth century to the beginning of the
            fifth. [1]

Stage II: Middle of the fifth century to the beginning of
            the sixth. [1]

Stage III: End of the sixth century to the beginning of the
            seventh. [1]

13. Bibliography.

1. Tsori, Nahum. "The Ancient Synagogue at Beth She'an."
        EI, VIII (1967), 149-167.

2. Idem. IEJ, 13 (1963), 148-149.

3. Idem. Qad., 3 (1970), 67-68.

4. Reeg, G. Antiken Synagogen. Vol. II, 571-577.

5. Naveh, Joseph. Personal interview. May, 1977.

6. Chiat, M. J. "Synagogue and Church Architecture in
        Byzantine Beit She'an." JJA 8 (1980), 6-24.

BETH SHE'AN B
B:4, I-3

1. Name of site and map reference.
    Beth She'an, Beit Se'an, Beisan, Bēsān, Bêshun, Scythopolis
    1969.2120 (6.28)
    Plan 17

2. Survey of site.
    The building complex, which includes the synagogue, is
    located within the Byzantine city wall surrounding Scythopolis.
    It was excavated by Dan Bahat, A. Druks, and M. Edelstein on
    behalf of the Israel Department of Antiquities and the American
    Union of Jewish communities.

3. Character and sections of the building as suggested by extant and identifiable remains.

The synagogue is a small room located south of the house of the wealthy Jew Kyrios Leontis, and across from what appears to be a joint courtyard identified as a "basilica court."[5] The synagogue has been described as a "small praying room."[1,2]

In the summer of 1974 the adjoining "basilica-court" was excavated; it has now been identified as a "possible" synagogue.[5] It is unclear if this "possible" synagogue is associated with the "small praying room," or is a separate entity; for that reason, the two structures are discussed jointly.[A]

BASILICA COURT PLAN

Evidence was found of several renovations. Five meters from the court walls and parallel to them is a low wall (stylobate ?) apparently intended to support an interior colonnade. Rooms adjoin the courtyard on its north, east, and west; it is unclear whether they opened onto the court.[5]

ENTRANCES

All entrances (three) were on the south.

PAVEMENT

The pavement was mosaic.

PRAYER ROOM PLAN

The room is irregularly square-shaped; its walls are not parallel or opposite one another.[2]

ENTRANCES

The prayer room's main entrance is through the basilica-court, on the north side. On the east is a smaller side entrance.

BENCHES

Benches were set along all the interior walls.

PAVEMENT

The pavement was mosaic.

4. Measurements.
Prayer room: ca. 7 x 7 m.[2]
Basilica court: ca. 30 m. long.[5]

5. Orientation.
Prayer room: the excavators postulate the direction of prayer on the direction the mosaic pavement was to be "read": south toward Jerusalem.[2]
Basilica-court: The entrances on the south face Jerusalem.[5]

6. <u>Character and form: apse, niche, Torah Shrine, bema, chancel</u>.
The excavators have assumed the existence of a niche in the
south wall of the prayer room; no evidence of it survives.[2]

7. <u>Auxiliary rooms/structures</u>.
The prayer room and basilica-court are part of a larger
building complex that includes the private house of Kyrios
Leontis.

8. <u>Ornamentation</u>.
In the basilica-court, a mosaic pavement was set in geometric
patterns. The prayer room[6] was paved with mosaic. A wide
border composed of four sections on three sides and two on
the north, encloses a large central field.
On the south border, a projecting section frames two lions
flanking a possible menorah. Then comes a narrow ribbon
border (#221) followed by a wide band of fleurons (#117)
interspersed with birds, fruits, and baskets. On the north,
in place of a wide border, a section of pavement is decorated
with an amphora flanked by two partridges; below this is an
Aramaic inscription (see no. 10). A narrow inner border is
composed of an inhabited vine rinceau issuing from amphorae
set in each corner. An inscription set within a <u>tabula ansata</u>
interrupts the design on the south (see no. 10).
The central field has a vine trellis forming nine medallions,
three to a row, issuing from a large amphora set in the center
of the north row; two medallions are destroyed.
The central medallion of the middle row is the most elaborate.
It is in the form of a double circle (wreath?) enclosing a
seven-branched menorah flanked by an ethrog and incense
shovels; other objects have been destroyed. A dove,
surrounded by grape clusters, is in the medallion to its
right; the left medallion has been destroyed. The medallion
above the menorah frames a peacock <u>en face</u>; to the left is a
buffalo; the right medallion has been destroyed. The spaces
between the medallions are filled with grape clusters, leaves,
vine tendrils, and birds.
On the east, a projecting portion of pavement contains a panel
decorated with two doves flanking a Greek inscription (see
no. 10).

10. <u>Inscriptions</u>.
1. The Hebrew word <u>shalom</u> above the menorah[2] is probably
part of a longer inscription, "Peace upon Israel" (see
Jericho, F:4, I-1).

2. A four-line Aramaic inscription is set in the south border.

> Remembered for good all the members of the
> holy community/ who contributed to repair
> the place/ the holy: peace be upon them
> and blessing, Amen./ . . . Peace, grace in
> peace.(2)

3. A four-line Aramaic inscription by the north entrance reads:

> Remembered/ be for good the artist/
> who made/ this work.(2)

4. A six-line Greek inscription by east entrance is set to be read from inside the hall.

> The gift of those of whom the Lord
> knows the names, He shall guard them,
> in times. . . .(2)

11. Donors or patrons.

The phrase, financed by the "holy community," may refer to the members of this particular congregation, not the entire Jewish community of Beth She'an. "Holy community" also occurs in a synagogue inscription at Jericho (F:4, I-1).[(A)]

12. Date.

Two stages are postulated for the prayer room:[(2)]

Stage I: The middle of the fifth to sixth centuries.

Stage II: Second half of the sixth century, when the new
           mosaic pavement was laid.

13. Bibliography.

1. Bahat, D. and A. Druks. "Beth Shean, Ancienne synagogue."
   RB, 78 (Oct. 1971), 585-586.

2. Idem. Qad., V, 2 (1972), 55-58.

3. Idem. HA, 41/42 (1972), 8f.

4. Idem. HA, 44 (1972), 9.

5. Idem. HA, 58/59 (1974), 44.

6. Idem. EAEh., pp. 227-228.

7. Hüttenmeister, F. Antiken Synagogen. Vol. I, pp. 58-67.

8. Chiat, M. J. "Synagogue and Church Architecture in
   Byzantine Beit She'an." JJA 8 (1980), 6-24.

MA'OZ HAYYIM
B:4, I-4

1. Name of site and map reference.
   Ma'oz Hayyim, Be'ela (?)
   2017.2110 (6.101)
   Plan 18

2. Survey of site.
   The synagogue site is located about 4 km. east of Beth
   She'an. Its mosaic pavement was exposed accidentally in
   1974; excavation and restoration continues under the direction
   of V. T. Tzfaris of the Israel Department of Antiquities and
   Museums.

3. Character and sections of the building as suggested by extant
   and identifiable remains.
   Only the wall foundations of the synagogue and fragments of
   its mosaic pavement are extant. [2]
   Evidence indicates three building stages. [4]
   STAGE I
   COURTYARD
   The court is adjacent to the basilica's east wall.
   PAVEMENT
   The floor was paved with limestone slabs.
   NARTHEX
   Running the full width of the basilica's north facade, the
   narthex adjoins the courtyard on the east.
   PLAN
   The main hall is divided into a central nave and two flanking
   aisles by two longitudinal rows of columns (five per row).
   ENTRANCES
   The north entrance was possibly a single door in the middle
   of the wall. On the east, two doors opened onto an adjacent
   court and room(s). The west side shows evidence of a door.
   BENCHES
   There may have been benches along the east and west walls.
   PAVEMENT
   The pavement was thick limestone slabs.
   STAGE II
   PLAN
   The basic plan remains unchanged, except for the addition of
   a raised apse projecting beyond the south wall (see no. 6).

PAVEMENT

A well executed mosaic pavement was laid in the main hall; it was placed over a foundation of broken roof tiles that may have come from an earlier building on the site, or an earlier stage of the synagogue. (A)

STAGE III

PLAN

The plan remains unchanged.

PAVEMENT

A second, crudely executed mosaic pavement was laid 0.50 m. above the Stage II pavement. (4)

4. Measurements. (5)

Stage I, Main hall: 13.0 x 12.5 m. (?)

Stages II, III, Main hall: 16 x 14 m.

5. Orientation.

STAGES II, III

Following the addition of the apse, the orientation was 180° south (see no. 6). (6)

6. Character and form: apse, niche, Torah Shrine, bema, chancel.

STAGE II

An external, semicircular apse, 0.20 m. above the nave's pavement, was added on the south. A long, stone-lined pit (genizah?) was uncovered in its southern corner. The apse was built partially of reused material, including a fragment of a marble chancel screen.

STAGE III

A foundation for some form of wall, the width of the nave, was added in front of the apse and appears to have projected into the nave up to the first pair of southern columns. (A)

7. Auxiliary rooms/structures.

A narthex adjoined the basilica's facade and a courtyard was adjacent to its east wall. Additional rooms may have been located south of the courtyard. (5)

8. Ornamentation.

STAGE I

The southern portion of a well-executed mosaic pavement has been exposed. (2) It is composed of a broad border subdivided into squares each of which frame a different geometric pattern or motif. On the south, the squares enclose a bird flanked by meanders (swastikas) and a seven-branched menorah flanked by a shofar.

The larger squares of the field contain designs of squares and lozenges giving the perspectival effect of square beams (#498).

STAGE III

A new pavement was laid 0.50 m. above Stage II. It is poorly preserved because an Early Arab structure was built on top of it, but it appears to have been composed of only geometric patterns.

9. Coins, ceramics and other artifacts found within building complex.

Not all of this material has as yet been reported. Five coins were uncovered, plus pieces of bronze, iron, glass, and clay lamps in the apse pit.[4] Pottery found on the surface has been dated to the eighth-ninth centuries.[2]

12. Date.

The following chronology is based on the preliminary report:[4]

Stage I: At the latest, this stage is dated to the fourth century.

Stage II: The mosaic pavement has been dated to the middle of the fourth century.

Stage III: The "new" pavement is dated to the fifth century; the synagogue was in use until the seventh century.

13. Bibliography.

1. Tzfaris, V. "Ma'oz Hayyim." HA, 50 (April 1974), 3 f.

2. Idem. IEJ, 24 (1974), 143-144.

3. Idem. Qad., VII, 3/4 (1974), 111-113.

4. Idem. HA, 50 (1974), 3.

5. Idem. HA, 53 (1975), 9.

6. Hüttenmeister, F. Antiken Synagogen. Vol. I, pp. 307-308.

7. Chiat, M. J. "Synagogue and Church Architecture in Byzantine Beit She'an." JJA 8, (1980), 6-24.

REHOV

B:4, I-5

1. Name of site and map reference.

Rehov, Farwāna, Tulūl Farwāna, Tell as-Sārim.

1967.2077 (6.128)

Plan 19

2. <u>Survey of site.</u>

The synagogue ruin is located six kilometers south of modern
Beth She'an, and 800 m. northwest of Tel Rehov, directly east
of the road from Beth She'an to Jericho. It was discovered
in a field in 1974; excavation under the direction of Fanny
Vitto of the Israel Department of Antiquities, is still in
progress.

3. <u>Character and sections of the building as suggested by extant
and identifiable remains.</u>

The building underwent at least three main building stages;
the precise sequence has recently been established.[11]

STAGE I

A structure, identified as a "prayer hall," was uncovered.
Some of its limestone material was reused in subsequent
rebuildings.[1,11]

PLAN

The main hall was divided into a central nave and two flanking
aisles by two longitudinal rows of limestone columns (five
per row) that stood on square basalt bases built on a stylobate made of one course of field stones laid below floor
level.[11]

ENTRANCES

On the north, three doors were in the facade. On the southeast, evidence is present of a small doorway opening onto an
aisle.

PAVEMENT

The floor was laid with polychrome mosaic; only the borders
in the aisles survive.[11]

STAGE II

Constructed following the destruction of most of Stage I by
a fire.[11]

PLAN

The general plan remains unchanged except for columniation
and the addition of a bema (see no. 6).

Square bases of the limestone Stage I columns were covered
over and replaced by two new rows of rectangular basalt
pillars set with a slightly different alignment. The pillars
rested directly on the pavement.[11]

PAVEMENT

Polychrome mosaic.

STAGE III

Numerous renovations were carried out over the next one
hundred plus years (see no. 12).[11]

NARTHEX

A narthex was added on the north end of the basilica. It extends 4 meters beyond the hall's east wall.[11] A court[1] or "corridor"[11] may have adjoined the narthex and ran the entire length of the hall's east wall. The narthex was entered by a single door in the middle of its north wall.

PLAN

Remained essentially the same except for changes to its south wall and bema. (See no. 6.)

BENCHES

A plastered bench adjacent to the east wall was placed over a Stage II or Stage III mosaic pavement.[1]

Evidence indicates an additional bench ran along the west wall.[1]

PAVEMENT

There is evidence of several phases of mosaic pavement and repairs made during Stage III (see no. 8).[1,11]

4. Measurements.

Main hall: 19 x 17 m.[11]

Narthex: ca. 3 m. deep.[2]

Bema: ca. 2.8 m. deep x 9 m. wide x 90 cm. high.[2]

West room: ca. 2.4 x ca. 3.3 m. wide.[2]

East room: ca. 2.4 x ca. 3.0 m. wide.[2]

5. Orientation.

The bema is built against the south wall, the direction toward Jerusalem.

6. Character and form: apse, niche, Torah Shrine, bema, chancel.

STAGE II

A bema was added on the south. It is raised ca. 90 cm. above the nave pavement, and is flanked on either side by three stairs that were plastered, but bear little evidence of wear. A square niche (genizah ?) was cut into the bema's eastern corner.[1]

STAGE III

The bema was enlarged by incorporating the two sets of original stairs into it. Three new steps were added in front of the bema's east and west corners; the center was left unencumbered. Walls were added that closed off the south ends of both aisles, creating small side chambers flanking the bema. An additional wall, 0.75 m. directly in front of the bema, was built upon undamaged mosaic pavement, forming an enclosed chancel area.[1,A] All the new walls were built in part of reused limestone material.[1]

7. <u>Auxiliary rooms/structures</u>.

STAGE III

The narthex and court/corridor were added during this stage.
Other structures may have adjoined the synagogue's east and
west walls, but apparently did not directly communicate with
it.[1]   A road of thick concrete surrounds the building.[11]

8. <u>Ornamentation</u>.

STAGE I

A limestone relief of a lion within a medallion was uncovered
near one of the building's entrances.[1]   It apparently is
part of a lintel.[11]

Pavement: polychrome mosaic.

STAGE II

The aisle pavement was replaced by a well executed polychrome
mosaic set in geometric patterns.[11]   No figurative motifs
survive, although evidence remains of areas of damage possibly
caused by iconoclastic mutilation.[1]   The aisle pavement was
repaired in Stage III.

STAGE III

The nave floor, other than its Stage II border, was bare; it
appears to have been prepared to receive a mosaic pavement at
the time of the synagogue's destruction. Piles of mostly
unused tesserae, divided according to color, were found on
the floor.[1,11]

NARTHEX

Paved in mosaic laid in a simple black geometric pattern on a
white ground. Two inscriptions were set into the pavement
(see no. 10).[11]

STAGE II

The walls of the hall were covered with white plaster and
painted: The west wall bore red stripes painted on a white
plaster ground. On the east wall, green frames, painted on
a white plaster ground, framed simple floral motifs. A
seven-branched menorah was enclosed with a floral frame. The
pillars had Hebrew and Aramaic inscriptions painted in red on
a white ground (see no. 10). Several inscriptions were
enclosed within <u>tabula ansatae</u>, framed by wreaths tied with
Hercules knots.[1]

STAGE III

The original pillar inscriptions were covered over with fresh
plaster and replaced with new ones painted in red and black
on a white ground.[1]   Marble fragments of a chancel screen

and its posts were found near Rehov;[3] matching fragments
were uncovered within the synagogue.[1,2] Carved in relief on
the front was a seven-branched menorah enclosed within a wreath
tied with a Hercules knot and terminating in ivy leaves. On
the back were four lilies issuing from a common source; they
are placed against a dressed background and surrounded on two
sides by a double border.[3]

9. Coins, ceramics, and other artifacts found within building
complex.
The final report has not yet been published. Potsherds, dated
to the sixth-seventh centuries, were reported found under the
mosaic pavement of the narthex (see no. 10). Clay lamps,
dated to the sixth century, and glass lamps and brass fittings
for polycandelons were found in the main hall.[1,11]

10. Inscriptions.
The inscriptions have not all been published.[1]
STAGE II
Hebrew and Aramaic inscriptions painted on pillars appear to
be lists of donors, benedictions, halakhic regulations and
"other texts" related to synagogue worship.[1,11] The scribe's
name appears on the bottom; two names thus far published are
"Yitzhok" and "Agrippa."[1]
STAGE III
The new inscriptions painted on the pillars are in a different
and "inferior" form of Hebrew script; they are not yet
published.[1]
A monumental inscription (2.75 x 4.30 m.) was set in the mosaic
pavement of the narthex; it contains about 360 words. It
represents the longest Hebrew/Aramaic inscription discovered
to date in Israel. It contains no dedicatory or memorial
information, nor any information regarding the synagogue
building proper. Rather, it consists of halakhic details
regarding the laws of the Sabbatical year and the setting
aside of tithes in the various regions of the Holy Land and
adjacent areas. The following summary of its contents is
based on Sussmann's report:[4]
Following the opening salutation "shalom" is a detailed list
of the fruits and vegetables and important halakhic obliga-
tions stemming from agricultural precepts indigenous with each
and every locality. The following standard formula is
generally used: "The products (listed below) are forbidden
in . . . during the sabbatical year, and during the other six

years are tithed out of uncertainty/ out of certainty . . .
(list of fruits and vegetables)." Then follows lists of
townships where these laws are to be obeyed and those areas
that are exempt. The rest of the inscription is divided into
eight paragraphs. Three contain lists of fruits and vegetables
forbidden within the limits of Beth She'an, Caesarea Philippi,
and Caesarea Maritima; three of the townships within the
limits of Hippos, Naveh, and Tyre; a list of the permitted
townships in Sebaste; and the text of the well-known blessing
concerning the boundaries of Eretz Israel.

Most of the inscription is known from talmudic literature;
however, there are important variations that deal with the
location, names, and outlying vicinities of the city-gates of
Beth She'an and the names of the eighteen townships within the
limits of Sebaste.

A second inscription was found set in the eastern portion of
the narthex pavement. Part of it was damaged by a later tomb.
It consists of four lines in Aramaic and apparently is a
dedication. [11]

11. <u>Donors or patrons</u>.

STAGE II

The synagogue had numerous donors, judging from the names
listed on the pillars. [1]

STAGE III

The covering up of the earlier names may reflect a change in
the congregation. The new congregants were responsible for
the lengthy Talmudic inscription; but the reasons for the
change are unknown. [A]

12. <u>Date</u>.

The following chronology is based on Vitto's latest published
report. [11]

Stage I: The limestone relief is described as "typically
           late Roman." On the basis of architectural frag-
           ments, coins and ceramics, this stage has been
           dated to the early fourth century.

Stage II: Dated to the late fourth or early fifth century on
           the basis of coins, pottery and the mosaic pave-
           ment's "style."

Stage III: Renovations to the building were carried out from
           the sixth to seventh century when the building was
           abandoned.

On the basis of pottery sherds found beneath it, the narthex pavement has been dated to the sixth-seventh centuries. A powerful earthquake shook this area in 748/9.

13. Bibliography.

1. Vitto, Fanny. Personal interview. 5, May, 1977.

2. Idem. "Excavation in the Beth Shean Valley." 'Atiqot, VII (1974), 100-104.

3. Bahat, Dan. "A Synagogue Chancel Screen from Tel Rehov." IEJ, 23, 3 (1973), 181-183.

4. Sussman, Y. "A Halakhic Inscription from the Beth-Shean Valley." Tarbiz, XLIII, 1-4 (1973/1974), 88-158.

5. Idem. Qad., 8 (1975), 123-128.

6. Vitto, Fanny. Qad., 8 (1975), 119-123.

7. Demsky, Aaron. "Permitted Towns in the Boundaries of Sebaste According to the Rehob Mosaic Inscription." Qad., XI, 2-3 (1978), 70-78.

8. Hüttenmeister, F. Antiken Synagogen. Vol. I, pp. 369-376, 528.

9. Demsky, Aaron. "The Permitted Villages of Sebaste in the Rehov Mosaic." IEJ, 29, 3-4 (1979), 182-193.

10. Chiat, M. J. "Synagogue and Church Architecture in Byzantine Beit She'an." JJA 8 (1980), 6-24.

11. Vitto, Fanny. "The Synagogue of Rehov, 1980." IEJ, 30, 3-4 (1980), 214-217.

TEL MENORA

B:4, I-6

1. Name of site and map reference.

Tel Menora, Tirat Zvi, Kefar Qarnaim, Tell Abū Faraǰ.

1994.2035 (6.152)

Plan 20

2. Survey of site.

The ruins of the synagogue are located 50 m. north of Tell Abū Faraǰ near the Kibbutz Tirat Zvi, 9 km. SSE of Beth She'an. Two distinct building periods could be distinguished: a rectangular structure dated to the Iron Age, and above it, a Byzantine synagogue.

3. Character and sections of the building as suggested by extant and identifiable remains.

Only the building's foundation is extant, built of medium and large size basalt ashlars. There is evidence that the synagogue underwent several building stages.[1,2]

STAGE I

PLAN

A four room house with an inner wall, aligned north-south, was built of large, well-hewn ashlars.[2]

STAGE II

PLAN

The house's interior wall was removed, transforming it into a large single room. No column bases or interior wall supports were recovered.[1,2]

PAVEMENT

The pavement is mosaic.

4. Measurements.

STAGE II: 10.60 x 11.30 m.[2]

5. Orientation.

The mosaic pavement is laid to be "read" facing north.[1,2]

7. Auxiliary rooms/structures.

"Later additions," uncovered along the building's west and north side are 40 cm. above the house's foundation.[2] No further information regarding their identity is available.[A]

8. Ornamentation.

The remains of a badly damaged mosaic pavement were uncovered in the center of the room; additional fragments were found to its north and west.[2] The surviving central panel is enclosed within a broad strip of black and ochre tesserae followed by a row of flowers. A seven-branched menorah, its base destroyed, is in the southwest corner of the preserved panel. A shofar flanks the menorah on the left; the right is destroyed. The remainder of the pavement is laid in geometric patterns (#344). One octagon frames the image of a defaced bird. An unusually large square, which may have marked the center of the pavement, frames a series of concentric circles. It overlaps a broad linear border that served to separate the menorah image from the octagonal field; the square's presence in this position disturbs the symmetry of the geometric pattern.[A]

12. Date.

The pavement has been dated to the sixth century, based upon the limited use of figurative motifs.[2,3,4]

13. Bibliography.

1. Goldschmidt, S. BIES, 19 (1955), 237.

2. Idem. "Synagogue Remains at the Mound of Kefar Qarnaim." EI, XI (1973), 39-40.

3. Avi-Yonah, M. "Places of Worship in the Roman and Byzantine Periods." Antiquity and Survival, II, 2/3 (1957), 271.

4. Hüttenmeister, F. Antiken Synagogen. Vol. I, pp. 435-436.

5. Chiat, M. J. "Synagogue and Church Architecture in Byzantine Beit She'an." JJA 8 (1980), 6-24.

KAFR DANNA
B:4, II-1

1. Name of site and map reference.

Kafr Danna.

1948.2244 (4.39)

2. Survey of site.

The site is located 13 kilometers northwest of Beth She'an. The lintel of a synagogue was reported found in the area; the location of the building is unknown.[1]

8. Ornamentation.

The basalt lintel is ornamented with a seven-branched menorah standing on a tripod base flanked by an ethrog and lulav. On the outer extremes are two effaced animals.[2]

12. Date.

Unknown.

13. Bibliography.

1. Author unknown. "Kafr Danna." HA 17.

2. Foerster, G. 'Atiqot 3 (Heb.) (1966), 66 f.

3. Hüttenmeister, F. Antiken Synagogen. Vol. I, p. 98.

Kefar Otnay (Caparcotnei) was a Jewish village located 24 Roman miles from both Caesarea and Scythopolis, and 16 Roman miles from Sepphoris. Following the second Jewish revolt (ended 135 C.E.), a second Roman legion was assigned to Palestine, the Legio VI Ferrata, and garrisoned at Capercotnei. The camp became known as Legio and the Jezreel Valley was made its estate. Diocletian gave the territory the additional name of Maximianupolis in honor of his co-ruler, Maximianus Herculius. (Jones, Cities, p. 279.)

Jewish people are known to have settled in this territory, but no material evidence has been uncovered attesting to their presence. (Paul Lapp, "Excavation at Taanach," BASOR, 183 (Feb., 1964), p. 4.) This may be owing, in part, to the lack of any detailed archaeological survey of the region.

C. COASTAL CITIES

DORA

C:1

The city of Dora, built on and around the mound known as
Khirbet el-Burg, is south of the Carmel headland on the
Mediterranean coast. It was first settled in the Late Bronze
Age, and was continuously occupied through the Byzantine period.

Although Josephus (AJ XIX:300-312) records the desecration
of the "chief synagogue" in Dora in 38 C.E., no evidence of
Jewish occupation has been uncovered. Until recently, only very
limited archaeological surveys and excavations have been conducted
in this region.

The port of Caesarea, originally known as Straton's Tower, was founded by the Sidonians at the end of the Persian era or the beginning of the Hellenistic period. The Hasmoneans controlled the city for a single generation until Pompey returned it to gentile control and made it part of the Province of Syria. The city was given to Herod the Great, who built its impressive artificial harbor and renamed it Caesarea in honor of his benefactor, Augustus. Caesarea always had a Jewish population, but only a limited number were granted Greek citizenship.

Evidence of four possible synagogues has been uncovered in the territory of Caesarea, but only two have been verified as synagogues: Caesarea and Husifah. The Babylonian Talmud (Shab. 116a, 152a) mentions Jewish "meeting places" in Caesarea where religious discussions were held. According to some scholars, one of these meeting places was converted into an odeum by emperor Vespasian; its location is not known.[1]

[1] Lee I. Levine. Caesarea Under Roman Rule (Leiden, 1975), p. 46.

1. Name of site and map reference.
   Caesarea.
   1402.2125 (5.34)
2. Survey of site.
   The exact location of the Jewish quarter in Caesarea has yet to be determined. Prior to the first revolt, the Jewish community comprised a wealthy minority. In the next century their numbers were greatly reduced, but increased again in the third to fourth centuries. Talmudic statements show that at least two schools co-existed in Caesarea's Jewish community, the "school of Bar Kappara" and the "school of Rabbi Hosaya" (JT Shab. passim).
   Babylonian Jews, brought to Caesarea by Herod the Great to act as his guards, may have formed a separate community.[10]

The ruins of a synagogue, reported uncovered in 1932, are
located on the city's north side near the aqueducts and within
the Roman wall. The site was partially excavated in 1945, and
underwent further clearance in 1956 and 1962 under the direction of Michael Avi-Yonah on behalf of the Department of
Archaeology, Hebrew University, Jerusalem. Five strata of
occupation were uncovered, the upper two occupied by the
synagogue.[7] The synagogue requires further excavation
before an accurate reconstruction of its plan can be made.
The following data are based on somewhat confusing published
reports.

STRATUM I

The foundations of Hellenistic houses are built on virgin
soil, 2.8 m. above sea-level. Artifacts found in them
include Megarian bowls and West Slope ware from the Athenian
Acropolis.

STRATUM II

A square building, one wall measuring 9 m. long was built
atop the houses. Its foundations are 3.9 meters high and
support five courses (each .27 m.) of hewn stones laid in
alternating headers and stretchers. Herodian lamps, spindle-
shaped bottles, and fragments of Herodian ware were found in
the debris. It has been postulated that the building may
have been a Second Temple Period synagogue.[1,9]

STRATUM III

Part of the Stratum II building was converted into a cistern.
In the fourth century C.E., the cistern was filled with
rubble, which included fragments of terra stigillata ware,
coins of the procurators, and Roman pottery.[1,9]

3. Character and sections of the building as suggested by extant
    and identifiable remains.

STRATUM IV

The synagogue built on the rubble-filled cistern of Stratum
III incorporated portions of the Stratum II building. Its
pavement was 4.9 m. above sea-level.[1,9]

PLAN

The building was described as long and narrow.[1]

ENTRANCE

An entrance was found on the east, suggesting that the
building may have been a broadhouse.[1]

PAVEMENT

The pavement is mosaic.

STRATUM V

A new synagogue was built on the ruins of Stratum IV.

NARTHEX

Its location is not given[9] but it was paved with mosaics.

PLAN

The building is described as a colonnaded basilica with a
gallery, as evidenced by marble columns and two sizes of
Corinthian style capitals found in the debris.[9]

PAVEMENT

Stone and mosaic formed the pavement.

4. Measurements.[9]

Stratum IV: Hall: 18 x 9 m.

Stratum V: Narthex: 11 x 2.6 m.

5. Orientation.

STRATUM IV

The orientation was "apparently south."[7]

STRATUM V

It was oriented north-south.[9] The synagogue at Husifah
(C:2, I-2) (and possibly Khirbet Semmâka, C:2, IIIA-1), also
within the territory of Caesarea, is oriented to the east.
No explanation has been offered to explain the lack of
uniformity in synagogue orientation in this territory.[7,9]
The door on the east may have been to conform to the disputed
ruling in T. Meg. 4:22, that states synagogue entrances must
be on the east, similar to the Temple's (see: Beth She'an A,
B:4, I-2, Eshtemoa, E:4, I-2, Khirbet Susīya, E:4, I-4,
Khirbet Semmâka, C:2, IIIA-1).[A]

6. Character and form: apse, niche, Torah Shrine, bema, chancel.

STRATUM IV

A "projection", form unknown, is described as being "nearer
the sea."[1] A coin hoard was hidden in its plastering. It
has been conjectured to be a Torah Shrine.[7]

STRATUM V

Small marble columns, fragments of a marble slab carved with
a menorah, and marble inlays found nearby may have come from
the synagogue's chancel screen.[9]

7. Auxiliary rooms and/or structures.

STRATUM IV

Small square foundations attached to the building's east
side may have been for shops.[7]

STRATUM V

A narthex, its location not given, is described as a long,
narrow entrance hall.[9]

8. Ornamentation.

   STRATUM V

   A corner fragment of a mosaic pavement was reported uncovered.
   It is composed of a broad border of dentils (#158), guilloche
   (#194), and squares containing assorted geometric patterns,
   including Solomon's knots (#54) and lozenges, enclosing a
   fragmentary Greek inscription (see #10).[4] Several of the
   capitals uncovered in the ruins are decorated with menorot,
   either incised or in relief.[4] The menorot have unadorned
   curved branches, joined by a bar and a tripod base.
   An additional capital bears two monograms in place of the
   menorot; they read: "Patricius" and "consul."[1]

9. Coins, ceramics, and other artifacts found within the
   building complex.

   STRATUM IV

   Lamps were uncovered decorated with seven-branched menorot.[7]
   The majority of coins found in the "projection" are dated to
   Constantius II (337-361); a few date to Julianus Caesar
   (Caesar in 355, named Augustus in 360). The coins are
   primarily of the feltempreparatio type, with a soldier
   spearing a fallen enemy.[7]

10. Inscriptions.

    STRATUM IV

    Three marble fragments are part of a single Hebrew inscrip-
    tion:[6] Fragment A was found near the synagogue. Fragment B,
    found 70 m. south of fragment 'A,' was reused in the marble
    pavement of a Byzantine house.
    Fragment C was picked up by chance on the surface in the
    city. The three fragments form part of a marble slab
    inscribed with a list of the Priestly Courses (I Chronicles
    25: 7-18) in their order, together with the Priest's surnames
    and the name of the locality that they had served after the
    destruction of the Second Temple.[6] (See Ascalon for a
    similar inscription (C:8, II-1)). The three fragments read:
    "[Ma]milah / Nazareth / Akhlah / [Mi]gdal."[6]

    STRATUM V

    A marble column carved with a five-line Greek inscription
    reads:

    > The gift of Theodorus son of Olympus
    > for the salvation of his daughter
    > Matrona.[1]

The name Theodorus is considered common among Jews, but
Olympus is unique. The Latin appellation Matrona is somewhat
common among Jews; it has been found in Jewish inscriptions
in Rome, Asia Minor and Africa.[1]

In the narthex, a six-line Greek inscription is set in the
mosaic pavement:

> Beryllos the head of the synagogue (?)
> and the administrator, the son of Iu[s]tus,
> made the mosaic work of the triclinium
> from his own means.[1]

Beryllos is a rare Jewish name; it was the name of a governor
of Nero, and a bishop of Bostra in the fourth century, neither
Jewish. Iustus is a common Jewish name; it usually serves as
a translation of Saddoq ("just").[1]

A triclinium in conjunction with a synagogue is also mentioned
in an inscription found in the synagogue at Stobi and in
Jerusalem (E:1, II-1). The Talmud (JT Ber. 3:6a) refers to
a room adjoining a synagogue that was used for honoring the
dead, study, prayer, and eating. The last-named function
usually is associated with a triclinium.[A]

A five-line Greek inscription was carved on a block of stone
with a hole in its center.

> God help us! Gift of the people in
> the time of Marutha.[3]

Another fragment also bore the name 'Marutha.' Its meaning
is uncertain.[3]

11. Donors or patrons.

The donation of a column (by Theodorus, see above) has been
found at other synagogue sites, for example Capernaum (B:3,
I-1). The "head of the synagogue and administrator" may refer
to the archisynagogos, a high synagogue functionary mentioned
in the talmud, but whose function is unknown.[A]

The congregants were probably Greek speaking, so it is not
unexpected that their inscriptions would be in Greek. The
Jerusalem Talmud (Sot. 7:1, 21b) records that the Jews in
Caesarea recited the supreme Jewish prayer, the Shema', in
Greek in their synagogues.[A]

12. Date.[9]

Stratum I: Hellenistic.

Stratum II: Herodian - ca. 66 C.E.

Stratum III: First to third century, C.E.

Stratum IV: Fourth century.

Stratum V: Fifth century, a dating based on the monogram
               of Patricius, who was consulate in 459 C.E.
               The synagogue was possibly destroyed by fire
               in the sixth century.

13. Bibliography.

1. Avi-Yonah, M. "The Ancient Synagogue of Caesarea:
         Preliminary Report." Bulletin Rabinowitz. Vol. III.
         (1960), pp. 44-48.

2. Schwabe, Moses. "The Synagogue of Caesarea and its
         Inscriptions." In Alexander Marx Jubilee Volume.
         New York: Jewish Theological Seminary, 1950,
         pp. 433-449.

3. Sukenik, E. "More About the Ancient Synagogue of
         Caesarea." Bulletin Rabinowitz. Vol. II. (June
         1951), pp. 28-30.

4. Goodenough, E. R. Jewish Symbols, Vol. I (1953), p. 263,
         Vol. III, figs. 996-998.

5. Avi-Yonah, M. "Caesarea." IEJ, 6 (1956), 260.

6. Idem. "A List of Priestly Courses from Caesarea." IEJ,
         12 (1963), 137-139.

7. Avi-Yonah, M. and A. Negev. "Caesarea." IEJ, 13 (1963),
         146 ff.

8. Lifshitz, B. Donateurs, #68.

9. Avi-Yonah, M. "Caesarea: The Synagogue." EAEh. 1975 ed.

10. Levine, L. I. "New Light on Caesarea." Qad., XI, 2-3
         (1978), 70-75.

11. Hüttenmeister, F. Antiken Synagogen. Vol. I, pp. 79-90,
         524.

HUSIFAH
C:2, I-2

1. Name of site and map reference.
    Husifah, 'Isfīyā, 'Usifīyā, 'Esfia.
    1565.2360 (3.74)
    Plan 21

2. Survey of site.
    The ancient village overlooks the Kishon (Belus) River 13 km.
    southeast of modern Haifa. A Hebrew elegy, discovered in the
    famed Cairo genizah, refers to the destruction of the Jewish
    settlement of Husifah.[3] Ancient Jewish graves and a hoard

of 4,560 silver coins were found near the village; the latest dated 50 to 53 C.E. [6] The synagogue was built on the highest level of the village, near the top of Mount Carmel. Excavations were carried out in 1933 by the Department of Antiquities of the Mandatory Government, under N. Makhouly and M. Avi-Yonah. Only half of the building could be excavated. [1]

3. <u>Character and sections of the building as suggested by extant and identifiable remains</u>.

The northern wall was cleared for its full length, but the east and west walls could be only partially exposed. The southern wall had completely disappeared under a modern house.

The eastern wall was cut into bedrock. No trace was found of any of the building stones other than three fragments of a straight rafter with turned up edges.

NARTHEX

Portions of the bedding of a mosaic pavement extended 1.60 m. west of the hall, suggesting the presence of a narthex. [1]

PLAN

The nearly square building was divided into a central nave and flanking aisles by two rows of pillars (columns ?, five per row). Traces of the north row, extending east-west, were uncovered; the intercolumnar spaces were irregular.

ENTRANCE

A threshold was found in line with the west wall.

PAVEMENT

The pavement was mosaic.

4. <u>Measurements</u>. [1]

Main hall: 10.10 x 10.7 m.
Nave: 4.30 m. wide.
North aisle: 2.60 m. wide.

5. <u>Orientation</u>.

The building has an inclination of 22° to the west from true magnetic north. [9] From the position of the threshold and an inscription, the excavators determined that the building was oriented toward the east. [1] The eastern orientation may have been required because Mount Carmel was on the seashore, considered the western boundary of Eretz Israel. According to this theory, the position of synagogues near the sea correspond to those on the shore directly west of Jerusalem. [1] It has been suggested, though, that the building was a broad-house; therefore, its focal point was the long southern wall facing toward Jerusalem. [7]

7. <u>Auxiliary rooms/structures</u>.
   A narthex may have adjoined the west facade.[1]

8. <u>Ornamentation</u>.
   The pavement of the main hall was laid with tesserae in six
   shades of limestone, blue marble chips, and green glass; the
   latter was possibly manufactured in a local glass
   factory.[1]
   The wide border is decorated with various geometric patterns,
   interrupted on the west by three square (1 meter each) panels.
   A wreath in the middle panel frames a Hebrew inscription[5]
   (see no. 10), and the side panels each contain a seven-
   branched menorah flanked by a shofar, lulab, ethrog, and
   incense shovel.[5]
   The main field is divided into three unequal panels. On the
   west, a narrow panel frames an inscription. The center is a
   narrow diagonal panel decorated with a vine trellis enclosing
   various birds. Two heraldic peacocks are above the inscription
   set in the west panel (see: Gaza A, C:9, I-1) (see no. 10).
   The panel contains fragments of a zodiac wheel. The outer
   circle measures 1.38 m. in diameter, the inner, 0.60 m. Only
   five zodiac signs survive; they are (clockwise) Saggitarius
   to Aries: Two horns of Capricorn are followed by a large
   amphora spilling water representing Aquarius, a fin of Pisces,
   and two hind legs of Aries. In the panel's only preserved
   corner is a female head adorned with a necklace and wearing
   a scarf. Near her head are pomegranates, dates (?), and
   possibly a sickle.[5] She apparently personifies autumn,
   although she is placed next to the spring months; similar
   dislocation occurs at Beth Alpha (B:4, I-1). The pavement
   is considered to be similar stylistically to the church at
   Shavey Zion in nearby Ptolemais.[1] Fragments of plaster
   were painted with a reddish color.[1]

9. <u>Coins, ceramics, and other artifacts found within building
   complex</u>.
   Fragments of ribbed Byzantine and painted Arab pottery were
   found in the ruins.[1]

10. <u>Inscriptions</u>.
    A two-line Hebrew inscription is enclosed within a wreath:

    Peace upon Israel.[A]

    A fragmentary Aramaic inscription, in a poorly executed
    script, is set in a <u>tabula ansata</u> in the west panel of the
    nave.

> . . . and blessed be . . . of the
> scholar . . . / . . . [honored be the
> memory of everyone who] promised and
> gave his donation, be [he blessed]
> . . . / . . . Honored be the memory
> of Josiah who gave . . . . [1]

11. Donors or patrons.

The female form of the word "blessed" in the Aramaic inscription has led to the theory the donor may have been a woman. [1]
A woman donor is known from an inscription at Na'aran (F:4, I-2).

12. Date.

The pavement has been dated to the late fifth or early sixth century because of its "analogy with Beth Alpha."[1] Ashes and discoloration of the tesserae indicate that the building may have been destroyed during a fire.[1]

13. Bibliography.

1. Avi-Yonah, M. and N. Makhouly. "A Sixth-Century Synagogue at 'Isfiya." QDAP, III (1933), 118-131.

2. Sukenik, E. Ancient Synagogues, pp. 85 f.

3. Assaf, S. "Cairo Genizah." BJPES, 7 (1948), pp. 62, 66.

4. Frey, J. B. CIJ, #884-885.

5. Goodenough, E. R. Jewish Symbols, Vol. I (1953), pp. 257-259, Vol. III, ills. 649-654, 658.

6. Kadman, L. "Silver Coin Hoard." Yediot Numismatiot I, (1962), pp. 9-12.

7. Foerster, G. "The Synagogues at Masada and Herodion." JJA, 3/4 (1977), 11.

8. Hachlili, Rachel. "The Zodiac in Ancient Jewish Art: Representation and Significance." BASOR 228 (Dec. 1977), 61-77.

9. Hüttenmeister, F. Antiken Synagogen. Vol. I, pp. 181-184, 525.

KHIRBET SEMMÂKA
C:2, IIIA-1

1. Name of site and map reference.
   Khirbet Semmâka, Horvat Summāqa.
   1538.2307 (3.146)

2. <u>Survey of site</u>.
   The ruins are on Mount Carmel, 2.5 km. south-southwest of
   Dalyiat al-Karmil. The name was translated by C. R. Conder
   as "the ruin of the Sumach tree."[1]
   The facade of a building was reported in 1873.[1] In the
   latter part of the nineteenth century, the site served as a
   quarry for local residents, and much of the architectural
   remains were destroyed. Kohl and Watzinger surveyed and
   cleared what remained.[2]

3. <u>Character and sections of the building as suggested by extant</u>
   <u>and identifiable remains</u>.
   The building was constructed of well-chiseled limestone
   ashlars.[2]

   PLAN
   A basilica was divided into a central nave and flanking aisles
   by two longitudinal rows of columns (six per row).

   ENTRANCES
   On the east, a large central door was flanked by smaller ones.
   A door may have opened off the north aisle.[2]

4. <u>Measurements</u>.
   Main hall: 19.3 x 14.8 m.[2]

5. <u>Orientation</u>.
   The building's facade was on the east. Because of the
   building's similarity to "early" type Galilean synagogues,
   Kohl and Watzinger assumed the facade determined its orientation.[1] See Caesarea (C:2, I-1) for an explanation
   regarding the orientation of synagogues built near the
   Mediterranean sea.

8. <u>Ornamentation</u>.
   The profile of the molding framing the central door is
   considered similar to that at Kefar Bar'am A (B:1, I-2).[2]
   Only the pilasters flanking the south door on the facade
   survive. Conder reported finding two lintels; the larger
   of the two, still <u>in situ</u> over one of the facade doors,[1]
   is decorated with two crudely carved lions (bulls ?) flanking
   a chalice; a second smaller chalice is above the animal on
   the left. The entire design is framed within a <u>tabula</u>
   <u>ansata</u>.[3]

12. <u>Date</u>.
   The building is considered contemporary to other so-called
   "early" Galilean synagogues;[2] see Kefar Bar'am (B:1, I-2)
   and Capernaum (B:3, I-1) for problems associated with their
   dating.

13. <u>Bibliography</u>.

1. Conder, C. R. "Notes from the Memoir," <u>PEFQS</u> (1877),
      pp. 179 f.

2. Kohl, Watzinger. pp. 135-137.

3. Goodenough, E. R. <u>Jewish Symbols</u>. Vol. I. (1953),
      p. 208, Vol. III, ills. 529, 536.

4. Hüttenmeister, F. <u>Antiken Synagogen</u>. Vol. I, pp. 419-420.

KHIRBET DŪBIL
C:2, IIIB-1

1. <u>Name of site and map reference</u>.
   Khirbet Dūbil, Davela.
   1542.2328 (3.43)

2. <u>Survey of site</u>.
   The ruins are on Mount Carmel, 500 m. south of Dalyiat al-
   Karmil, 20 km. south-southeast of Haifa.

3. <u>Character and sections of the building as suggested by extant
   and identifiable remains</u>.
   A report filed in the archives of the Mandatory Government of
   Palestine records the discovery of cisterns, mosaic pavement,
   column fragments, and a Greek inscription on land belonging
   to Sheikh Azzam. The remains are not identified as a
   synagogue.[2]

8. <u>Ornamentation</u>.
   L. Oliphant, in 1884, reported two lintels recovered at the
   site. One is decorated with a stylized rosette set in the
   center, the other with an eagle, an unidentified object, and
   a wreath flanked by rosettes and trees (?).[4] It is uncertain,
   however, whether the lintels came from a synagogue.[1,3]

10. <u>Inscriptions</u>.
    A fragment of a seven-line Greek inscription carved on a
    stone is set within a <u>tabula ansata</u> and decorated with an
    image of a cross. Its attribution is not known.[A]

13. <u>Bibliography</u>.

1. Oliphant, L. <u>PEFQS</u> (1884), pp. 32 f.

2. Mandatory Government of Palestine. Archives. Rockefeller
      Museum, Jerusalem.

3. Avi-Yonah, M. <u>QDAP</u>. 13 (1948), 145.

4. Goodenough, E. R. Jewish Symbols. Vol. I. (1953),
        p. 225, Vol. III, ills. 596-598.

5. Hüttenmeister, F. Antiken Synagogen. Vol. I, p. 102 f.

APOLLONIA
C:3

Apollonia is located on the same stretch of Mediterranean coast as the port of Caesarea. The city may have received its Hellenized name following its transformation into a port by the Greeks sometime during the Hellenistic period. Apollonia has not been extensively excavated. The ruins of a Samaritan synagogue have been uncovered at Ramat Aviv.

RAMAT AVIV
C:3, IIIA-1

1. Name of site and map reference.
   Ramat Aviv.
   1311.1678 (7.1026)
   Plan 22

2. Survey of site.
   Many Samaritans spread into the coastal cities after the second Jewish revolt (end 135 C.E.); evidence of their occupation remains in Apollonia. A building recently uncovered on the slope of a hill north of modern Tel Aviv near the entrance of the Ha'aretz Museum was initially identified as a Samaritan church or synagogue.[2] In a 1978 report, it is identified as a church.[3] The building is being excavated by the Israel Department of Antiquities and Museums under the direction of H. and J. Kaplan.

3. Character and sections of the building as suggested by extant and identifiable remains.
   Only the south wall and one row of columns are extant.
   PLAN
   Two rows of columns (three per row) divided the building's interior into a wide central nave flanked by narrow side aisles.[2]
   ENTRANCES
   An "opening" is described as "facing" east.[2]
   PAVEMENT
   The pavement is mosaic.

5. Orientation.
   The building is oriented east-west.[2]

8. Ornamentation.

About one-third of a multicolored mosaic pavement has survived;
it is described as decorated with geometric designs and plant
motifs.[2]

9. Coins, ceramics, and other artifacts found within building
complex.

Pottery and a single bronze coin have been reported found.[2]

10. Inscriptions.

Three inscriptions are set in the mosaic pavement; two are in
Greek and one in Samaritan.

1. Of the first Greek inscription, set in a tabula ansata
near the building's "opening," only half is preserved.

> In the rule of count [comes] Urbicus,
> as an offering of . . . , son of
> Agatheus for the salvation of his most
> God-loving children, the structure with
> phosisterion [baptistry ?] is [dedicated]
> to the Lord.[6]

The term comes also appears at Hammat Gadara (G:8, I-2) and
Sepphoris (B:2, II-6).[A]

2. The second Greek inscription is set in a medallion.

> Blessing and Peace on Israel and on the
> place. Amen.[2]

3. The Samaritan inscription, set in one of the aisles,
consists of four lines in Aramaic characters. A
translation has not been published.

11. Donors or patrons.

It has been suggested, because of the building's orientation
to the east, that the structure was not a synagogue but a
church built by Samaritan Christians.[5]   Another possible
Samaritan Christian church has been uncovered at Salbīt
(E:3, I-1), but this attribution is also questionable.[A]
Plummer[5] is incorrect in assuming that the orientation of
a building can serve as positive identification of a church
or a synagogue when other signs are lacking. The debatable
term phosisterion in inscription 1, if the translation as
baptistry is accepted, would be more certain proof of the
building's use by Christianized Samaritans.[6,A]

12. Date.

On the basis of the pottery and the bronze coin (see above,
no. 9), the structure had been dated to the end of the
sixth or the beginning of the seventh century.[2]

13. Bibliography.

1. Kaplan, H. and I. HA 54/55 (July, 1975), 15.

2. Idem. IEJ, 22, 1 (1977), 55.

3. Idem. "A Samaritan Church on the Premises of Museum Ha'aretz," Qad., XI, 2-3 (1978), 78-80.

4. Reeg, G. Antiken Synagogen. Vol. II, pp. 631-632.

5. Plummer, Reinhard. "New Evidence for Samaritan Christianity," Catholic Biblical Quarterly, 41, 1 (Jan., 1979), 112-117.

6. Kraabel, A. Personal interview. August 7, 1979.

ANTIPATRIS
C:4

Antipatris, a city founded anew by Herod the Great, had its
name changed numerous times throughout its history. The city was
located near the source of the Yarkon (Yarqon) River, which
accounts for its Hellenistic name, Pegae, or "sources." In the
time of Pompey, the city may have been called Arethusa. The name
changes reflect the various peoples who fought to control this
strategic location on the Via Maris (Coastal Road). The city,
although technically not on the coast, has been geographically
included with the coastal cities.

No evidence of Jewish occupation has yet been uncovered,
although Josephus (BJ II:513) records a Jewish community in the
city.

JOPPA
C:5

The ancient port of Joppa is built on a high promontory
jutting into the Mediterranean sea. Its harbor, protected by a
chain of rocks forming a breakwater, was at the foot of the
promontory. The port has been occupied since the second half of
the 17th century B.C.E.; the scene of the Greek legend regarding
Perseus and Andromeda was the sea off Joppa.

The city's Jewish population can be traced back to the reign
of the Hasmonean Jonathan in 142 B.C.E. They are reported to have
been hostile to Herod's claim to be King of Jews. In response,
Herod built the port of Caesarea, thus depriving Joppa and its
Jewish population of its primary means of livelihood (Avi-Yonah,
Holy Land, p. 94).

Although Joppa retained its Jewish community throughout the
Roman and Byzantine periods, no evidence of a synagogue has yet
come to light.

JAMNIA

C:6

Jamnia (Yavneh) is known in Jewish sources as the
city where Yohanan ben Zakkai set up his rabbinic academy
following his secret departure from Jerusalem during the first
Jewish revolt (J. Neusner, A Life of Yohanan ben Zakkai, 2nd ed.
[Leiden: Brill, 1970, p. 148]). Jews may have first settled in
the city during the reign of the Hasmonean King Simon. During the
first Jewish revolt, the city became a refuge for pro-Roman Jewish
loyalists (Avi-Yonah, Holy Land, p. 111). After the second revolt,
the city became home to numerous Samaritans.

Although Jamnia was the center of Jewish scholarship and de
facto government during the period between the two revolts, and
its many synagogues and schools receive numerous mentions in the
two talmudim, no foundations of any of these buildings have been
found.

The only evidence of a synagogue is a column fragment containing a Hebrew/Aramaic inscription dated to ca. 600, long after
the city's heyday as a center of Jewish scholarship. A Samaritan
inscription is evidence of that community's occupation of the
territory in the period following the second revolt.

HORVAT HABRĀ

C:6, II-1

1. Name of site and map reference.
    Horvat Habrā, Khirbet Hebra.
    1285.1398 (10.61)

2. Survey of site.
    Horvat Habrā is located on the eastern border of Jamnia, near
    the territory of Lydda Diopolis. In 1931, a fragment of a
    column was discovered carved with part of a Hebrew or Aramaic
    inscription. It was postulated that the column was part of a
    no longer extant synagogue.[3] Earlier, in 1902, an inscrip-
    tion was found engraved on what apparently was a tombstone.[1]

10. Inscriptions.
    The Hebrew/Aramaic inscription inscribed on the column has
    four lines, the first line missing.

> [Blessed be the memory of] Judah the
> son of . . . from Beth She'an [who
> made this column] and repaired [it].[3]

The tomb inscription has one line in Hebrew and three lines
in Greek.

> Hebrew: "Peace to Israel. Forever."
> Greek: "Abram, son of the deceased Ruben
> the Pharbetis."[2,4]

The word "Pharbetis" suggests that Ruben was a native of that
city in Lower Egypt.[1]

12. Date.

The column inscription has been dated on the basis of its
letter forms to ca. 600;[3] an earlier date, the end of the
fifth century or early sixth, has also been proposed.[5]

13. Bibliography.

1. Vincent, L. "Notes épigraphiques," RB (1902), 436 f.

2. Avi-Yonah, M. QDAP III (1934), 120.

3. Schwabe, M. BJPES 11 (1944/1945), 31-33.

4. Frey, P. J.-B. CIJ #1175.

5. Hüttenmeister, F. Antiken Synagogen. Vol. I, pp. 149-150.

JAMNIA

C:6, II-2

1. Name of site and map reference.
    Jamnia, Yavne, Yabneh, Jabne.
    1262.1415 (7.1037)

2. Survey of site.
    The town is located 22 km. south of Tel Aviv, and 7 km. south-
    west of Rehovot. Following the first Jewish revolt, Jamnia
    became the center of Jewish culture and remained so until the
    end of the second revolt in 135 C.E., when it became a
    Samaritan and Christian village.

10. Inscriptions.
    A marble slab bearing a Samaritan inscription was uncovered
    east of the old mosque in Jamnia. It contained 20 lines
    inscribed in Samaritan characters. The inscription opens
    with the phrase: "Praise be to God who read (the Ten
    Commandments to Moses), be (His Name) praised forever."[3]
    These words are followed by the commemoration of the erection

of a synagogue by Qorah and a summary of the Decalogue
according to the Samaritan version. It concludes with the
words: "Let the Lord arise."[1] The precise wording is in
doubt.[2,3]

12. Date.
The inscription has been dated on the basis of its letter
forms to the late Byzantine or Early Arab period.[1]

13. Bibliography.

1. Kaplan, J. BIES, 13 (1946/1947), 165 f.

2. Ben-Zvi, I. BIES, 13 (1946/1947), 671-673.

3. Ben-Haim, V. Z. BIES, 14 (1947/1948), 49 f.

4. Reeg, G. Antiken Synagogen. Vol. II, pp. 671-673.

AZOTUS
C:7

Azotus comprises two cities: Azotus Mesogaeus, or Hippenus, and the harbor city, Azotus Paralius (Jones, Cities, Appendix IV, Table XXXIX). Before the Hellenistic and Roman periods, the inland city was known by the name Ashdod and the harbor as Ashdod-Yam. At the beginning of the Hasmonean period, Azotus was a gentile city; this character changed after the Hasmonean expansion onto the Coastal Plain, when Jews were encouraged to settle in the region.

Although the Jewish community in Azotus suffered great losses during the first Jewish revolt, many chose to remain in the city during the ensuing years. Samaritans began moving into the Coastal Plain following the Jewish exodus from the region at the end of the second revolt. Evidence of the existence of both these religious communities has been uncovered in the territory; however, the actual locations of their houses of worship have not been found.

AZOTUS MESOGAEUS/HIPPENUS
C:7, II-1

1. Name of site and map reference.
   Azotus Mesogaeus/Hippenus, Ashdod, Isdūd, Ašdod.
   1178.1293 (10.11)
2. Survey of site.
   During the Byzantine period the inland city became a semi-agricultural settlement. A marble slab containing Jewish symbols and a Greek inscription has been found in the area.[1]
8. Ornamentation.
   Kohl and Watzinger published a photograph of a fragment of a marble slab, which they suggested was part of a cabinet similar to those found in early Christian churches.[1] Sukenik, upon examining the slab, declared it was part of a synagogue chancel screen.[2] A second marble fragment, acquired by the Oslo Nasjonalgalleriet, fits into the upper left hand corner of the Kohl and Watzinger slab.[5] The slab is decorated with a Lesbian cyma enclosing a wreath tied with a knot whose two ends terminate in leaves. The

wreath frames a seven-branched menorah, flanked by a shofar and lulab. Only five flames are seen; the outermost flames are covered by the wreath.[4]

10. Inscriptions.

Above the cyma is a Greek inscription, followed by the Hebrew word shalom. Nine more letters of the inscription are on the Oslo fragment; thus scholars were able to reconstruct a complete translation.

> Lord remember for good and blessing.
> Peace.[5]

An alternative reading has been suggested.

> Let . . . be remembered for good and for
> blessing on the N. N. Peace.[7]

12. Date.

The slab has been compared stylistically to a marble panel reused in the Mosque of Omar on the Temple Mount in Jerusalem that is believed to have come from Justinian's basilica, now the el-Asqa mosque.[1] It has a similar Lesbian cyma frame enclosing two wreaths tied with knots whose ends terminate in heart-shaped leaves. This type of decoration was popular in Northern Syria and the Hauran region during the Roman and Byzantine periods.[1] Because of the similarity of the two panels, the Ashdod slab has been dated to the fifth century.[1]

13. Bibliography.

1. Kohl, Watzinger, p. 160.

2. Sukenik, E. The Ancient Synagogue of el-Hammam, pp. 61-67.

3. Frey, J. B. CIJ, #961.

4. Goodenough, E. Jewish Symbols. Vol. I. (1953), p. 218, Vol. III, ill. 571.

5. Avi-Yonah, M. "A New Fragment of the Ashdod Chancel Screen." Rabinowitz Bulletin. Vol. III. (Dec. 1960), pp. 69-70.

6. Dothan, M. "Ashdod II, III." 'Atiqot 9-10 (1971), p. 191.

7. Lifshitz, B. Donateurs, #69.

8. Hüttenmeister, F. Antiken Synagogen. Vol. I, pp. 19-21, 523.

AZOTUS MESOGAEUS/HIPPENUS - SAMARITAN
C:7, II-2

1. Name of site and map reference.
   Azotus Mesogaeus/Hippenus, Ashdod, Isdūd, Ašdod.
   1178.1289 (10.11)

2. Survey of site.
   The inland city of Azotus lies about 4 km. east of the
   Mediterranean coast. It never recovered from the debilitating
   effects of the first and second Jewish revolts and is described by Eusebius as a "townlet" (Onom. 20:18, 22:11). Its
   greatly decimated Jewish population was partly replaced by
   Samaritans.

10. Inscriptions.
    A marble fragment, bearing a Samaritan inscription, was found
    near the hill opposite the ancient acropolis. The beginning
    letters are from the Samaritan text of the biblical passage
    Exodus 15:18. It has been postulated that the inscription
    adorned a Samaritan synagogue in Ashdod. [1]

13. Bibliography.

    1. Dothan, M. 'Atiqot, 9-10 (1971), 191.

    2. Reeg, G. Antiken Synagogen. Vol. II, p. 553.

Ascalon retained its independence throughout the period of
Hasmonean expansion and was not included in the territory ruled
by Herod the Great (Josephus, AJ XV:217). The city, however, was
favored by Herod because it was his birthplace. During the Roman
and Byzantine periods, Jews lived in the city, although it was
considered to be outside the borders of Eretz Israel (Josephus,
BJ III:1-3).

Although no foundation has been uncovered of a building that
could be identified as a synagogue, considerable other archaeological evidence has come to light attesting to the existence of
synagogues within Ascalon. This material includes stones decorated with Jewish motifs and synagogue inscriptions.

ASCALON
C:8, II-1

1. Name of site and map reference.
   Ascalon, Ashkelon, Aschkelon, 'Asqalān.
   Tel Ashkelon: 107.119 (10.12)

2. Survey of site.
   About 75 years ago, several stones decorated with Jewish
   motifs and/or inscriptions were found in the area of
   Ascalon. [2,3] Three additional polished marble stones found
   in a nearby tomb were thought to be from the same building
   because of their similarity in height and thickness. [3] A
   decorated marble pedestal was found nearby in 1958. [5]

8. Ornamentation.
   The three marble stones found in the tomb are cut with
   lengthwise grooves that indicate they were designed to
   receive a screen.

   1. One stone is carved on both faces with a seven-branched
      menorah. [5] One menorah has its seven lamps shown as
      triangles resting on a horizontal bar; the other has
      four clusters of three leaves emerging from its horizontal
      bar. Both menorot are flanked by lulab and ethrogs to
      their right and shofars to the left.

2. A marble pedestal, 70 cm. high, is decorated on one side with a seven-branched menorah; the other three sides have been effaced. The menorah is flanked by a shofar and an ethrog that appears to be attached to the menorah's stand.

10. Inscriptions.

1. A marble fragment inscribed with a Hebrew inscription is now lost. The inscription may have been part of the list of the 24 Priestly Orders[1] (see Caesarea, C:2, I-1).

2. A badly damaged Hebrew inscription is now in the Louvre.

> Remembered be for good . . . , who
> offered . . . for the glory of
> Heaven.[1]

3. A column contains a Greek inscription.

> For the Salvation of Menahem and
> his wife Mairona and their son
> Samuel.[1]

4. Two screen fragments are carved with a two-line Greek inscription on both sides; a narrow bar separates the lines. The letters are cut out flush with the stone.

> To the Helping God, we Kyria Domna,
> Daughter of Ju[lian ?] and Kyrios
> Mari, son of Nonnos, in gratitude
> present. Kyrios . . . the son
> of . . . the grandson of Helikios,
>
> has presented to God and to the Holy
> Place for his salvation. Kyrios
> Kommodus has presented for his
> salvation . . . life. Year 709.[1]

The date 709 may be in the Seleucid era, therefore 397 C.E.[2] "Kyria Domna" has been postulated to be Empress Julia Domna, and "Kyrios Kommodos," Emperor Commodus. Others suggest that the date refers to the era of Ascalon, 604 C.E.[1,3] The phrases "Holy Place" and "in gratitude" (also translated as "sign of respect") occurs in a synagogue inscription at Gaza A (C:9, I-1).

11. Donors or patrons.

The suggestion regarding the identity of the empress and emperor has not been generally accepted.[2] A Jewish inscription possibly honoring a Roman emperor and his family has been found at Qazyon (B:1, IIIB-9).

12. Date.

The inscription refers to either the late fourth century or the early seventh. The pedestal has been dated to the fourth century.[6]

13. Bibliography.

1. Sukenik, E. The Ancient Synagogue of el-Hammeh, pp. 62-67.

2. Dalman, K. O. ZDPV, (1903), pp. 22-28.

3. Clermont-Ganneau, C. "Sur diverses inscriptions de
   Palestine publiees par M. Dalman." RAO, VI (1905),
   169-172.

4. Frey, J. B. CIJ, #962.

5. Goodenough, E. R. Jewish Symbols. Vol. I (1953),
   pp. 219-221; Vol. III, ills. 575-576.

6. Avi-Yonah, M. "Ascalon." Bulletin Rabinowitz. Vol. III.
   (Dec. 1960), p. 61.

7. Lifshitz, B. Donateurs, #70-71.

8. Hüttenmeister, F. Antiken Synagogen, Vol. I, pp. 21-26,
   523.

GAZA

C:9

Gaza, the ancient gateway to the desert and beyond, to Egypt, the Mediterranean world, and Palestine, retained its importance throughout much of its long history. It withstood a seige by Alexander the Great for five months before finally succumbing. Gaza was conquered by the Hasmonean king Alexander Janneaus and repopulated by Jews (Josephus, AJ, XIII:15-16; BJ, II:87). The city, however, retained its pagan character until the fifth century, when Bishop Porphyry destroyed its last remaining temple. (See Life of Porphyry, Bishop of Gaza, transl. by G. F. Nill (Oxford, 1913), Chapt. 75.)

Jews have resided in Gaza since the days of the Hasmonean conquests of Alexander Jannaeus; that the Jewish community prospered in this important commercial city is evident from the remains of a large synagogue found in Constantia Neapolis, the port of Gaza. Additional architectural fragments decorated with Jewish symbols and inscriptions found in the city and in the area between Gaza and Joppa would indicate that other synagogues existed in the territory; however, their locations remain unknown. Also unknown are the locations of the Samaritan synagogues to which a series of Samaritan inscriptions undoubtedly belong.

GAZA A

C:9, I-1

1. Name of site and map reference.

   Gaza, Gaza Mauimas, Constantia Neapolis, Gazza.

   0958.1033 (10.55)

   Plan 23

2. Survey of site.

   The synagogue, about 300 m. south of the city's modern harbor, was built over the remains of an older building. Its mosaic pavement was discovered by 1965, and its identity as a synagogue was established in 1967. Further excavations were conducted by Asher Ovadiah in 1976, on behalf of the Israel Department of Antiquities.

3. <u>Character and sections of the building as suggested by extant and identifiable remains</u>.

   PLAN

   The exact plan of the building is unknown, but it is postulated to have been a basilica with a central nave flanked by two aisles on each side separated by four rows of columns (10 per row).[1-4]

   ENTRANCES

   Three entrances are on the west side, a large central door opening onto the nave, flanked by two side entrances opening onto the inner north and south aisles. An additional entrance is postulated on the south.

   PAVEMENT

   Originally the synagogue was paved with mosaic (see no. 8); it was later repaved with marble slabs; several are <u>in situ</u>.

4. <u>Measurements</u>.[1]

   Main hall: ca. 30 x 26 m.

   Apse: Theorized as 3 m. deep. Not extant.

5. <u>Orientation</u>.

   The building is aligned east-west. The pavement is positioned to be read while the worshipper is facing east. See Caesarea (C:2, I-1) for a discussion of the orientation of synagogues on the Mediterranean coast.

6. <u>Character and form: apse, niche, Torah Shrine, bema, chancel</u>.

   It has been suggested that the building had an external raised semicircular apse off its east wall.[1] The published plan indicates an area in front of the apse that is as wide as the nave and that extends to the first pair of inner columns; it is enclosed by a chancel screen and railing.

7. <u>Auxiliary rooms/structures</u>.

   Two squares excavated in an area adjacent to and east of the synagogue revealed two packed earth floors laid on a sand base and separated by a kurkar wall. The floors are on the same level as the synagogue pavement, and may be part of the synagogue complex.[1] Byzantine sherds found on the floors and the evidence of fire suggest this area was destroyed at the same time as the synagogue.[4]

8. <u>Ornamentation</u>.

   A portion of the nave and southernmost aisle mosaic pavement has survived; it is considered to be the work by a Gaza based atelier of mosaicists.[8] See Ma'on, F:1, I-1.

In a central panel located in the westernmost portion of the nave is an image of King David wearing a crown and holding his lyre; he is seated on a throne surrounded by wild animals. Above the lyre, in square Hebrew script, is the name "David."[7] David as Orpheus also appears on a wall painting in the synagogue at Dura Europos; however, he is not crowned.[9] The Gaza image is the only one known where David is represented as both royalty and Orpheus.[7]

On the south aisle,[8] a guilloche border (#196) frames a field of an inhabited vine trellis, three medallions per row. The animals and birds are placed symmetrically in heraldic poses facing the figures in the central medallions. Two peacocks face an inscription (see no. 10) and two doves (?) flank a bird in a cage. These motifs were also popular for contemporary church pavements; for example, see nearby Beth Gubrin and Shellal.[8]

Hundreds of fragments of four marble chancel screens, window grills, and bone plaques were recovered near the east end of the synagogue.[1] The decorated fragments were all carved in the drill technique. Several screens are decorated with motifs similar to those of the aisle pavement, others with bunches of grapes, pomegranates, and rosettes. Red paint, found on some fragments, was the base for a gold-leaf overlay. Two large marble basins found in the ruins may have stood in the center of the synagogue's courtyard.[1]

9. Coins, ceramics, and other artifacts found within building complex.

Finds of artifacts have not yet been fully published; however, shoe-type Sassanian lamps were reported found on the hall pavement.[4]

10. Inscriptions.

A Greek phrase is inscribed on one of the marble basins.

> For the Salvation of Roubelos and
> Isses and Benjamin.[1]

A ten-line Greek inscription is set in the southern aisle's pavement; a portion is missing.

> Menahem and Yeshua the sons of the late
> Isses, wood merchants, as a sign of
> respect for a most Holy Place, have
> donated this mosaic in the month of
> Loos, 569.[1,6]

The phrases "Holy Place" and "sign of respect" (or "in gratitude") occur at Ascalon (C:8, II-1) and on a slab found between Gaza and Joppa (C:9, II-1).

11. Donors or patrons.

The names mentioned in the inscriptions are common Jewish names. It has been suggested that the donors of the mosaic pavement were wealthy wood importers.[8]

12. Date.

The month of "Loos" is August; the year 569 is in the era of Gaza, equal to 508/509. The synagogue probably was begun ca. 500 and completed at the time of the dedication of the mosaic pavement.[1] It was destroyed sometime in the first half of the seventh century, either during the Sassanian invasion (thus explaining the shoe lamps), or following the Muslim conquest in 635.[1]

13. Bibliography.

1. Ovadiah, A. "Excavations in the Area of the Ancient Synagogue at Gaza." IEJ, 19, 4 (1969), 193-198.

2. Idem. Qad., I (1968), 124-127.

3. Idem. "Gaza." EAEh. 1976 ed.

4. Idem. IEJ, 27, 2-3 (1977), 176-178.

5. Philonenko, M. "David-Orphée sur une mosaïque de Gaza." Revue d'Histoire et de Philosophie Religieuse, 47 (1967), 355-357.

6. Lifshitz, B. Donateurs, #73, 73a.

7. Barasch, M. "The David Mosaic at Gaza." EI, 10 (1971), 94-99.

8. Avi-Yonah, M. "Une École de Mosaïques a Gaza au Sixième Siècle." La Mosaïque Greco-Romaine II (Paris, 1975), pp. 377-383.

9. Kraeling, C. H. The Excavations at Dura Europos, Final Report. Vol. VIII, Part I: The Synagogue. New Haven: Yale Univ. Press, 1956, pp. 223-225.

10. Hüttenmeister, F. Antiken Synagogen. Vol. I, pp. 130-137.

11. Finney, Paul Corby. "Orpheus-David: A Connection in Iconography Between Greco-Roman Judaism and Early Christianity." JJA, 5 (1978), 6-15.

GAZA B

C:9, II-1

1. <u>Name of site and map reference</u>.

   Gaza, Gazza.

   099.101 (10.55)

2. <u>Survey of site</u>.

   Architectural fragments have been found in the area between
   Gaza and Joppa; no building foundations have been uncovered,
   however, other than at Gaza A (C:9, I-1). A large column
   decorated with a menorah and an inscription is in secondary
   use in the great mosque in Gaza.[1]

8. <u>Ornamentation</u> and 10. <u>Inscriptions</u>.

   1. The column reused in the mosque was found by Clermont-
   Ganneau in 1873.[1] It measures over 4 meters in height and
   is crowned with a Corinthian style capital. A bas-relief
   carved on the column shows a wreath framing a menorah, flanked
   by what appears to be an ethrog, oil jug, shofar, or sacrifi-
   cial knife. The wreath is of laurel leaves with an egg-shaped
   (almond ?) gem at its top; it is tied at the bottom with a
   ribbon terminating in ivy-leaves. A large trefoil is at the
   bottom of the wreath. Below the wreath is a <u>tabula ansata</u>;
   its <u>ansae</u> appear to be each decorated with a seven-branched
   "tree" (menorah ?). A three-line inscription within the
   <u>tabula ansata</u> is in Hebrew and Greek:

   > Hebrew: "Hannaniah son of Jacob."[1]

   > Greek: "To Ananias, son of Jacob."[1]

   The Hebrew inscription uses the Aramaic <u>bar</u> for the Hebrew
   term <u>ben</u>, meaning "son."

   2. A fragment of a lattice chancel screen was found somewhere
   between Gaza and Joppa. Traces of Greek lettering in the
   screen's upper lefthand corner cannot be deciphered. The
   screen is superficially incised with a seven-branched menorah
   flanked by a shofar and lulab.[6]

   3. A second slab, containing a five-line Greek inscription,
   was found in the same area. Two translations have been
   proposed:

   > For the salvation of Jacob the son of
   > Lazarus, X, his son, in gratitude to
   > God has renovated the structure of the
   > apse of this Holy Place together with
   > its screen from the ground up in the
   > month of March, indiction . . .(4)

> For the salvation of Jacob, Lazarus, and
> Marina (?) in gratitude renovated the
> [construction ?] of the apse of God in
> this Holy Place [in the synagogue ?] . . .(7)

Several of the phrases ("Holy Place," "in gratitude") are
similar to the inscription at Gaza A (C:9, I-1). It has been
postulated that the inscription does not refer to an "apse"
but, literally, to a "mussel shell," suggesting that the
donors renovated a screen and its shell ornament.(6)

12. Date.

The column has been dated to the second to third century,(1)
and the screen inscription to the sixth century.(7)

13. Bibliography.

1. Clermont-Ganneau, C. ARP, II. (1873-1874), pp. 392-396.

2. Reinach, J. "Chandeliers a Sept Branches." REJ, 19
   (1889), 100 f.

3. Durand, G. RB, I (1892), 248 f.

4. Sukenik, E. The Ancient Synagogue of el-Hammeh, pp. 62,
   68.

5. Frey, J. B. CIJ, #967-969.

6. Goodenough, E. R. Jewish Symbols. Vol. I. (1953),
   p. 223; Vol. III, ill. 583.

7. Lifshitz, B. Donateurs, #72.

8. Hüttenmeister, F. Antiken Synagogen. Vol. I, pp. 135-136.

GAZA C
C:9, II-2

1. Name of site and map reference.

   Gaza, Gazza.

   097.103 (10.1012)

2. Survey of site.

   Six Samaritan inscriptions and three marble pillars are among
   the evidence of the Samaritan occupation of the Gaza region.
   They were all uncovered about one km. from the sea shore;(1-6)
   no evidence of any Samaritan building(s) foundations have been
   found, however.(1-6)

10. Inscriptions.

    The inscriptions are in Samaritan script and are mainly texts
    from the Samaritan version of the Torah. It is assumed they
    came from synagogues in Gaza.(1)

12. Date.

The inscriptions have been dated from the fifth century[4-6] to the period of the Arab occupation.[2]

13. Bibliography.

1. Pirchett. "Note on the Newly Discovered Samaritan Stone." PEFQS (1873), p. 118.

2. Ganneau-Clermont, C. AEH II, p. 430.

3. Idem. "Inscription Samaritaine de Gaza et Inscriptions Greque de Bersabee." RB, 15 (1906), 84-91.

4. Taylor, W. R. "Samaritan Inscription from Gaza." JPOS, X (1930), 18 f.

5. Idem. JPOS, XVI.

6. Idem. "A New Samaritan Inscription." BASOR, 81 (Feb. 1941), 5.

7. Reeg, G. Antiken Synagogen. Vol. II, pp. 585-587.

RAPHIA
C:10

Raphia is the southernmost city on the Mediterannean coast
of ancient Palestine and is on the Palestine border with Egypt.
The city came under the control of the Hasmoneans, but was
restored to the gentiles by the Roman general Pompey (Josephus,
AJ XIV:88, BJ I:87).

No excavations have been undertaken in this region.

D. SAMARIA

SEBASTE

D:1

The Romans formed the city-territory of Sebaste from the
northern portion of the country called Samaria that had been
controlled by the Samaritans since the time of the Assyrian
conquest of Israel. Herod refounded the city in 27 B.C.E. and
renamed it Sebaste, in honor of the emperor. He subsequently
transformed it into a Hellenistic stronghold (Josephus, AJ VIII:
15, BJ I:21).

No Jewish evidence has been uncovered in the territory.

The formation of the city-territory of Sebaste by the Romans
left the southern area of ancient Samaria in the control of the
Samaritans. Because Samaritans chose not to support the Jews in
the first revolt, Vespasian rewarded them by founding a new city
in their territory, Flavia Neapolis, on the site of ancient
Maabartha (Josephus, BJ IV:499). The new city territory became
known as Neapolis.

Only one site in Neapolis, Shiloh, has been suggested as
having evidence of a Jewish house of worship, but the attribution
is based on questionable evidence. Whereas no physical remains
of a Samaritan synagogue have been uncovered in the territory,
there is considerable epigraphic evidence confirming their
existence.

SHILOH
D:2, IIIB-1

1. Name of site and map reference.
   Shiloh, Šilo, H. Selūn, Seiloun, Siloun.
   1778.1621 (8.143)
2. Survey of site.
   Shiloh is situated eighteen km. north-northeast of Ramallah,
   on the border of Neapolis and Aelia Capitolina. It has a
   long history as a sacred site.
3. Character and sections of the building as suggested by extant
   and identifiable remains.
   A little southeast of the Christian chapel at Shiloh, on a
   site considered holy by the Muslims, Jamia (Wali) Sitīn, are
   the ruins of a building whose identity remains uncertain. It
   has been suggested that the building was originally a synagogue, later reused as a mosque. The building has a niche in
   its southern wall, the direction toward Mecca, as well as
   toward Jerusalem. The niche has been described as larger
   than the usual Arab mihrab. [1] A window in the western wall
   has been closed off. Fragments were found of four different
   Corinthian-style columns that apparently carried vaults.
   The columns may have been spoils from one of the nearby

churches. [2] East of this building are the foundations of a
smaller building possibly built at a later date. It too has
a niche in its southern wall. [4] There is no evidence to
indicate either of the buildings were used as synagogues.

8. Ornamentation.
A large lintel, found near the Muslim building's northern
entrance (possibly one of three entrances in the north wall),
is decorated with a relief of an amphora flanked on either
side by a wreath and a horned altar. [3]

12. Date.
The pre-Muslim building may date to the fourth century;
however, there is evidence it underwent numerous
rebuildings. [1,2] The columns, which may be spoils from the
nearby Christian building, appear to date prior to a seventh
century renovation of the Muslim structure. [2,5]

13. Bibliography.

1. Kjaer, Hans. "The Danish Excavations of Shiloh: Prelimi-
    nary Report." PEFQS (1927), p. 212.

2. Idem. "Shiloh: A Summary Report of the Second Danish
    Expedition: 1929." PEFQS (1931), p. 86.

3. Goodenough, E. Jewish Symbols. Vol. I. (1953), p. 213;
    Vol. III, ill. 556.

4. Yeivin, Z. "Shiloh." HA 41/42 (April, 1972), p. 18.

5. Hüttenmeister, F. Antiken Synagogen. Vol. I, p. 396-398.

E.   JUDAEA

AELIA-CAPITOLINA
E:1

The territory of Aelia-Capitolina, as Jerusalem was known in
the Roman period, was carved out of a section of ancient Judaea
(Judah), the southern half of David and Solomon's United Monarchy.
It was refounded and renamed by Emperor Hadrian in 132 C.E., and
was composed of four Judaean toparchies: Oreine, Gophitica,
Herodium, and Bethleptepha. Hadrian expelled all Jews from the
territory, but they were apparently allowed to return after his
death (Smallwood, Jews, pp. 478-479).

The Babylonian Talmud (Ket. 105a) gives the number of synagogues in Jerusalem at the time of the first Jewish revolt
(66-70 C.E.) as 394; the Jerusalem Talmud (Meg. 3:1) gives the
number as 480. The Talmudim both refer to a synagogue built on
the Temple Mount (JT Sot. 7:7-8, Yom. 7:1), but its existence is
controversial (Sidney B. Hoenig, "The Supposititious Temple-
Synagogue," JQR, LIV, 2 (Oct., 1963), 115-131).

The only certain evidence of a synagogue in the territory is
the famed Theodotos inscription found in the Ophel section of
Jerusalem (E:1, II-1). Other sites suggested as possible locales
of synagogues are: David's Tomb (E:1, IIIA-1); a rock hewn cavern
in the Mamillah cemetery (not in Handbook); and Herodium (E:1,
IIIA-2).

JERUSALEM
E:1, II-1

1. Name of site and map reference.
    Jerusalem, al-Quds, Aelia-Capitolina.
    1725.1313 (11.79)
2. Survey of site.
    An inscribed limestone block was found in 1913 among other
    architectural remains discovered in an ancient cistern in the
    Ophel section of Jerusalem.[1] What was unusual about the
    find was the manner in which the ruins of the demolished
    building had been carefully piled and stored in the cistern,
    rather than thrown haphazardly.[3] L. Vincent suggested the
    ruins were of a synagogue destroyed in 70 C.E.; their orderly
    storage occurred either because the congregants had hoped to

return and rebuild their synagogue, or because they desired
to preserve its remnants from profanation.[5]

10. Inscriptions.

The limestone block was carved with a ten-line Greek inscription. It measured 75 x 41 x 20 cm. and apparently was meant
to be built into a wall. A few letters have been defaced.

> Theodotus, son of Quettenos (Vettenos),
> priest and archisynagogus, son of an
> archisynagogus, grandson of an archi-
> synagogus, built this synagogue for the
> reading of the Law and for the teaching
> of the Commandments, and the hostel and
> the chambers and the water fittings for
> the accomodation of those who [coming]
> from abroad have need of it, of which
> [synagogue] the foundations were laid by
> his fathers and by the Elders and
> Simonides.[6]

11. Donors or patrons.

Theodotus may have been the descendant of a synagogue
official taken prisoner by Pompey in 64 B.C.E. and sent to
Rome. The grandson had enough money to build a synagogue and
hospice on the site of his ancestor's earlier foundation.[4,5]

12. Date.

The inscribed block and the other architectural fragments
found with it have been dated to the first century of this
era.[3,5] The date is supported by the inscription's letter
forms, which are of a type that purportedly date to before
70 C.E.[4]

13. Bibliography.

1. Weill, M. R. CRABL (1914), pp. 333f.

2. Idem. REJ, LXX (Jan.-June, 1920), Annexe, Pl. XXVa.

3. Weill, M. R. PEFQS (Jan. 1921), p. 22.

4. Clermont-Ganneau, C. Syria, I (1920), p. 191.

5. Vincent, L. "Découverte de la 'Synagogue des Affranchis'
   à Jérusalem." RB, (April, 1921), p. 247.

6. Fitzgerald, G. M. PEFQS, (1921), pp. 175-181.

7. Sukenik, E. Ancient Synagogues, pp. 69 f.

8. Frey, J. B. CIJ, #1404.

9. Lifshitz, B. Donateurs, #79.

10. Hüttenmeister, F. Antiken Synagogen. Vol. I, pp. 192-195,
    525.

DAVID'S TOMB
E:1, IIIA-1

1. Name of site and map reference.
   David's Tomb.
   1717.1310 (11.79)

2. Survey of site.
   The building connected with David's Tomb and the Cenacle on
   Mount Zion were inspected in 1949 for signs of damage.[1]
   In the course of a thorough examination of the burial hall
   and its various building phases, a high "apse" was discovered
   behind David's cenotaph.[1]

3. Character and sections of the building as suggested by extant
   and identifiable remains.
   The three outer walls of the "tomb" (north, south, east) are
   built of ashlar stones and date to the building's first
   phase. The present west wall, and the vault between it and
   the east wall, are dated to the Mameluke period.[1] The
   cenotaph is Crusader.[5]
   Twelve centimeters beneath the modern pavement is a layer of
   plaster on the same level as the base of the cenotaph; 48 cm.
   below this are the remains of a colored mosaic pavement set
   in geometric patterns. Another layer of plaster 10 cm. below
   the mosaic pavement may belong to an earlier stone or mosaic
   pavement.[1] The first phase walls were plastered; traces of
   Greek letters have been found on plaster fragments.[1]

4. Measurements.[1]
   Main hall: 10.50 m. long.
   Niche: 2.48 m. wide x 1.20 m. deep x 2.44 m. high.

5. Orientation.
   The niche(s) points towards the north with an eastern deviation of several degrees (10° N), toward the Temple Mount.[1]

6. Character and form: apse, niche, Torah Shrine, bema, chancel.
   The high internal "apse" was reportedly in the form of a
   niche cut into the thick (2.80 m.) north wall.[1] Recently
   two, and possibly three, niches have been discovered in the
   wall.[5] The floor of the niche(s) is 1.92 m. above the
   hall pavement.[1] This is similar to the placement of the
   three niches in the synagogue at Eshtemoa (E:3, I-2).

7. Auxiliary rooms/structures.
   The hall has undergone numerous rebuildings. The Coenaculum
   built above the tomb is oriented east.[4] (See no. 11.)

8. <u>Ornamentation</u>.
   The later mosaic pavement is set in geometric patterns.

11. <u>Donors or patrons</u>.
   The Cenacle is the traditional Christian site of the Last
   Supper; therefore, some scholars suggest it became a center
   for the Primitive Church and a cult center for "Judeo-
   Christians."[2,4]   See too Kafr Kannā (B:2, II-5) and
   Nazareth (B:2, IIIB-2). There is insufficient evidence to
   indicate what the building's function was or what group
   built it.[A]

12. <u>Date</u>.
   The original building, of which three walls survive, has been
   dated to the Late Roman Period.[1]   Historically, the most
   likely time for the construction of a synagogue in Jerusalem
   would be during the brief reign of Emperor Julian (361-363).[5]

13. <u>Bibliography</u>.

   1. Pinkerfeld, J. "David's Tomb: Notes on the History of the
      Building, Preliminary Report." <u>Rabinowitz Bulletin</u>.
      Vol. III (Dec., 1960), pp. 41-43.

   2. Finegan, Jack. <u>The Archaeology of the New Testament</u>.
      Princeton, 1969, pp. 149-151.

   3. Hirschberg, H. "The Remains of Ancient Synagogues in
      Jerusalem." <u>Qad</u>. I, 1-2 (1968), 56-62.

   4. Bagatti, B. <u>The Church from the Gentiles in Palestine</u>.
      Jerusalem: Franciscan Press, 1973, p. 25.

   5. Avi-Yonah, M. "Jerusalem." <u>EAEh</u>. 1976 ed.

   6. Hüttenmeister, F. <u>Antiken Synagogen</u>. Vol. I, pp. 196, 526.

HERODIUM
E:1, IIIA-2

1. <u>Name of site and map reference</u>.
   Herodium, Herodion, Jebel Fureidis, Ǧabal Furēdis.
   1731.1193 (11.68)
   Plan no. 24

2. <u>Survey of site</u>.
   Located 12.5 km. south of Jerusalem near Tekoa, the palace
   fortress was set within a cone of an artificial hill, 758
   meters above sea-level. V. Corbo, on behalf of the Franciscan
   Custody of the Holy Land, partially excavated the site between
   1962 and 1967,[1,2] and clearance was continued under the

direction of G. Foerster on behalf of the Isarel Department
of Antiquities and Museums.[3,5]

Herod built the fortress at the spot where he supposedly
routed his pursuers during his flight in 40 B.C.E. from
Jerusalem to Masada; it was intended to serve as a fortress,
a capital of a toparchy, and his mausoleum. During the first
revolt, Herodium, Masada, Machaerus, and Jerusalem were the
last zealot holdouts against Rome. Herodium fell first,
captured by the Romans following the fall of Jerusalem in
August, 70 C.E.; later, it served as a command post for rebels
led by Bar Kochba during the second Jewish revolt.

The Herodium plan consists of two areas; a main complex on
top of the hill and a second building complex at its base.
The building on the summit was a circular fortress palace
surrounded by two parallel circular walls (outer wall is 62 m.
in diameter) with four towers, one round and three semicircular.[4] The circular palace area is divided into two sections,
the western half containing service rooms and dwellings
separated by a possible court. A triclinium, located in the
southern portion of the western half, is surrounded by four
small rooms that abut the inner circular wall. Another room
adjoins the triclinium on the north. These rooms may have had
upper stories.[4] The zealots transformed the triclinium into
an assembly hall that has been identified by some scholars as
a synagogue.[1-6] A miqvah was added in front of the
building.

Corbo and Foerster disagree as to the triclinium's original
form and later alterations. Both theories are presented
below (no. 3).

3. <u>Character and sections of the building as suggested by extant
and identifiable remains.</u>

<u>Corbo.</u>[1,2]

STAGE I

PLAN

Tetrastyle triclinium: two rows of columns, three columns
each, divide the interior into three aisles.

ENTRANCES

On the east, a single main entry was flanked on either side
by a window. Doors, located in the north and south walls
opened onto two loci.

STAGE II

PLAN

The basic layout of the hall remains unchanged.

BENCHES

Three tiers were added along the north, south and west walls, and possibly flanking the main entrance.

Foerster. [3-5]

STAGE I

PLAN

The building was a rectangular hall without interior columns.

ENTRANCES

On the east were a single main entry and two windows. An additional entrance on the north leads into an adjoining room.

STAGE II

PLAN

Four columns were now added, one in each corner; they do not rest on a stylobate, but are on a layer of soil 10 cm. thick, laid over the now destroyed original pavement. The column bases and shafts may have been spoils from the western wing of Herod's great peristyle.

BENCHES

Three tiers were added along the north, south, and west walls.

4. Measurements.

HALL: 14 x 10 m. [1]

15 x 10.5 m. [5]

15.15 x 10.6 m. [4]

5. Orientation.

The building's main entrance and facade are on the east. The orientation has contributed to the building's identification as a synagogue. [3,5] This attribution is based upon the disputed ruling in T. Meg. 4:22: "One does not place the entrance to synagogues except in the east, for we find that in the Temple the entrance faced the east." It must be noted, however, that the building has its western corner and adjoining room built into the interior circular wall, so that the most practical position for its entrance is on the east. [7]

See Masada, F:IIIA-1.

6. Character and form: apse, niche, Torah Shrine, bema, chancel.

It has been suggested that the Torah Scrolls were stored in the small room adjoining the hall on the north, and were brought into the building only on those days when they were used. [3,5] There is no evidence to support this theory (see Masada, F:IIIA-1). [A]

7. <u>Auxiliary rooms and/or structures</u>.

The hall is surrounded by four small rooms, none of which had access into it. Only the room adjoining the hall on the north opened directly into it.

8. <u>Ornamentation</u>.

The building was a simple hall without ornament. The walls were stuccoed.[4]

11. <u>Donors or patrons</u>.

STAGE I

It was built as a triclinium or assembly hall by Herod the Great.[1-7]

STAGE II

The building was altered by zealots during the first Jewish revolt.[1-6] Whether the alterations were intended to transform the building into a synagogue, a Jewish house of worship, has not as yet been proved.[3,5,7] The question of the existence of synagogues as early as the first century is still disputed.[7]

12. <u>Date</u>.

Stage I: Following Herod's victory in 40 B.C.E.[1-7]
Stage II: First Jewish revolt: 66-70 C.E.[1-6]

13. <u>Bibliography</u>.

1. Corbo, Virgil. "L'Herodion de Gebal Fureidis." <u>LA</u> XVII (1967), pp. 101 ff.

2. Idem. "The Excavation at Herodium," <u>Qad.</u> I, 4 (1968), 132-136.

3. Foerster, G. "The Synagogues at Masada and Herodium," <u>EI</u> XI (1973), 224-228.

4. Idem. "Herodium." <u>EAEh</u>. 1976 ed.

5. Idem. "The Synagogues at Masada and Herodium." <u>JJA</u> 3/4 (1977), 6-11.

6. Hüttenmeister, F. <u>Antiken Synagogen</u>. Vol. I, pp. 173-174.

7. Chiat, Marilyn. "First Century Synagogues: Methodological Problems." <u>Ancient Synagogues: Current Stage of Research</u>. Edited by Joseph Gutmann. Brown Judaic Studies 22. Chico: Scholars Press, 1981, pp. 49-60.

LYDDA/DIOSPOLIS
E:2

Following the first Jewish revolt, the town of Lydda became
a center of Jewish scholarship ("Talmud, Jerusalem," EJ, 1972 ed.).
The city was refounded ca. 200 C.E. by Septimius Severus and
granted full city rights (Smallwood, Jews, p. 491). Its Jewish
population diminished, but the city remained an important and
flourishing center of trade.

Samaritans moved into the territory in the fourth century and
evidence of their presence has been uncovered at several sites,
although the precise locations of their synagogues remain unknown.
One building, at Huldah, may have belonged to the Samaritan community; however, the evidence is inconclusive.

Lydda was a center of Jewish scholarship, home to numerous
schools and synagogues; however, no evidence has been recovered
that can be attributed to a Jewish synagogue. Excavation is
difficult in the city because it has been continually occupied
since the Roman period.

HULDAH
E:2, I-1

1. Name of site and map reference.
   Huldah, Hulda, H. ar-Raqadīya, H. ar-Ruqqadīya.
   1474.1385 (10.1015)
2. Survey of site.
   The ruin is located 8.5 km. southeast of Rehovot, near the
   northwestern border of Lydda and Azotus. The building was
   excavated in 1953 by J. Ory, on behalf of the Israel Department of Antiquities.
3. Character and sections of the building as suggested by extant
   and identifiable remains.
   PLAN
   The rectangular building is divided into two rooms by a cross-
   wall 30 cm. thick.[1,2] In the north room; two niches were in
   each of the three external walls; each niche was provided
   with a sump and was paved with mosaic.[1,2] (See nos. 6 and
   8.) The south room contained a round cistern with plastered
   walls sunk into the mosaic pavement in the center of the room.

Three semicircular steps descended into the pool. The pool
was connected on the east by a conduit (lead pipe) to a
smaller and shallower square pool that was paved with mosaic
and had a sump in its center.[2]   (See no. 8.)

ENTRANCES

On the south side, a threshold was uncovered in the center
of the wall.[1]

4. Measurements.[2]

Rectangular building: 12.20 x 7.00 m.

North room: 4.60 x 7.00 m.

South room: 5.30 x 7.00 m.

Niches: 1.00 x 0.60 m. (each)

Large pool: 2.50 m. in diameter.

Small pool: 1.10 meters square.

5. Orientation.

The inscriptions (see no. 10) set into the mosaic pavement are
to be read facing north; this has led to the suggestion that
the building was Samaritan.[4]

6. Character and form: apse, niche, Torah Shrine, bema, chancel.

The function of the six niches in the north room is not known.
It has been suggested that they were related to a miqvah.[2]

8. Ornamentation.

The north room is paved with coarse white tesserae set in the
form of three squares, one within the other. The south room
also is paved with coarse white tesserae; facing the entrance
is an oblong panel of finer tesserae. The panel has a single
line of black tesserae that frames an inscription (see no. 10)
and a seven-branched menorah flanked on the right by a shofar
and on the left by a lulab, ethrog, and incense shovel. East
of the panel is another one with a square border enclosing a
circle (1.16 m. in diameter) that frames a wreath. A Greek
inscription within the wreath is in black, except for the
names, which are in red tesserae. (See no. 10.)

9. Coins, ceramics, and other artifacts found within building
complex.

Fragments of large jars were found within each niche in the
north room.[2]

10. Inscriptions.

Two are in Greek. In the menorah panel, there are three lines:

Blessing to the people.[2]

This has been compared with an inscription found at Ramat
Aviv (C:3, IIIA-1).

Within the wreath are six lines:

> Good luck to/Eustochios/and Hesychios/
> and Euagrios/the founders.[2]

The phrase "good luck" is unusual in Jewish inscriptions. The
names Eustochios and Euagrios are rare, Hesychios is known
from a Jewish epitaph found at Joppa (CIJ, #922).[2]

11. Donors or patrons.

The three individuals named in the inscription must be considered the major patrons of the building, whatever its
function.[A]

12. Date.

The building has been dated to the fifth century, because of
the letter forms of the inscriptions.[2]

13. Bibliography.

1. Ory, J. "Huldah." IEJ, 3 (1953), 133-134.

2. Avi-Yonah, M. "Various Synagogal Remains: Huldah."
       Bulletin Rabinowitz, Vol. III. (1960), pp. 57-59.

3. Lifshitz, B. Donateurs, #81.

4. Reeg, G. Antiken Synagogen. Vol. II, p. 602.

KEFAR BILU

E:2, II-1

1. Name of site and map reference.

Kefar Bilu, H. al-'Asafīra.

1329.1428 (7.1018)

2. Survey of site.

The site is located one km. south of Rehovot on the ancient
border of Jamnia and Lydda/Diospolis. A fragment of a marble
tablet engraved with an eleven-line Samaritan inscription
found here may come from a neighboring site named Khirbet
'Asabirah.[1] The inscription contains the initial words of
the verses of the Samaritan Decalogue; the opening line is
the first two words of Genesis.[2]

12. Date.

The inscription has been dated to the Byzantine period,
although it may be as late as the Early Arab.[1,2]

13. Bibliography.

1. Ben-Zvi, I. <u>BIES</u>, 18 (1954), pp. 223-229.

2. Ben-Zvi, I. <u>IEJ</u>, 5 (1959), p. 199.

3. Reeg, G. <u>Antiken Synagogen</u>. Vol. II, pp. 612-613.

NA'ANEH

E:2, II-2

1. <u>Name of site and map reference.</u>
   Na'aneh, Na'āna, Ni'āna, Nīana.
   1381.1422 (7.1022)

2. <u>Survey of site.</u>
   Located six km. south of Ramlah, this town receives no
   mention in the two talmudim.[4]

8. <u>Ornamentation.</u>
   A fragment of a bronze plate and two square capitals were
   random finds in the village.[1]
   Bronze Plate
   The plate was reported found by Clermont-Ganneau, who
   suggested it served a religious purpose similar to the
   paten in the Eucharist.[1] It has also been attributed
   to a synagogue or tomb. The plate is round, 50 cm. in
   diameter; one-third is missing. The rim is decorated with
   projecting beads, followed by an interlaced vine rinceau
   framing flowers (rosettes). Within one vine medallion is
   a seven-branched menorah standing on a tripod base, with a
   horizontal crossbar joining the branches. To the menorah's
   right within a second medallion is a gabled Torah Shrine
   with two closed doors that are divided into two panels with
   a circle in the center. The center of the plate is divided
   into quarters by the curling tendrils of four plants; the
   design is considered similar in style to designs carved
   on Jewish ossuaries.[5] Between the plants, in each of
   four openings, are a pair of palm branches (?) emerging
   from an amphora.
   Capitals
   The capitals are squared in form; one is decorated on one
   face with what appears to be an ivy plant with two branches

terminating in heart-shaped leaves. A second face is decorated
with an acanthus leaf as seen from above, flanked by a small
trefoil.[5]

10. Inscriptions.

The second capital has a short Greek inscription set within
a wreath: "Heis Theos," translated as "one God" or "God is
one." A similar inscription, carved on a capital was found
along with a Samaritan inscription at 'Imwas (Emmaus E:3, II-1).
This has led to the suggestion that the capitals and bronze
plate are from a lost Samaritan synagogue at Na'aneh.[4] The
phrase "Heis Theos" also was popular in Christian use, suggesting the capitals may have come from a church, and the
bronze plate from a synagogue, possibly Samaritan.[1,2,6]

12. Date.

The capitals are dated to the fifth-sixth centuries.[3]

13. Bibliography.

1. Clermont-Ganneau, Charles. PEFQS, (1882), p. 18.

2. Clermont-Ganneau, Charles. "Rapports sur une Mission en
     Palestine et en Phénicie." Archives des Missions
     scientifiques et littéraires. Series III, vol. XI
     (1885), pp. 184, 185.

3. Dussaud, Rene. "Les monuments palestiniens et judaïques."
     Départment des antiquités orientales. Paris: Musée
     des Louvre, 1912. Nos. 95-97, pp. 75-77.

4. Sukenik, E. The Ancient Synagogue of Beth Alpha. Jeru-
     salem: Univ. Press, 1932, pp. 23-24.

5. Goodenough, E. Jewish Symbols. Vol. I, (1953), pp. 173,
     225; Vol. III, ills. 590-591.

6. Reeg, G. Antiken Synagogen. Vol. II, pp. 621-622.

NICOPOLIS/EMMAUS
E:3

The Roman Emperor Elagabalus formed the city-territory of Nicopolis from an urbanized land located in the toparchy of Emmaus (Smallwood, Jews, n. 48, p. 343; n. 24, p. 492). It is uncertain whether this is the same Emmaus named in Luke (24:13-35) as the site of a resurrection-appearance of Jesus. Earlier, Vespasian had transformed Emmaus, which he may have renamed Nicopolis, into one of the camps (campus legionis) encircling Jerusalem (Smallwood, p. 311).

The city's Jewish community receives mention in both talmudim (BT Shab. 147b, JT Ber. 4:27d); however, no evidence of a synagogue has been found. A Samaritan synagogue at Salbīt has been uncovered; a second one, located at Emmaus, is known only from inscriptions.

SALBĪT
E:3, I-1

1. Name of site and map reference.
   Salbīt, Sa'alavim, Selebi, Selbît, Shaalbim, Shelbit, Sche'Albim.
   1488.1419 (8.1028)

2. Survey of site.
   The ancient village of Salbīt receives mention in the Bible under the name of Shaalbim (Jos. 19:42; Judg. 1:35; I Kings 4:9). It is located 3 km. south of el-Qubab, a village on the Jerusalem to Ramleh highway, on a hillock overlooking the Ayalon Valley. The city of Emmaus was 3.5 km. to the north.

   A mosaic pavement was uncovered in the courtyard of a modern village house; the site was excavated in 1949 by E. Sukenik on behalf of the Archaeological Institute of Hebrew University, Jerusalem.

3. Character and sections of the building as suggested by extant and identifiable remains.
   NARTHEX
   There may have been a narthex on the south. [1]

PLAN

The building was a rectangular hall; no evidence of columns or of an interior partition have been found. [1]

PAVEMENT

Two super imposed mosaic pavements were found. [1]

4. Measurements. [1]

Main hall: 15.40 x 8.05 m.

5. Orientation.

The building is aligned northeast-southwest; the facade is oriented to the northeast in the direction of Mount Gerizim, the holy mountain of the Samaritans. [5]

7. Auxiliary rooms and/or structures.

Remains found adjacent to the hall's west and north walls suggest the existence of rooms possibly associated with the synagogue. [5]

8. Ornamentation.

Of the two mosaic pavements, one 15-28 cm. above the other, [1] the lower [3] originally covered the entire floor area of the hall, but only three large areas and several smaller fragments survive. One area consists of a border of dentils (#158) and four-petaled flowers (#109) that frame a large rectangular panel (6 m. long x 3.20 m. wide). In the center of the panel a fragment of a medallion (1.45 m. in diameter) frames the last two lines of a Greek inscription (see no. 10). Below it a stylized mountain (Mount Gerizim ?) is awkwardly flanked by two seven-branched menorot, one larger than the other.

The upper pavement has been almost entirely destroyed; the surviving fragments indicate it was crudely executed and contained mainly floral and geometric patterns.

9. Coins, ceramics, and other artifacts found within building complex.

Late Roman, Byzantine, and Early Arab pottery fragments were found on top of the upper pavement; below it were fragments of Late Roman ware. [1]

10. Inscriptions.

The precise translation of the two-line Greek inscription in the medallion is not possible, but it refers to the restoration or renovation of the building. Line 3 contains the name of the building restored, eukterion, frequently found in Christian inscriptions. [4]

A one-line Samaritan inscription, in Hebrew characters, reads:

The Lord shall reign for ever and ever.[1]

This is followed by the Samaritan's recension of Exod. 15:18.
A second Samaritan inscription, in fragmentary condition,
contains three lines and several "signs." Translation is
not possible.[1]

11. Donors and patrons.

It has been suggested, because of the use of the term
eukterion in the Greek inscription, that the building may
have been renovated by Samaritan Christians, that is, it
was a church, not a Samaritan synagogue.[7] See Ramat Aviv
(C:3, IIIA-1) for another possible Samaritan church.

12. Date.

The lower panel has been dated to the fourth century on
archaeological grounds (Late Roman ware[1]) and historical
facts: in the fourth century, under the leadership of Baba
Rabbah, the Samaritans were said to have experienced a
rebirth of faith. The lower mosaic pavement has been assigned
to the fifth century, a dating based on its style.[5] The
Greek inscription has been dated to the sixth century;[4]
however, this is contrary to another theory that the building
was destroyed in the fifth or early sixth century during a
Samaritan uprising.[1]

13. Bibliography.

1. Sukenik, E. "The Samaritan Synagogue at Salbit: Prelimi-
      nary Report." Rabinowitz Bulletin. Vol. I. (Dec.,
      1949), pp. 26-30.

2. Tod, Marcus N. "On the Greek Inscription in the Samaritan
      Synagogue at Salbit." Rabinowitz Bulletin. Vol. II
      (June, 1951), pp. 27 f.

3. Goodenough, E. R. Jewish Symbols. Vol. I (1953),
      pp. 262-263; Vol. III, ills. 661, 663, 665.

4. Lifshitz, B. Donateurs, #80.

5. Barag, Dan. "Shaalbim." EAEh. 1978 ed.

6. Reeg, G. Antiken Synagogen. Vol. II, pp. 635-637.

7. Plummer, Reinhard. "New Evidence for Samaritan
      Christianity." Catholic Biblical Quarterly, 41,
      1 (Jan. 1979), 112-117.

EMMAUS

E:3, II-1

1. Name of site and map reference.
    Emmaus, 'Imwās, 'Amwās, Nicopolis.
    1494.1386 (11.1016)

2. Survey of site.
    Four Samaritan inscriptions have been uncovered in the city,
    but the location of the synagogue(s) is not known. [1]
    Clermont-Ganneau reported finding an Ionic capital among the
    ruins of a Crusader church; the capital bears a Samaritan
    inscription. [1] A decade later an inscribed limestone block
    was found near the same church. [1]

10. Inscriptions.

    1. On the "Ionic" capital, in Samaritan characters, the
        inscription reads:

        Blessed be His name forever. [2]

        The other side has in Greek: "Heis Theos" ("one God" or
        "God is one." A similar inscription is on a capital from
        nearby Na'aneh (E:2, II-2).

    2. On the limestone block is a four-line inscription from
        the Samaritan version of Exod. 15:3-13, Gen. 24:31,
        Deut. 33:26. The block may have been an amulet. [2]

    3. A Samaritan inscription on a doorpost contains the verse
        from Exod. 13:23. [2]

    4. Another Samaritan inscription with the text of Exod.
        15:3-11, may also have been an amulet. [3]

12. Date.
    The "Ionic" capital has been dated to the fifth or sixth
    centuries, [1] but the form of the Samaritan characters
    suggests an earlier date, in the first to second centuries. [3]
    The second and fourth inscriptions are dated to the fifth
    century, and the third is considered contemporary to the
    first. [3]

13. Bibliography.

    1. Clermont-Ganneau, C. PEFQS, (1882), pp. 22-34.

    2. Frey, J. B. CIJ, #1186-1188.

    3. Reeg, G. Antiken Synagogen. Vol. II, pp. 603-609.

BETHGABRA/ELEUTHEROPOLIS
E:4

Bethgabra (Beth Guvrin), later renamed Eleutheropolis, was a prominent city in the years following the first Jewish revolt (Avi-Yonah, Holy Land, p. 112). It was apparently refounded by Septimius Severus and encompassed the single largest region in Roman Palestine. After the Second Revolt, Jews were allowed to continue to live in the territory although they were expelled from much of Judaea. They formed a sizable percentage of the territory's population, although technically the region was considered outside Eretz Israel (Eusebius, Onom. 26:11, 88:16, 92:19-21, 108:8).

Four synagogues have been uncovered in Eleutheropolis; two, Eshtemoa and Khirbet Sūsīya, are close geographically and have similar architectural characteristics. The third, at En-Gedi, differs from these, except for its orientation and use of mosaic. Horvat Rimmon appears to be a rectangular basilica paved with flagstone.

Two sites contain synagogue fragments, but the foundations of the buildings have not been found. Three other sites are considered as possible synagogue locations, but their evidence is inconclusive.

EN-GEDI
E:4, I-1

1. Name of site and map reference.
    En-Gedi, Ein-Geddi.
    1874.0965 (16.47)
    Plan 25
2. Survey of site.
    En-Gedi is an oasis in a valley on the west shore of the Dead Sea. The combination of a tropical climate and an abundant water supply enabled the inhabitants to develop the cultivation of balsam plants for which the village gained fame.
    Tel Goren, the most prominent site in the oasis, was occupied continuously from 630 B.C.E. through the sixth century. From the Herodian period onward the center of settlement was on

the plain east and northeast of the Tel, between Nahal David
and Nahal 'Arugot.[2,8] A Roman bathhouse, dated 70-130 C.E.,
was built in the center of a plateau between the two rivers,
about 200 meters west of the Dead Sea. This structure was
built over an earlier installation that may have served as a
miqvah.[2] The earlier installation consisted of two
adjoining pools. The southern pool, at the bottom of a
flight of stairs, has been dated, with the help of coins
found there, to the reign of Agrippa I.[2] The synagogue
ruins are located in an area northeast of Tel Goren. Its
mosaic pavement was uncovered in 1966; the building was
excavated in 1970-1972 by Dan Barag for the Institute of
Archaeology of Hebrew University and the Israel Department
of Antiquities.

Three strata were cleared, the third divided into two stages.
The top stratum, Stratum I, contained disturbed remains dating
from the eighth century C.E. to the present. The other two
strata were the synagogue.[1-3]

3. Character and sections of the building as suggested by extant
and identifiable remains.

STRATUM IIIA/STAGE I

PLAN

A simple, irregularly shaped rectangular hall had no interior
colonnades. The irregular shape may have been due to the
location of pre-existing buildings.[1]

ENTRANCES

Two entrances were on the north, one door in the center of
the wall, the other to its east.

PAVEMENT

Large white tesserae formed the pavement.

STRATUM IIIB/STAGE II

NARTHEX

Added along the full length of the west wall, the narthex was
separated from the main hall by pillars placed directly on
the mosaic pavement.[1]

PLAN

The hall was rectangular, divided by a single longitudinal
row of pillars to the east and a single large reinforced
pillar on the south, forming a nave, a flanking aisle, and a
transverse south aisle. The pillars rest directly on the
mosaic pavement.

ENTRANCES

Entrances were on the west, opening off the narthex.

BENCHES

Three tiers of benches were added along the hall's south wall.

CHAIR OF MOSES

A double-tiered bench is located east of the northern niche.
(See no. 6.)

PAVEMENT

The pavement is mosaic.

STRATUM II/STAGE III

NARTHEX

A new narthex (see below) was added on the west, entered from
the outside by a door in its north and south walls. It is
paved with mosaics. [1]

PLAN

The original narthex was transformed into the main hall's west
aisle, thus surrounding the nave with aisles on three sides. [1]

ENTRANCES

On the west side, three opened off the adjoining narthex.

GALLERY

A monumental staircase uncovered west of the narthex's north
entry may have led to a gallery located over the narthex and
hall's south end. [1]

4. Measurements. [2]

    Strata III A and III B: Stages I and II.

        Main Hall: ca. 15.5 m. x 10 m.

    Stratum II: Stage III.

        Main Hall: 13.5-16 m. x 12.5 m.

        Narthex: 4 m. wide.

5. Orientation.

The synagogue's north wall is directed toward Jerusalem.

6. Character and form: apse, niche, Torah Shrine, bema, chancel.

STRATUM III A

None.

STRATUM III B/STAGE II:

The central door in the north wall was blocked and transformed
into a niche; a "Chair of Moses" was to its east. [1]

STRATUM II/STAGE III:

The niche was closed and a large (1.5 x 3.25 m.) wooden cupboard was added that projected into the hall. Fragments of
its wooden posts were in situ. A semicircular niche was
built into the cupboard; the remainder of its interior space

was apparently used for storage.[1]

An ambo or bema (ca. 4 x 2 m.) was located in front of the cupboard; its foundation is _in situ_.[1]

7. Auxiliary rooms and/or structures.

STRATUM II/STAGE III

A small room was added in the southwest corner of the hall; a second room adjoined the northeast corner; it was entered from the east aisle.[1-3] A house to the northwest was separated from the synagogue by a monumental staircase; a piazza was next to the staircase.[1]

8. Ornamentation.

STAGES I and II

The nave is paved with large white tesserae; in the center of the pavement is a large black frame in the shape of a rectangle (ca. 3 x 8 m.) divided into three squares (ca. 1.4 m. each); in the south square is a black swastika.

STAGE II

In the nave,[2] a second mosaic pavement was laid over the first and is made of finer, smaller multicolored tesserae. A wide frame of black lines and a dentil pattern (#161) enclose a field composed of a regular pattern of four-petaled flowers (#109). In the center of the field a large square frames a circular medallion placed within a lozenge and a square (#587); the medallion frames two pairs of birds; in each corner of the large square are a pair of peacocks grasping grape bunches in their beaks. The bema bears a similar design; a bird rests in the center of the circular medallion; three small menorot are in the pavement's border, directly in front of the bema's foundation. The west aisle is paved with various decorative designs, including the fish-scale pattern (#448); five inscriptions are set into the pavement (see no. 10). The east aisle was accidentally destroyed.[1]

9. Coins, ceramics, and other artifacts found within building complex.

1. A bronze menorah was found near the north wall.[1]

2. A small lamp decorated with a cross found on the nave pavement may have been dropped during the deliberate burning of the synagogue.[1]

3. Scorched scrolls, coins, a bronze beaker, and glass and pottery lamps were found in the area of the wooden cupboard.[2]

10. Inscriptions.

STAGE III

West aisle: An 18-line Aramaic and Hebrew inscription is divided into five sections. The first two sections are in Hebrew, the first from I Chron. 1:1-4; the second lists the names of the 12 signs of the zodiac, then the 12 months of the year starting with Nissan, followed by the names of the three patriarchs and the three companions of Daniel, and ends with "Peace unto Israel": [2,14]

1. Adam Seth Enosh Kenan Mahallalel Jared/Enoch Methuselah Lamech Noah Shem Ham and Japheith.
2. Aries Taurus Gemini Cancer Leo Virgo/Libra Scorpio Saggittarius Capricornus and Aquarius Pisces/ Nissan Iyyar Siwan Tammuz Av Eillul Tishri Marheshwan Kisleiw Teveit Shevat/ and Adar Abraham Isaac Jacob Peace/ Hanaiah Mishael and Azariah. Peace unto Israel.
3. Of blessed memory are Ysa and 'Eiron and Hizzikiyyo the sons of Hilfi/ Anyone causing a controversy between a man and his fellows or who [says] slanders his friends before the gentiles or steals/ the property of his friends, or anyone revealing the secret of the town/ to the gentiles -- He whose eyes run to and fro through the whole earth/ and who sees the concealed, He will set his face on that/ man and on his seed and will uproot him from under the heavens/ and all the people shall say: Amen and Amen, Selah.
4. (Added later) Rabbi Yosa the son of Hilfi and Hizzikiyyo the son of Hilfi of blessed memory/ The upper [great ?] step was made by them in the name of the Merciful. Peace.
5. Remember to the good all the people of this city. [Remainder uncertain: mentions the hazan, a synagogue official.]

11. Donors or patrons.

The three brothers named in the inscription were probably the major patrons of the synagogue. They may have engaged in the lucrative balsam industry, perhaps the "secret of the town" to be kept from gentiles. [A]

12. Date.

The following chronology is based on Barag's reports. [1-4]

Stratum III A, Stage I: Late second or early third century.

Stratum III B, Stage II: End of third or early fourth century.

Stratum II, Stage III: Second half of the fifth century.

It has been suggested the synagogue was destroyed during the period of Justinian's persecutions of the Jews. [1]

13. Bibliography.

1. Barag, Dan. Personal interview. May, 1977.

2. Barag, Dan and B. Mazar. "En-Gedi." EAEh. 1967 ed.

3. Barag, D. and Y. Porat. "The Synagogue at En-Gedi." Qad., III, 3 (1970), 97-101.

4. Barag, D. and E. Netzer. "En-Gedi." RB 79 (1972), 581-583.

5. Barag, D. "Kertah in the Inscriptions from the Synagogue of En-Gedi." Tarbiz 41 (1972), 453-454.

6. Barag, D. and Y. Porat. "En-Gedi." RB 81 (1974), 96-97.

7. Barag, D., Y. Porat and E. Netzer. "The Second Season of Excavations in the Synagogue at En-Gedi." Qad. V, 2 (1972), 52-54.

8. Feliks, Jehuda. "Concerning the Expression 'Hei Ganeiv Zevtei De-Havrei' in the En-Gedi Mosaic Pavement." Tarbiz 40, 2 (Jan., 1971), 257.

9. Lieberman, Saul. "A Preliminary Remark to the Inscription of En-Gedi." Tarbiz 40, 1 (1970), 24 f.

10. Mazar, Benjamin. "Excavations at the Oasis of Engedi." Archaeology, 16-17 (1963-1964), 99-107.

11. Idem. "The Inscription of the Floor of the Synagogue in En-Gedi." Tarbiz 40, 1 (1970), 18 f.

12. Mirsky, A. "Aquarius and Capricornus in the En-Gedi Pavement Inscription." Tarbiz 40, 3 (April, 1971), 376 f.

13. Sarfatti, Gad Ben-Ami. "The Hebrew Translation of the En-Gedi Synagogue Inscription." Tarbiz 40, 2 (Jan., 1971), 255.
14. Urbach, Ephraim E. "The Secret of the En-Gedi Inscription and its Formula." Tarbiz 40, 1 (1970), 27 f.

15. Hachlili, Rachel. "The Zodiac in Ancient Jewish Art: Representation and Significance." BASOR 228 (Dec., 1977), 72.

16. Hüttenmeister, F. Antiken Synagogen. Vol. I, pp. 108-114, 524.

ESHTEMOA

E:4, I-2

1. Name of site and map reference.

Eshtemoa, as-Samū, es-Semou'a, Samoa.

1564.0898 (15.50)

Plan 26

2. <u>Survey of site</u>.

The site of Biblical Eshtemoa (Josh. 15:50, I Chron. 6:42, I Sam. 30:28) is identified with the small Arab village named as-Samū located 6 km. south of Jatta, 15 km. south of Hebron. A century ago explorers reported seeing stones decorated with menorot rebuilt into the village's modern dwellings. The ruins of a synagogue were found during a 1934 survey of the village conducted by L. Mayer and A. Reifenberg; the synagogue was cleared in 1935-1936 on behalf of Hebrew University. Salvage excavations and partial restorations were carried out in 1969-1970 by Z. Yeivin.

The synagogue stands on an elevated site in the southern part of the village; it is built at an oblique angle to a piazza that apparently antedated the synagogue. [1]

3. <u>Character and sections of the building as suggested by extant and identifiable remains</u>.

STAGE I

Portions of all four walls of the synagogue are preserved, the west wall to a height of 8.5 m. The walls are built of two faces of dressed stone set in alternating courses of medium and large stones, with headers and stretchers irregularly distributed. The stones are set without mortar; a rubble core separates the two faces.

NARTHEX

The narthex is two steps above the piazza. It is described as being distyle in antis[1] or as having four columns between two pillars. [3-5] The columns were crowned with Corinthian style capitals and stood on square pedestals.

PAVEMENT

The pavement is multicolored mosaic.

PLAN

The main hall is in the form of a broadhouse without interior colonnades.

ENTRANCES

On the east are three entrances in the hall's facade.

BENCHES

Double-tiered benches are set along the north and south walls; additional benches may have rested against the west wall. [3]

PAVEMENT

The pavement is possibly mosaic.

ROOF

The roof is of red tile. [1]

STAGE II

The building remains essentially the same except for changes in its north wall. (See no. 6.)

4. Measurements. [1]

Narthex: 13.33 x 4.10 m.

Main hall: 13.33 x 21.30 m. wide.

Width of walls: East and west: 1.2 - 1.5 m.

North and south: 3.0 - 3.5 m.

Portals: Central: 173 cm. wide.

North: 124 cm. wide.

Niches, Stage I: Central: 173 cm. wide x 86 cm. deep, opening into a rectangle 211 cm. wide x 73 cm. deep.

West: 85 cm. wide x 47 cm. deep, open into a rectangle 81 cm. wide x 63 cm. deep.

East: Unknown.

Niches, Stage II: Central: 203 cm. wide x 102 cm. deep.

Bema (Stage II): ca. 5.5 x 2 m. [5]

5. Orientation.

The wall with the niches and bema is facing 340° north-northwest, toward Jerusalem. [8] The hall's entrances are on the east, possibly to conform to the disputed ruling in T. Meg. 4:22 that synagogue entrances were to conform to those of the Temple (see Khirbet Sūsīya, E:4, I-4).

6. Character and form: apse, niche, Torah Shrine, bema, chancel.

STAGE I

Three niches are located high (208 cm. above pavement level) on the north wall. They have semicircular interiors formed of carefully worked stone. [1]

STAGE II

A stone double-tiered bema was added in front of the niches; it had wooden or stone steps that ascended to the niches. At a later date the central part of the bema may have been rounded off and the steps made semicircular. [3] Mayer and Reifenberg report a second "wall of poor construction" built between the west wall and the bema, which contained a "cupboard" with grooves for shelves. [1] Yeivin did not find any evidence of this construction. [3]

7. Auxiliary rooms and/or structures.

A large room possibly contemporary with the synagogue, adjoins its northwest corner. [1,5]

8. Ornamentation.

Of a mosaic pavement, little is preserved except for a fragment of a geometric patterning and floral motifs. About a
dozen carved stones, presumably from the synagogue, have been
reused in the village's dwellings.[1] Several fragments are
also reused in the synagogue, but none are in situ.[2]

1. A lintel fragment is decorated with a menorah standing
    on a tripod base; to the menorah's right is a rosette;
    the left side of the lintel is destroyed.

2. A stone fragment, decorated with a menorah in a different
    style, is flanked by a column to its right that appears
    to support a ball wreathed in garlands.

3. A lintel is divided into three sections by columns: In
    the central section is a spoked wheel; the flanking
    sections each contain a gadrooned amphora and grapevine
    flanking a six-pointed star.

4. A lintel decorated with two conch shells separated by a
    rosette may have been part of a chancel screen.

5. A window (?) lintel now set above the synagogue's central
    entrance is decorated with a small conch shell.

6. Below the conch lintel now over the central entrance,
    another lintel (?) is decorated with a wreath tied with a
    Hercules knot. It is flanked by two rosettes on one side,
    and an unusual geometric pattern on the other.

The style and quality of decoration of the stones indicate
they are the work of more than one artisan. Several stones
still bear evidence of red paint.

9. Coins, ceramics, and other artifacts found within building
    complex.

A treasure was uncovered below the pavement of the room northwest of the synagogue, including five pottery jugs containing
about 25 kg. of silver jewelry and ingots. The treasure has
been dated to the 9-8th centuries B.C.E.[7]

10. Inscriptions.

An Aramaic inscription is preserved in the narthex pavement.

> Remembered be for good Eleazar the
> Priest and his three sons who donated
> one tremissis to the synagogue.
> [Third line]incomplete (3)

An inscription in Hebrew characters west of the central niche
has not been translated.[3]

11. Donors or patrons.
    A tremissis is equal to a third of a gold denarius. It would
    appear that the synagogue was built with the help of a series
    of small donations such as from Eleazar's family, not by a
    single, large contributor or several major donors.[A]
12. Date.[5]
    Fourth century: Synagogue built.
    "Byzantine period": Remodeled.
    Seventh century: Seized by Arabs; transformed into a mosque.
13. Bibliography.

    1. Mayer, L. and A. Reifenberg. "The Synagogue of Eshtoemo'a:
        Preliminary Report." JPOS, XIX (1941), 314-326.

    2. Goodenough, E. R. Jewish Symbols. Vol. I, pp. 232-236;
        Vol. III, ills. 605-616.

    3. Yeivin, Ze'ev. Letter to author. 5 August 1977.

    4. Idem. RB, 3 (July, 1970), 400-401.

    5. Idem. Qad., 5 (1972), 43-45.

    6. JSG, ‖235, p. 79.

    7. Barag, D. "Eshtemoa." EAEh. 1976 ed.

    8. Hüttenmeister, F. Antiken Synagogen. Vol. I, pp. 117-121.

HORVAT RIMMON
E:4, I-3

1. Name of site and map reference.
   Horvat Rimmon, Hurvat Rimmon, Khirbet Umm er-Ramāmīn,
   Khirbet Umm er-Ramālī.
   1372.0868 (14.129)
2. Survey of site.
   The site is located 10.5 km. south of Hebron near Kibbutz
   Lahav. A Jewish burial cave was found nearby at Horvat Tilla
   (Khirbet Khueveilifa, 1375.0881).[2]
   Eusebius described Rimmon as a large Jewish village located
   16 miles south of Beth Guvrin in the Daromas (Onom. 88:17;
   146:25). The village was an important trade center in the
   Roman and Byzantine periods.[1]
   Two seasons of excavations have been carried out at the site
   under the direction of Amos Kloner of the Israel Department of
   Antiquities and Museums. The following is based on his
   preliminary report.[1]

3. Character and sections of the building as suggested by extant and identifiable remains.

The building apparently underwent at least two building stages. Sometime in the early Byzantine period, the entire building was surrounded by an "enclosure wall" (see no. 7).

STAGE I

PLAN

The building was constructed on bedrock. It may have had a rectangular plan similar to Stage II. Its floor was composed of a layer of compressed plaster on a foundation of carefully laid small stones.

STAGE II

NARTHEX

A narthex was added adjoining the hall's south wall. It was paved with stone slabs.

PLAN

A rectangular hall divided into a central nave and two aisles by two longitudinal rows of columns (five columns each).

Five square column bases, in situ, rest on bedrock.

ENTRANCES

There are three entrances on the south, a large central portal flanked by two smaller doors.

PAVEMENT

The hall is paved with limestone slabs laid in rows over a foundation of closely packed stones (see no. 8).

4. Measurements.[1]

Main hall: ca. 13.5 x 9.5 m.

Narthex: 16 m. W-E x 3.5 m. N-S.

Enclosure wall: 34 x 30 m.

5. Orientation.

The building faces north toward Jerusalem.

6. Character and form: apse, niche, Torah Shrine, bema, chancel.

The existence of a bema is "assumed" in the north. All but one stone of it had been pillaged.

7. Auxiliary rooms and/or structures.

An enclosure wall was added around the building. Between it and the west wall of the main hall was a row of rooms. One room was equipped with an oven.

Rooms to the synagogue's north and south had remains dated to the Second Temple period and contemporary with the synagogue.

8. Ornamentation.

Many decorative architectural fragments were reported found that have been dated to Stage I. These include pieces of stone doorposts, friezes composed of parallel rows of flowers, rope-like designs, vine trellis with grape clusters, double meander (see: Kefar Bar'am A, B:1, I-2 and Naveh, G:3, I-1). All are carved in local sandstone.

STAGE II

The pavement of the main hall, in the center of the nave, is incised with rosettes and a seven-branched menorah.

9. Coins, ceramics, and other artifacts found within building complex.

1. Coin of Emperor Justinian found in the cement foundation of Stage II pavement.

2. Coin hoard in enclosure wall room: sixty coins found in a hole in the room's wall.

3. Two coin hoards found in an adjoining room. They were in ceramic vessels placed upside down in the ground.

4. Numerous bronze objects, including parts of a candelabrum, vessel stands and a lamp.

12. Date.

STAGE I: Synagogue first built on the site at the end of the third century C.E.[1]

STAGE II: Dated to the end of the sixth century.[1]

The enclosure rooms were in use until the seventh century.[1]

The coin hoards are dated to the early sixth century.[1]

13. Bibliography.

1. Kloner, Amos. "Hurvat Rimmon, 1979." IEJ, 30, 3-4 (1980), 226-228.

2. Idem. "A Lintel with a Menorah from H. Kishor." IEJ, 24, 3-4 (1974), 200.

3. Hüttenmeister, F. Antiken Synagogen. Vol. I, pp. 376-377.

KHIRBET SŪSĪYA
E:4, I-1

1. Name of site and map reference.

Khirbet Sūsīya, Khirbet Susiyah, Khirbet Sūsye.

1598.0905 (5.149)

Plan 27

2. Survey of site.

The abandoned village located at this site receives no mention in any of the ancient texts. L. Mayer and A. Reifenberg

reported finding the remains of a broadhouse synagogue here
in 1937; excavations were carried out in 1970, 1971 by
Z. Yeivin and S. Guttman on behalf of the Israel Department
of Antiquities.

3. Character and sections of the building as suggested by extant
    and identifiable remains.
    The plan of the building remained unchanged throughout its
    long history except for alterations to its north wall and the
    addition of a gallery.[1] The original building was constructed
    of well-cut ashlar blocks; the later gallery addition was built
    in a cruder rubble wall technique.[1]

    COURTYARD
    The court is located east of the synagogue. It's pavement is
    raised three steps above street level, and it is surrounded
    on three sides (north, south, east) by porticoes roofed with
    stone arches supported on square columns.[11] The west side
    of the court is open and has five broad steps that ascend
    1.5 m. to a narthex.[11]

    COURT PAVEMENT
    In the northeast and southeast angles of the court are two
    square sections of pavement plastered and paved with white
    tesserae. The southern portico is paved with mosaics; the
    northern has a floor of beaten earth. A pit cut into the
    bedrock leads from the eastern quadrant of the court into a
    series of grottoes that have not been fully explored.[1]

    NARTHEX
    The narthex, directly before the synagogue's facade, has four
    columns between antae; a portion of its architrave survives.
    The unfluted columns, crowned with crudely carved Corinthian-
    type capitals, rest on Attic-type bases.

    PAVEMENT
    The pavement is multicolored mosaic.

    PLAN
    The synagogue is in the form of a broadhouse without
    interior colonnades.

    ENTRANCES
    A large central door flanked by two smaller ones are on the
    east side.

    BENCHES
    Multitiered benches are along the length of the south and
    west walls and along a section of the north wall.[1]

PAVEMENT

Five layers of mosaic constitute the pavement.[1]

ROOF

Flat and convex tiles made of burnt coarse clay were used for the roof.[1]

GALLERY

The gallery was a later addition; it was built over the hall's western wall, which was reinforced to support the added weight.[1] The gallery is reached by two staircases: One ascends from the southeast corner of the narthex; the other is in the southwest corner of the synagogue complex.

4. **Measurements.**[2]

Main hall: ca. 9 x 16 m. wide.

5. **Orientation.**

The broad north wall with the two bemas is facing 0° north, toward Jerusalem.[10]

6. **Character and form: apse, niche, Torah Shrine, bema, chancel.**

A large elaborate bema is located in the center of the north wall and a smaller one is to its east. The larger bema bears evidence of numerous rebuildings; its precise form is not known. Five curved stairs may have ascended to a niche set high in the northern wall above the bema (for an analogy see Eshtemoa, E:4, I-2).[1] The stairs were faced with marble veneer; grooves and postholes cut into them were intended to receive the posts and panels of several chancel screens. Hundreds of marble fragments found in the debris came from the screens and posts.[6] A bench may have abutted the bema on the west.[1] The smaller bema is raised one step above the hall's pavement. It is plastered and has evidence of a post, in situ, in its southeast corner.

7. **Auxiliary rooms and/or structures.**

Several annexes adjoined the main hall's south wall. A doorway on the extreme south of the facade led to a passageway that ran the full length of the wall. Further south, at street level, is an entrance leading to a second passageway, which led to the gallery's southwest staircase. To the stair's left is a small enclosed room entered through a door on its east.

8. **Ornamentation.**

The narthex was paved in three colors (black, red and beige) of tesserae set in an interlace pattern (#481) framed by a guilloche border (#194).

In the main hall the pavement is divided into three panels (east - west):

1. The east panel is set directly in front of the east bema. It contains an image of a Torah Shrine flanked by two menorot and a lulab and ethrog placed between columns. Flanking the columns are two deer or rams (?) shown in an abbreviated landscape of semicircular hills and sticklike trees.

2. The center panel is separated from the east panel by a wide border of alternating swastikas (#39) and grape clusters set within squares. The panel is partially destroyed but appears to have been decorated with geometric patterns. Directly in front of the main bema is a geometric composition (#350) interrupted by a large multicolored spoked wheel (#556); it may represent a zodiac wheel surrounded by a wreath.[11]

3. All that remains of the west panel is a fragment of a scene; its subject matter is uncertain, but it may be Daniel in the Lion's Den,[1] or an Orans figure. (See Na'aran F:4, I-2.)

9. Coins, ceramics, and other artifacts found within building complex.
    Coins and ceramics were reported found in the ruins; however, their descriptions have not been published. Moreover, they were not found stratigraphically and therefore cannot be used for dating.[1]

10. Inscriptions.
    Four inscriptions are set into the narthex and hall's mosaic pavements. Nineteen fragmentary inscriptions were also found on pieces of marble. An Arabic inscription on plaster fragments was found in the southern portion of the courtyard, which had been converted into a mosque in the tenth century; the inscription is dated 905.

    1. In the southeast corner of the narthex pavement are six lines set within a tabula ansata. The inscription is described as being in an "elegant and perfect Hebrew."[7]

        > May be remembered for good the saintly
        > master teacher/ Isi the priest the honored
        > eminent scholar made/ this mosaic and
        > covered its walls/ with plaster as he
        > vowed at the feast of Rabbi Yochanan/ the
        > eminent priestly scribe/ His son. Peace
        > upon Israel. Amen.[7]

2. A fragmentary six-line Hebrew inscription is set in the pavement inside the central entry into the main hall.

> Remembered be for good and for blessing/
> Who donated and made . . . / In the
> second year of the Sabbatical . . . / in
> the year 4000 . . . / Since the world was
> created/ Shalom.(9)

3. A fragmentary one-line Aramaic inscription is set in the middle of the narthex pavement.

> Remembered . . . Yoshua . . . Yehudan
> . . . [Mena]huma . . .

4. A fragmentary Aramaic inscription is set in the north end of the narthex pavement.

> Well remembered Menahem (?) . . . Yeshua
> that . . . Menahem that g . . .

The inscriptions on the marble fragments are in Hebrew or Aramaic; one is complete.

> Remembered be for good Lazar and Isai
> sons of Simeon son of Lazar.(6)

A fragmentary Hebrew inscription reads:

> Yudan the Levite son of Simeon made
> the . . .(6)

Several of the inscriptions contain the popular form:

> Remembered be for good all the people
> of the town who endeavored . . .(6)

Another mentions "The holy congregation"; this phrase appears again at Jericho (F:4, I-1).

11. <u>Donors or patrons</u>.

This beautifully endowed synagogue was apparently supported by contributions from the village's Jewish population.(A)

12. <u>Date</u>.

The synagogue was built at the end of the fourth century or the beginning of the fifth and continued to be used and renovated by the Jewish community until the ninth century. At that time it fell into disuse (no sign of destruction) until the tenth century, when a portion of its courtyard was transformed into a mosque.(11)

13. <u>Bibliography</u>.

1. Yeivin, Ze'ev. Personal interviews. July, 1975; May, 1977.

2. Idem. Letter to author. 5 August 1977.

3. Guttman, S. "Sousiyeh: Synagogue." RB, 3 (July 1972),
       421 f.

4. Guttman, S., Z. Yeivin and E. Netzger. "Excavations in
       the Synagogue at Khirbet Susiya." Qad., 5 (1972),
       50-51.

5. Idem. HA, 38 (1971), 21-22.

6. Yeivin, Z. "Inscribed Marble Fragments from the Khirbet
       Susiya Synagogue." IEJ, 24 (1974), 201-209.

7. Safrai, S. "The Synagogues South of Mount Judah."
       Immanuel, 3 (Winter, 1973-1974), 44-50.

8. JSG, #230, p. 77.

9. Naveh, J. Personal interview. May, 1977.

10. Hüttenmeister, F. Antiken Synagogen. Vol. I, pp. 422-432,
       528.

11. Guttman, S., E. Netzger, and Z. Yeivin. "Khirbet Susiya."
       EAEh. 1978 ed.

BETH GUVRIN
E:4, II-1

1. Name of site and map reference.
    Beth Guvrin, Bēt Gibrīn, Beth Govrin, Beit Jirbrin, Bethgabra,
    Eleutheropolis.
    140.112 (11.24)

2. Survey of site.
    The ancient village is located 37 km. southwest of Jerusalem.

8. Ornamentation.
    Three finds reported uncovered in the village are allegedly
    from a local synagogue. [1]

    1. A Corinthian style capital is decorated with a seven-
        branched menorah standing on a tripod base. [7] The
        menorah's style has been compared with that of one
        carved on a lintel from nearby Horvat Kishor (E:4, II-2)
        and one from a capital from Caesarea (C:2, I-1).

    2. A small pillar is decorated with a double interlacing vine
        rinceau growing out of a gadrooned amphora; the vine forms
        three medallions framing grapes and a grape leaf. [7]

    3. A marble colonette, probably part of a chancel screen, was
        also found.

10. Inscriptions.

   1. A seven-line Aramaic inscription is set within an ellipsoid circle on a limestone drum; its left side is damaged. The translation is uncertain.

> Remembered be/ for good Kyrios/ . . . ,
> peace upon his soul; the son of Auxentios/
> who built (?) this column/ in honor of
> the synagogue/ Peace.[2]

The Aramaic term kenoeshtah is used here for synagogue, a form that occurs in both talmudim.[2] The Greek term kyrios occurs again at Hammat Gadara (G:8, I-2), Ascalon (C:8, II-1) and Beth She'an (p. 127); it may be a proper name and not a title.[5,9] A second translation of the text reads:

> Remembered be/ for good Kyrios/ son of
> Sh'ai (?) peace upon his soul/ son of
> Auxentios, who built this column/ in
> honor of the synagogue/ Peace.[9]

   2. An Aramaic inscription is carved on a marble colonette.

> Remembered be for good/ Severus (?) son
> of Jo[na]than / son of . . . (fourth
> line missing.)[9]

11. Donors or patrons.

Inscription No. 1 mentions the name of a synagogue donor and his father and grandfather. This form occurs at several other synagogues, for example: Kafr Kannā (B:2, II-5), Sepphoris (B:2, II-6), and Capernaum (B:3, I-1). The term "built" refers to the donation, not fabrication, of a column.

12. Date.

The inscriptions have been dated to the fourth-sixth centuries.[9,10]

13. Bibliography.

   1. Clermont-Ganneau, C. ARP II (1896), p. 442.

   2. Sukenik, E. "A Synagogue Inscription from Beit Jibrin." JPOS X (1930), 76-79.

   3. Idem. Ancient Synagogues, p. 72.

   4. Idem. The Ancient Synagogue of el-Hammeh, pp. 60 f.

   5. Klein, S. "The Inscription from Beit Jibrin." JPOS XII (1932), 271.

   6. Frey, J. B. CIJ, #1195 (inscription 1).

7. Goodenough, E. R. Jewish Symbols. Vol. I, p. 212;
   Vol. III, ills. 537, 542.

8. Negev, A. "The Chronology of the Seven-branched Menorah."
   EI 8 (1967), 193-210.

9. Barag, D. "An Aramaic Synagogue Inscription from the
   Hebron Area." IEJ, 22, 2-3 (1972), 147-149.

10. Hüttenmeister, F. Antiken Synagogen. Vol. I, pp. 51-53.

HORVAT KISHOR
E:4, II-2

1. Name of site and map reference.
   Horvat Kishor, H. Kišor, H. Umm Kašram.
   1364.0970 (14.93)

2. Survey of site.
   The ruins of the village are located 25.5 km. north-northeast
   of Beersheba. A Jewish cemetery in the village has not been
   excavated.[1] In 1958, a limestone lintel decorated with a
   menorah was found reused in a ruined building in the
   village.[3]

8. Ornamentation.
   The menorah carved on the lintel has seven branches joined by
   a horizontal cross-bar with ends projecting. From the ends
   hang what appear to be clusters of grapes or lamps; similar
   objects, but reversed, flank the menorah's central stem. The
   menorah's style is considered similar to ones found decorating
   a lintel at Beth Guvrin (E:4, II-1) and a capital at Caesarea
   (C:2, I-1).[3]

12. Date.
    The lintel has been dated to the second half of the fourth or
    early fifth centuries because of the menorah's form;[1]
    however, the use of a horizontal bar is thought to represent
    the last stage of development in the form of the menorah, so
    the lintel could date somewhere between the fifth and seventh
    centuries.[3]

13. Bibliography.

    1. Kloner, Amos. "A Lintel with a Menorah from H. Kishor."
       IEJ, 24, 3-4 (1974), 197-200.

    2. Idem. Qad., IX, 2-3 (1971), 181.

    3. Negev, A. "The Chronology of the Seven-branched Menorot."
       EI, 8 (1967), 193-210.

    4. Hüttenmeister, F. Antiken Synagogen. Vol. I, p. 271.

HORVAT KARMIL
E:4, IIIB-1

1. Survey of site and map reference.
   Horvat Karmil, Khirbet Kermel, Kurmel, Chermela, el-Karmil,
   al-Birka.
   1628.0925 (15.86)

2. Survey of site.
   The site is located 11 km. south of Hebron. The remains of a
   Roman fort found within the village indicate that it was at
   one time a military garrison.[1]

8. Ornamentation.
   A small decorated stone was found reused in a modern house;
   it is decorated on its right and left with rosettes. The
   central design has been effaced, but may have been a
   menorah.[1] What may have been a date has been obliterated by
   an Arab house number, and the evidence is too inconclusive to
   make an attribution.[2,3,A]

13. Bibliography.

   1. Avi-Yonah, M. QDAP 19 (1944), 140.

   2. Goodenough, E. R. Jewish Symbols. Vol. I (1953),
      p. 213; Vol. III, ill. 554.

   3. Hüttenmeister, F. Antiken Synagogen. Vol. I, p. 253.

   4. JSG. #222, p. 76.

HORVAT MIDRAS
E:4, IIIB-2

1. Name of site and map reference.
   Horvat Midras, Khirbet Durusiya.
   143.118 (11.24)

2. Survey of site.
   The large ruined ancient town was excavated in 1976 by Amos
   Kloner on behalf of the Israel Department of Antiquities. He
   reported finding a Jewish burial cave, dated to the "Second
   Temple Period," located on the western side of a hill near the
   village. A second rock-cut burial cave was uncovered 15 m. to
   the south; it has been identified as a Christian tomb dated to
   the Byzantine period.[1] The Christian tomb is decorated with
   sixteen crosses and with Greek inscriptions incised on the
   walls.

8. Ornamentation.

A stone lintel found in the northern part of the town is decorated with a relief of a wreath tied with a Hercules knot. Stylistically, the decoration is considered similar to other ancient synagogue lintels found in the territory.[1] The evidence is too inconclusive to make an attribution.[A]

13. Bibliography.

1. Kloner, Amos. "Horvat Midras." IEJ, 27, 4 (1977), 251-253.

KHIRBET 'AZIZ
E:4, IIIB-3

1. Name of site and map reference.
   Khirbet 'Aziz, Khirbet el-'Uzeiz, H. al-'Uzēz.
   1578.0932 (15.88)

2. Survey of site.
   The village is located 10.5 km. south of Hebron. On the southwest side of a hill is an outline of a rectangular building oriented east to west; its west wall is best preserved. A large limestone column fragment was found near the building's northwest corner. At the building's eastern end, along its southern side, are two standing limestone pillar fragments and other architectural fragments.[1] A capital found in the debris was considered to be similar to one found at Khirbet Sūsīya (E:4, I-4).[1]
   A street leading eastward down the hill passes the ruins of other buildings, including one that has two rows of standing and fallen columns running east to west.[1] It has been suggested that the two buildings could have been ancient synagogues;[1] however, their east to west orientation would also be appropriate for churches.[A] Synagogues in the south generally were oriented north, although several (Eshtemoa, E:4, I-2) and Khirbet Sūsīya (E:4, I-4) do have their facades on the east.[A]

12. Date.
    The date is unknown; the excavation report identifies the pottery as "Roman."[1]

13. Bibliography.

1. British Mandatory Government Archives. Jerusalem: Rockefeller Museum.

2. Hüttenmeister, F. Antiken Synagogen. Vol. I, pp. 255-256.

3. JSG, #218, p. 75.

F.   LIMES PALAESTINAE

LIMES PALAESTINAE: SALTUS CONSTANTINIACES   F:1
                     SYCOMAZON   F:2
                     SALTUS GERARITICUS   F:3

The date of the formation of the Roman limes in Palestine
(Limes Palaestinae) is uncertain. Soon after the first Jewish
revolt, the Romans developed a line of forts along the Herodian
frontier between Idumaea and Nabataea (Gechon Tiordeckai, "The
Military Significance of Certain Aspects of the Limes Palaestinae,"
in Seventh International Congress of Roman Frontier Studies, 1967
[Tel Aviv, 1971], p. 191). The number of forts was increased at
least twice more, until the entire Sinai region was turned into a
Roman militarized zone intended to defend against Saracen attack.
The forts, manned by military colonists who enjoyed a special
status within the province, introduced a foreign element into an
area already populated by Jews.

The only confirmed synagogue in the limes is at Ma'on; the
zealot's hall at Masada is of questionable attribution. A chancel
screen pillar inscribed with an Aramaic inscription was reported
found at Beersheba; the location of the building it came from is
unknown.

MA'ON
F:1, I-1

1. Name of site and map reference.
    Ma'on, Ma'in, Nirim, Khirbet al-Ma'īn.
    0937.0822 (13.100)
    Plan 28
2. Survey of site.
    The ancient village of Ma'on is located about 20 km. southwest
    of Gaza, 5 km. southwest of Kibbutz Nirim; it is now known as
    Khirbet al-'Ma'īn. In the Roman period, it formed the western
    boundary of the limes Palaestinae. A mosaic pavement was
    accidentally uncovered in 1957 during the construction of a
    side-road from Nir-Yishaq to the Magen-Nirim highway in the
    Gaza strip. The synagogue was excavated in 1957 and 1958 by
    the Israel Department of Antiquities, S. Levy, director of
    excavations.

3. Character and sections of the building as suggested by extant and identifiable remains.

A section of the hall's northeast wall, built of ashlars, is in situ.[3]

PLAN

As judged by meager remains, the synagogue appears to be in the form of a basilica divided by two longitudinal rows of columns (four ? per row), forming a central nave and flanking aisles.[3]

An alternative plan has been proposed[5] and is presented here; however, it is generally considered unacceptable.[2] The plan suggests that the synagogue was of a unique "one room-type" surrounded on three sides by a solid wall, strengthened by columns. East and west of the main hall were open courts; thus a very narrow main hall (5.30 m. wide) was surrounded by disproportionately large courts. The unusual plan supposedly was adapted to the "local climate and geography," as well as "the accepted ritual of the time."[5]

ENTRANCES

On the southwest, three entrances are postulated in the facade wall. On the east, a single entrance may have opened onto an aisle.

PAVEMENT

The aisles and southern half of the nave were paved with limestone slabs. The remainder of the nave is paved with mosaic.

4. Measurements.[1]

Main hall: ca. 19 x 15 m.

Apse: 3.20 m. wide x 1.80 m. deep.

Bema: 0.75 x 0.60 m.

Cistern: 3.50 m. in diameter.

Square pool: 2.50 x 2.25 m.

5. Orientation.

The apse is on the northeast (50° north), the direction toward Jerusalem.[10]

6. Character and form: apse, niche, Torah Shrine, bema, chancel.

An external semicircular apse built of ashlar projects beyond the northeast wall. A pit cut in its pavement may have been a genizah.[1] A small platform in front of the apse, also built of ashlars, may have been a bema;[9] the excavator, however, suggests that it formed the base for the Ark of the Law.[1] In front of the platform a layer of Byzantine sherds (sixth century) were covered over with a mosaic pavement; four post-holes are still visible cut into the pavement. [1]

7. <u>Auxiliary rooms and/or structures.</u>

A water channel, built of limestone and plastered on the inside and rim, is located 0.40 m. from the synagogue's east wall. It runs in a curved line from the southeast corner of the building to a cistern on the northeast. The cistern, built of limestone ashlars, also collected water from another channel located to the synagogue's north; it was set below the pavement and partly covered over by stones and slabs. A square pool east of the synagogue is plastered on the inside and has three steps descending into it; it may possibly have been used as a miqvah. [1] It is not certain, however, whether the pool and cistern were part of the original synagogue complex. [9]

8. <u>Ornamentation.</u>

The whole width of the synagogue nave and the area in front of the apse was paved with mosaic. The pavement was laid after the synagogue's walls were up, and after the platform was built. [3]

The pavement of the nave has a border of interlacing flowers facing alternately inward and outward (#286). The main field forms a single panel composed of a vine trellis forming 55 circular medallions, five per row; 18 medallions are partially or completely destroyed. The vine emerges from an amphora placed in the center of the bottom row; a peacock, which flanked it, survives.

The top two medallions of the axial row frame a seven-branched menorah standing on a lion claw base. Flanking the menorah are ethrogs and shofars; one shofar appears to have an ethrog attached to it. Next to the menorah in the top row are two stylistically dissimilar lions. Other motifs include birds flanking palms and the popular bird in the cage (see Gaza A, C:9, I-1).

9. <u>Coins, ceramics, and other artifacts found within building complex.</u>

Small objects that were found on the apse pavement may have been stored in the genizah; they include several coins and scores of small inscribed metal cylinders, possibly amulets. Pieces of bone and ivory may have adorned furniture; iron nails suggest the presence of wooden cupboards or chests. Approximately 80 coins were recovered, dating from Constantine I (306-337) to Mauritius Tiberias (584-585). [6]

10. Inscriptions.

A four-line Aramaic inscription is framed within a tabula ansata set in the mosaic pavement in front of the apse. The poor quality of its Hebrew characters had led to the suggestion the artist was either a Christian or a Greek-speaking Jew.[3]

> Remembe[red] for good be the whole
> congregation/ [who ha]ve contributed
> this mosaic/ [and furtherm]ore Daisin
> and Thoma and Judah/ who have donated
> [the] sum [of] two denarii.[7]

11. Donors or patrons.

Two denarii are a considerable sum of money for three members to donate. The honored position of the inscription, set in the pavement directly in front of the apse, evidences the congregations' recognition of the donors' generosity.[A]

12. Date.

The synagogue was built over the ruins of an earlier building possibly dated to the fourth century. The present building may have been finished by 528 and remained in use until 585. The dates are based on coins, the paleography of the inscription, fifth century ceramics, and the similarity of the style of the mosaic pavement to the dated example at Gaza A (C:9, I-1).[1,3,6,7]

13. Bibliography.

1. Levy, Shalom. "The Ancient Synagogue of Ma'on (Nir'im): Excavation Report." Rabinowitz Bulletin. Vol. III. Dec. 1960, pp. 6-13.

2. Avi-Yonah, Michael. "Editor's note." Rabinowitz Bulletin. Vol. III, pp. 22-24.

3. Avi-Yonah, Michael. "The Mosaic Pavement of Ma'on Synagogue." Rabinowitz Bulletin. Vol. III, pp. 25-35.

4. Dunayevsky, I. "Reconstruction II." Rabinowitz Bulletin. Vol. III, p. 22.

5. Hiram, A. S. "Reconstruction I." Rabinowitz Bulletin. Vol. III, pp. 19-21.

6. Rahman, L. Y. "The Small Finds and Coins." Rabinowitz Bulletin. Vol. III, pp. 14-18.

7. Yeivin, S. "The Inscription." Rabinowitz Bulletin. Vol. III, pp. 36-40.

8. Levy, Shalom. "The Ancient Synagogue of Ma'on (Nir'im)." Seventh Annual International Congress of Roman Frontier Studies. Tel Aviv: Tel Aviv Univ. Press, 1971, pp. 206-210.

9. Barag, D. "Ma'on." <u>EAEh</u>. 1977 ed.

10. Hüttenmeister, F. <u>Antiken Synagogen</u>. Vol. I, pp. 302-306.

BEERSHEBA

F:II-1

1. <u>Name of site and map reference</u>.
    Beersheba, Beerscheva, Bīr as-Saba'.
    130.072 (14.19)

2. <u>Survey of site</u>.
    Beersheba is known in the Bible as the chief city of the
    Negeb and as a sacred site; it is the symbol of the southern
    boundary of Eretz Israel (Judges 20:1; I Kings 19:3). In
    1904, L. Vincent copied a fragmentary Aramaic inscription
    found on a portion of a chancel screen pillar built into a
    window of a village house. Portions of three lines survive.
    The inscription was published by E. Sukenik.[1]

10. <u>Inscriptions</u>.
    Line one: ends with the name "Joshua."
    Line two: ends with "upon his soul." This may be equivalent
               to "for his life" used on Palmyrene votive
               inscriptions.[1]
    Line three: Has two surviving words: the common Palestinian
               name "Tanhum," and ends with "his son."[1]
    Lines two and three have been compared with an inscription
    found at the synagogue of Hammat Gadara (inscription #1, G:8,
    I-2).[1]

12. <u>Date</u>.
    Unknown.[1-4]

13. <u>Bibliography</u>.

    1. Sukenik, Eleazar. <u>The Ancient Synagogue of El-Hammeh</u>.
        Jerusalem: Rubin Mass, 1935, pp. 67-68.

    2. Goodenough, Erwin. <u>Jewish Symbols</u>. Vol. I. (1953), p. 253.

    3. Frey. <u>CIJ</u>, #1196.

    4. Hüttenmeister, F. <u>Antiken Synagogen</u>. Vol. I, pp. 39-40.

MASADA

F:IIIA-1

1. Name of site and map reference.
   Masada.
   1837.0807 (16.105)
   Plan 29

2. Survey of site.
   Masada is a fortress palace built by Herod the Great atop a
   rock cliff on the western shore of the Dead Sea, about 25 km.
   south of En-Gedi. The cliff's top is rhomboid in shape,
   measuring about 600 m. north to south, and 300 m. east to
   west at its widest. [1]
   Josephus (BJ VII:285) states that the Hasmonean High Priest
   Jonathan built the first fortress on the site and gave it the
   name Masada, Aramaic for "fortress." A second version is
   given by Josephus in BJ IV:399, where he attributes the
   fortress' foundation to unnamed "ancient kings." Herod
   rebuilt Masada as a fortress of refuge for himself and his
   family. A Roman garrison that was stationed on Masada after
   Herod's death was captured by the Jewish rebel leader
   Menahem at the inception of the first Jewish revolt (BJ II:
   408, 433). Following Menahem's murder in Jerusalem, his
   nephew Eleazar became the leader of the zealots at Masada.
   Jerusalem and the Jewish nation succumbed to the Romans in
   70 C.E.; however, the zealots at Masada resisted the Romans
   for three more years before they committed suicide rather than
   surrender to the Roman governor Flavius Silva (Josephus, BJ
   VII:252-254, 275-280, 304-306).
   Two Americans, E. Robinson and E. Smith, were the first to
   identify Masada as the site mentioned in Josephus. By the
   mid-nineteenth century several expeditions were made to the
   top of the cliff. In 1953, Israeli archaeologists began a
   systematic examination of the site. Excavations were begun
   in October, 1963, under the direction of Y. Yadin; they
   continued until 1965. [1]
   Herod made the fortress self-sufficient. The cliff, lacking
   natural water supplies, needed cisterns to catch the runoff
   of rain water. Storehouses were built for food and weapons.
   A casement wall enclosed the fortress on all sides except
   the northernmost tip; the outer wall is 1.4 m. thick, the
   inner, 1 m. thick. Towers, four gates, and 70 rooms were

built into the wall.[1,2] A large bath house located in the
northern complex south of the upper terrace consisted of a
large open court, entered from the northeastern corner, and
four rooms: the _apodyterium_, _tepidarium_, _frigidarium_, and
caldarium. Its plan has been compared with those of Herodian
bath houses at Jericho and Herodium, and Roman bath houses at
Pompeii and Herculaneum.[2] The walls and possibly the
ceilings of the bath were covered with frescoes simulating
marble panels and decorated with geometric and plant designs.
The pavement, originally mosaic, was later replaced with
black and white triangular tiles.[1] The bath's open court
was surrounded on the west, north, and east by a covered
portico. The capitals of the portico's pillars have been
described as in the "Nabataean style."[1]

Herod built four groups of palaces on Masada: 1. The palace-
villa (North Palace); 2. the ceremonial and administrative
palace (West Palace); 3. three small palaces near the West
Palace; and 4. several elaborate buildings adjoining the
West Palace. During the zealots' occupation of Masada they
reused and rebuilt many of Herod's abandoned buildings. Two
miqvahs were added. The building included in this Handbook
and identified by Yadin as a synagogue was built into the
northwest portion of the surrounding casement wall, one of
70 rooms built into the wall. The original function of the
building is unknown; Yadin suggests it may have been built as
synagogue for the Jewish members of Herod's family and
entourage;[1] but there is no evidence to support his
theory.[6]

3. Character and sections of the building as suggested by extant
    and identifiable remains.

The remains provide evidence that the building underwent two
stages of construction.[1]

STAGE I

A rectangular building was divided into two principal but
unequal parts by a cross-wall. The smaller southern section
formed an anteroom to the larger main hall.

PLAN

The main hall had three pillars along the west and an additional pillar on the north. Broader than its length, it gives
the appearance of being a broadhouse.

ENTRANCES

A single entrance was located in the middle of the exterior southeast wall. A door in the middle of the cross-wall provided access into the main hall from the anteroom.

STAGE II

The cross-wall was removed and the building transformed into a single rectangular hall with two rows of columns.

PLAN

The original five pillars were removed and replaced by five round columns, two on the north and three on the south. A "cell" added in the hall's northeast corner was entered through a door located next to the west column of the south row.

ENTRANCES

The single entrance in the southeast wall remained intact.

BENCHES

Four tiers of benches were added along all the walls, except the "cell" wall, which had a single tier.

PAVEMENT

The floor was raised above the level of the Stage I pavement.

4. <u>Measurements</u>.
   Hall: 12 x 15 m. [3]
         10.5 x 12.5 m. (internal measurements). [1]
   Cell: 5.5 x 3.6 m. [1]

5. <u>Orientation</u>.
   That the hall had its facade and entrance on the southeast is one factor that has led to the identification of the building as a synagogue; it conforms to the ruling in T. Meg. 4:22, which states synagogue entries should conform to the Temple's. [1] It should be noted, however, that the building's entrance could not be located elsewhere because of the building's location in the casement wall (see Herodium, E:1, IIIA-2). [6]

6. <u>Character and form: apse, niche, Torah Shrine, bema, chancel</u>.
   The "cell" added in Stage II apparently was a storage room for Scrolls and other ritual objects; see no. 9. [1]

7. <u>Auxiliary rooms and/or structures</u>.
   A plastered pool north of the building may have been associated with it, but it was not a miqvah (see no. 2). [1]

9. <u>Coins, ceramics, and other artifacts found within building complex</u>.
   Broken jars and wine jugs belonging to Herod were reported found; several are dated with the name of the Roman consul

C. Sentius Saturninus, the Roman consul in 19 B.C.E. One jug is inscribed: "To King Herod of Judaea."[1]

CELL

Fragments of glass and bronze vessels were reported found.[1] The two pits cut into the floor may have been genizahs. They contained fragments of scrolls; however, these included no complete Torah Scroll, but rather excerpts from the Book of Psalms, the noncanonical Book of Jubilees, and the Book of Ecclesiastes.[4] Over 700 Hebrew names were written on ostraca.[1]

10. Inscriptions.

Only on ostraca (see no. 9).

11. Donors and patrons.

STAGE I

The structure was built by Herod the Great; its function is unknown.

STAGE II

The building was altered by zealots as an "assembly room." There is no certain evidence to suggest the building was used as a synagogue, a Jewish House of Worship; this attribution is controversial.[6]

12. Date.

Stage I: 37-31 B.C.E.[1]

Stage II: 66-73 C.E.[1]

13. Bibliography.

1. Yadin, Yigael. Masada. New York: Random House, 1966.

2. Idem. "Masada," EAEh. 1977 ed.

3. Foerster, Gideon. "The Synagogues at Masada and Herodium." JJA 3/4 (1977), 6-11.

4. Mirsky, Norman. Unorthodox Judaism. Columbus: Ohio State University Press. 1978, pp. 151-171.

5. Hüttenmeister, F. Antiken Synagogen. Vol. I, pp. 314-315.

6. Chiat, Marilyn. "First Century Synagogues: Methodological Problems." Ancient Synagogues: Current Stage of Research. Edited by Joseph Gutmann. Brown Judaic Studies 22. Chico: Scholars Press, 1981, pp. 49-60.

The earliest remains found at Jericho are in the area near
the north end of the main mound of the oasis, Tell es-Sultān;
they have been dated by Carbon-14 to the period between 9687-
7770 B.C.E. Jericho has been continuously occupied with periodic
abandonments until the present day. Its unfortified position on
an open plain has always made it an easy prey for marauders. The
region was not urbanized by the Romans, but remained an imperial
estate (Smallwood, Jews, p. 340).

Two synagogues have been uncovered in the region of Jericho:
one near the modern town, the other at the nearby oasis of Na'aran.
These two towns were at one time bitter enemies, because of
Jericho's diversion of the Na'aran water supply. Their two synagogues bear little resemblance to one another, either in their
architectural form or their decoration.

JERICHO
F:4, I-1

1. Name of site and map reference.
   Jericho, Tell es-Sultān, Arīhā, Tall al Ǧurn.
   1928.1428 (9.78)
   Plan 30

2. Survey of site.
   A mosaic pavement was accidentally uncovered as trenches were
   dug for bananas near Tell es-Sultān, ancient Jericho, about
   2 km. northeast of the modern town. The site was cleared by
   D. C. Baramki in 1936, on behalf of the British Mandatory
   Government.

3. Character and sections of the building as suggested by extant
   and identifiable remains.
   PLAN
   A basilica was divided into a central nave and two lateral
   aisles by two longitudinal rows of square pillars (four per
   row). The northernmost pillars abut the wall; the southernmost
   abut the wall and the sides of the apse steps. The pillars
   rest directly on the pavement.

ENTRANCES

A single entrance is in the center of the northeast wall. A
step flanked by two columns (the right column base is in situ)
was in front of the entrance.

PAVEMENT

The pavement is mosaic.

4. Measurements.

Main hall: 13 x 10 m. [1,3]

5. Orientation.

The apse point 230° southwest, directly toward Jerusalem. [4]

6. Character and form: apse, niche, Torah Shrine, bema, chancel.

A raised semicircular external apse projected off the southwest side. Its walls were not bonded to the synagogue's.
The apse is not extant.

8. Ornamentation.

The entire basilica is paved with mosaic.

The nave pavement is divided into three panels enclosed within
a guilloche border (#194). [2]

The north panel is a narrow strip in the center of which is
an Aramaic inscription framed by grape vines and pomegranates.

The central panel is a square and contains 64 alternating
squares and circles (#482) filled alternately with circles
and lozenges.

The south panel is divided into lozenges by diagonal lines
of floral shapes forming "Maltese crosses." Superimposed on
the field are two insets: One is a circle framing a seven-
branched menorah flanked by a lulab and shofar; below it is
a Hebrew inscription (see no. 10). The second inset frames
a representation of a Torah Shrine standing on four legs
surmounted by a conch shell but without a pediment. The
aisles are paved in geometric panels of octagon and squares
(#350) and squares crossed with diagonal lines (#312).

9. Coins, ceramics, and other artifacts found within building
complex.

Found in a 65 cm. gap between the wall and the pavement of
the north aisle were nine Kufic coins dated to the early
eighth century, a badly worn Roman coin, three whole glass
bottles, and pieces of bronze including a fragment believed
to be part of a menorah. [1]

10. Inscriptions.

Below the menorah, in Hebrew, an inscription reads "Peace to Israel."[(A)]

A six-line Aramaic inscription set in the pavement near the entrance reads:

> May they be well remembered, may their
> memory be for good, all [the] holy
> community, its elders and its youth,
> whom [the] King of [the] World helped
> and who exerted themselves and made the
> mosaic. He who knows their names and
> the names of their children and the
> names of the people of their households,
> shall write them in the Book of Life
> together with the just. They are
> associates with all Israel. Peace.
> [Amen, Selah].(1)

Only the phrase "Book of Life" is in Hebrew. The phrase "holy community" also occurs at Beth She'an B (B:4, I-3).

11. Donors or patrons.

The anonymity of the donors as noted in the inscription is unusual, but not unknown in Palestinian synagogue inscriptions (see Table 17). It may suggest a need for secrecy regarding the congregation's identity. It would appear that the entire community contributed to the synagogue, not a single large donor.[(A)]

12. Date.

The synagogue has been dated to the eighth century on the basis of the Kufic coins, the style of the pavement, the paleography of the inscription, and the basilical form of the building.[(1)] An earlier date, the end of the sixth or early seventh century, also has been proposed.[(3)]

13. Bibliography.

1. Avi-Yonah, M. and D. Baramki. "An Early Byzantine Synagogue near Tell es-Sultān, Jericho." QDAP, VI (1938), 73-77.

2. Goodenough, Erwin R. Jewish Symbols. Vol. I. (1953), pp. 260-262; Vol. III, ills. 655, 657, 659, 666.

3. Foerster, G. and G. Bacchi. "Jericho, the Synagogue." EAEh. 1976 ed.

4. Hüttenmeister, F. Antiken Synagogen. Vol. I, pp. 189-192.

NA'ARAN

F:4, I-2

1. Name of site and map reference.

Na'aran, Na'aram, Na'ana, Naarah, Noarath, 'Ein-Duq, Ain Douq.

1901.1448 (9.109)

Plan 31

2. Survey of site.

The oasis of Na'aran is located about 5.5 km. northwest of modern Jericho. Eusebius (Onom. 136:24) describes Na'aran as a large Jewish village.

A shell fired during the British and Ottoman battle in September, 1918, accidentally exposed a mosaic pavement. It was investigated by two English archaeologists serving in the British army; following the end of hostilities, it was excavated by L. J. Vincent on behalf of the École Biblique et Archéologique Francaise of the Dominicans in Jerusalem. The building's plan was not published until 1932; Vincent's report of the excavation was published posthumously in 1961. [3]

The synagogue was part of a large building complex consisting of courts and annexes completely surrounded by a wall. [3,12]

3. Character and sections of the building as suggested by extant and identifiable remains.

COURT

An L-shaped court located north and northwest of the main hall had a single entrance in its diagonal northern wall. A loggia (2.65 m. wide) faced with two pilasters was built against the court's northwest wall. A square pool or fountain was in the center of the court immediately in front of the entrance into the adjoining narthex. [12]

NARTHEX

An L-shaped narthex adjoined the main hall's north wall; it turns at a right angle along the court's east wall. The narthex had a single entry opening off the court paved with white tesserae framed in black.

PLAN

Two longitudinal rows of columns (pillars ?, 6 per row) divide the hall's interior into a central nave flanked by aisles. The southern end was destroyed, but may have terminated in a straight wall with a transverse aisle created by a single column. [3] (See no. 6.)

ENTRANCES

On the north side, one large door is flanked by two smaller ones. On the west, a door opened onto the aisle.

PAVEMENT

The entire hall was paved with mosaic.

4. Measurements.

Court: Long arm (north-south): 10.25 m. wide.
         Short arm (west-east): 8.7 m. wide.[12]

Narthex: Long arm (along hall's facade): 17.4 x 3.65 m. wide.[12]

         Short arm (north-south): 10.2 x 3.58 m. wide.[12]

Main Hall: 21 x 14.80 m.[8]
            21.94 x 14.94 m.[3]

Central door: 2.20 m. wide.[3]

West door: 1.42 m. wide.[3]

East door: 1.40 m. wide.[3]

5. Orientation.

The basilica's southern wall faces 180° south, toward Jerusalem.[14]

6. Character and form: apse, niche, Torah Shrine, bema, chancel.

Although the southern end of the building is destroyed, a semicircular apse has been postulated as projecting beyond the wall.[8,12] The published reconstruction of the synagogue shows a straight south wall, with a single column between the two rows of columns.[3]

7. Auxiliary rooms and/or structures.

The side door of the west aisle opened onto a room that was divided into three aisles by two longitudinal rows of columns (pillars ?, three per row). The endmost columns abutted the north and south walls. The room was paved with mosaic. The function of the room is unknown.

8. Ornamentation.

The narthex is paved with white mosaic set in a black frame. In the pavement directly in front of the hall's main entrance was a rectangular panel framing a highly stylized menorah surrounded by various floral motifs.[11] The menorah appears to have eight branches formed by semicircular bands and supporting eleven lamps. Its wide central stem is decorated with a guilloche pattern (#194); the base appears to emerge from three semicircular shapes, possibly meant to represent hills. The menorah is flanked by an Aramaic inscription (see no. 10).

The nave pavement is divided into three panels surrounded by a single broad border consisting of wave crest (#190), double guilloche (#202), and second wave crest patterns. [11] The first panel, on the north, occupies one half of the total floor space of the nave. A field of polygons, circles, and semicircles are bound by bands of guilloche (#194), lotus flowers (#286), and bands of colors. The geometric forms frame images of various animals, including a hare, jackal, and the popular bird in the cage, and various fruits and vegetables. Many of the animal motifs are mutilated.

Panel 2 contains remnants of a badly damaged zodiac circle set within a square frame. A smaller inner circle frames an image of Helios driving his quadriga. The figures of the zodiac were later effaced, but their Hebrew names were left intact. The four seasons, one in each corner of the square, go counterclockwise, whereas the zodiac signs go clockwise. A similar disorientation occurs at Beth Alpha (B:4, I-1) and Husifah (C:2, I-2).

Panel 3, scene 1, is separated from the zodiac panel by two lines. Two lions approach a central figure of a man; all three images have been almost completely obliterated. The male figure appears to have been in an orans pose with arms upraised. Above and to his right is the name "Daniel"; the scene has been identified as Daniel in the lion's den. [12] A similar scene has been identified at Khirbet Sūsīya (E:4, I-4).

Panel 3, scene 2, depicts a Torah Shrine with closed double doors flanked by two seven-branched menorot; the Shrine's sole decoration is circles placed above the diagonal lines of its gabled roof. Glass lamps in the shape of canthari hang from the menorot's two outer branches; [12] they are similar to the lamp that hangs on the Torah Shrine at Beth Alpha (B:4, I-1).

10. Inscriptions.

Ten Aramaic inscriptions were set in the mosaic pavements.

1. In the narthex above the menorah are three lines:

> Remembered be for good Phineas the
> Priest the son of Justos who gave/
> the price of this mosaic/ and this
> basin from his substance. [8]

The term "basin" is uncertain. [8]

2. In the narthex on either side of the menorah are the words:

> Remembered be/ for good/ Rivkeh
> the wife of Pinchas.

3. In the northern border of the nave, the inscription reads:

> Honored be the memory of Halifu,
> daughter of Rabbi Safrah,/ who
> has shared in this Holy Place,
> Amen.(6)

4. Zodiac panel: Twelve signs and four seasons were in Hebrew.
5. Daniel panel: Above the male figure: "Daniel Peace."
6. Daniel panel: Below the figure: "Remembered be for go[od], Samuel."
7. Daniel panel: Between the figures of the man and the lion at the left are two inscriptions; their translation is uncertain. The first consists of three lines:

> Remembered be for good/ Benjamin the
> parnas/ the son of Jose.(8)

8. The second part has six lines:

> Remembered be for good every one/ who
> donates and contributes/ or who gave
> to this Holy/ Place gold or/ silver,
> or other valuable objects/ who brought
> their share/ to this Holy Place./ Amen.(5)

Line six has also been translated as follows:

> Let them . . . their part (?) in
> this Holy Place.(6)

> whatsoever, or any that brought their
> contribution.(8)

9. On panel 3, scene 2, above the menorot and to the right is a four-line inscription; the translation is uncertain:

> Remembered be for good, Maruth . . .
> Ketina and Jacob his son who donated
> to this place, Amen.(6)

10. Panel 3, scene 2: To the left is a three-line inscription, its translation uncertain:

> Remembered be for good, Mar . . . son
> of Chrospedah, who brought their share
> to this Holy Place, Amen.(6)

The term "Maruth" means lordship or honored. It is used as a proper name at Caesarea (C:2, I-1).

11. Donors or patrons.

The long inscription in the Daniel panel may indicate community
ownership of the synagogue rather than a single individual
donor or group. [8]

12. Date.

The pavement was originally ascribed to the first century
C.E., a dating based on its so-called "Augustan" style. [1,2]
Later this early date was amended to the second half of the
third century. [3] The pavement has since been dated to the
fifth [18] or sixth century. [14]

13. Bibliography.

1. Vincent, L. H. "Le Sanctuaire Juif d' 'Ain Douq." RB,
    28 (1919), 532-563.

2. Vincent, L. H. and B. Carriere. "La Synagogue de Noarah."
    RB, 30 (1921), 579-601.

3. Vincent, L. H. "Un Sanctuaire dans la Region de Jericho,
    La Synagogue de Na'arah." RB, 65 (1961), 163-173.

4. Benoit, Pierre. "Note Additionelle." RB, 65 (1961),
    174-177.

5. Klein, Samuel. Corpus, pp. 69-74.

6. Avi-Yonah, Michael. "Mosaic Pavements in Palestine."
    QDAP, 11, 2-4 (1932), #69.

7. Krauss, Samuel. "Nouvelles descovertes archaeologique de
    Synagogues en Galilee." REJ, 89 (1930), 395-405.

8. Sukenik, E. L. The Ancient Synagogue of Beth Alpha,
    pp. 50-55.

9. Idem. Ancient Synagogues, pp. 38-41; 72-76.

10. Frey, J. B. CIJ, #1197-1207.

11. Goodenough, E. R. Jewish Symbols. Vol. I. (1953),
    pp. 253-257, Vol. III, ills. 642-647.

12. Avi-Yonah, M. "Na'aran." EAEh. 1977 ed.

13. Hachlili, Rachel. "The Zodiac in Ancient Jewish Art:
    Representation and Significance." BASOR 228 (Dec.
    1977) 61-77.

14. Hüttenmeister, F. Antiken Synagogen. Vol. I, pp. 324-334.

G.   EAST OF THE JORDAN RIVER

CAESAREA-PHILIPPI
G:1

    After the death of Agrippa I, the Romans made the territory
of Caesarea-Philippi part of the Province of Syria where it
remained until it was later transferred to Phoenicia (Jones,
Cities, pp. 287-288). The city controlled a large expanse of
territory that included a Jewish constituency; however, the city
and territory were considered pagan in character (Jones, Cities,
p. 282).
    No Jewish material has been uncovered in the territory. A
lintel decorated with a cross and menorah was found at Burīqa,
but its attribution is unknown.

BURĪQA
G:1, IIIB-1

1. Name of site and map reference.
    Burīqa, Burēqa, al-Buraika, el-Breikah.
    2314.2717 (2.32)
2. Survey of site.
    A Circassian village was built atop ancient ruins located at
    the northern foot of Tell el-Akkaseh. A lintel found at this
    site was decorated with a menorah in combination with a cross
    flanked by two other circles enclosing crosses.[1,2] The
    combination of a cross and menorah was also found on a stone
    uncovered at Kafr el-Ma (G:2, IIIB-9). The evidence is too
    inconclusive to make an attribution.[A]
13. Bibliography.

    1. Schumacher. Jaulan, pp. 113-115.

    2. Goodenough, E. R. Jewish Symbols. Vol. I. (1953), p. 222;
            Vol. III, ill. 587.

    3. Hüttenmeister, F. Antiken Synagogen. Vol. I, p. 76.

Gaulanitis and its neighbor to the west, Tetracomia, shared many cultural characteristics. Foremost among these were their large conservative Jewish populations; for that reason, Rome did not grant the two regions status as city-territories. The Romans did allow the Jews living in the two regions a certain amount of internal autonomy, which enabled them to maintain their own ethnic identity separated from the prevailing Greco-Roman culture.

Many of the Jewish people expelled from Judaea at the end of the Second Revolt (135 C.E.) sought refuge in Tetracomia and Gaulanitis. Considerable archaeological evidence attests to the Jewish presence in Gaulanitis, but the material has yet to be adequately evaluated. A preliminary assessment of the synagogue evidence can be proposed on the basis of published accounts and personal observation.

Only two sites can be considered validated (category I): Qisrin and Mazra'at Kanef. Thirteen other sites are placed in category II. Two sites, ed-Dikke and Gamla, are considered to be certain (validated) synagogues, but no Jewish inscriptions and/or motifs have been uncovered that would confirm their identities.

Seventeen other sites have either the remains of buildings or architectural fragments attributed to synagogues, although none bear Jewish inscriptions and/or motifs.

MAZRA'AT KANEF
G:2, I-1

1. Name of site and map reference.
    Mazra'at Kanef, Mazra'at Qanaf, Khirbet Kanef.
    2145.2531 (4.102)

2. Survey of site.
    The site is located on a high bluff that separates two wadis 21 km. north of Hammat Gadara. In 1885, L. Oliphant reported discovering here a corner of a monumental building, which he identified as a synagogue.[1] The ruins were reexamined by E. Sukenik in 1932,[2] but the site has not undergone a systematic excavation.

3. Character and sections of the building as suggested by extant and identifiable remains.

A row of five column fragments had been reused to support a cowshed in the modern village; about 15 m. away was the corner of an ancient building incorporated into a modern dwelling. The ancient wall was constructed of well-cut basalt blocks of uneven size set without mortar.[2] The reused column fragments may have come from the ancient building.

COURT

A stone floor uncovered north of the ancient building may have been part of its court.[2]

ENTRANCES

Remains of lintels, doorposts, and jambs found west of the ancient building suggest an entrance on that side.[2]

4. Measurements.[2]

North wall: 16.30 m. long (surviving).

West wall: 11 m. long (surviving foundation).

5. Orientation.

The facade of the building was possibly on the west and determined the building's orientation.[2,5]

8. Ornamentation.[4]

Numerous stone fragments carved in relief were found nearby: One stone was decorated with rows of leaves, eggs, string of beads, a guilloche pattern, and a grapevine issuing from an amphora. A smaller stone had similar decoration plus two squares circumscribed by a circle and inscribed with a rosette. A stone in secondary use showed traces of a gable inscribed with a wheel set in its pediment.

10. Inscriptions.

An Aramaic inscription is carved on what appears to have been a lintel; only half of the inscription survives:[2]

> . . . the blessing. Remembered for good
> Yose bar Halfo bar Han . . .

The donor's name has also been translated as "Yose bar Helbo," who may have been the son of the Amora Rabbi Helbo bar Hanan.[3]

11. Donors or patrons.

The only name known is the one mentioned above.[A]

12. Date.

No date has been proposed for the ruins. Evidence suggests the building was destroyed by an earthquake.[2,5]

13. <u>Bibliography</u>.

1. Oliphant, L. <u>PEFQS</u> (1886), pp. 75 f.

2. Sukenik, E. <u>The Ancient Synagogue of El-Hammeh</u>, pp. 87-91.

3. Frey, J. B. <u>CIJ</u>, #94.

4. Goodenough, E. <u>Jewish Symbols</u>. Vol. I. (1953), pp. 212-213; Vol. III, ills. 547, 549, 550, 551, 553.

5. Hüttenmeister, F. <u>Antiken Synagogen</u>. Vol. I, pp. 308-310.

QISRIN

G:2, I-2

1. <u>Name of site and map reference</u>.
Qisrin, Qasrīn, Kitzrin.
2161.2661 (2.121)

2. <u>Survey of site</u>.
Qisrin is an abandoned village located about 8 km. east of the Daughters of Jacob (<u>Benoth Ya'akov</u>) bridge over the Jordan River. The ruin was discovered during a 1967 survey of the region conducted by the Israel Archaeological Survey Society.[7] Part of the building was excavated by Dan Urman in 1971 and 1972 on behalf of the Israel Department of Antiquities; the building is currently being further excavated.

The structure, which appears to have been part of a large complex, has evidence of numerous renovations. Steps nearby descend to a perennial spring.[6]

3. <u>Character and sections of the building as suggested by extant and identifiable remains</u>.
The building was constructed of well-dressed smooth basalt ashlars set without mortar. Its western wall, preserved to a height of 3 m., does not appear to follow the general plan of the hall; it turns in a southerly direction.

PLAN

The exact plan of the building is unknown, but it possibly was a broadhouse.[6] Monolithic columns and capitals found in the ruin suggest that it was colonnaded.

ENTRANCES

A single large entrance, its doorposts <u>in situ</u>, is on the north. A second entrance is in the southern quadrant of the east wall.

BENCHES

Benches are set along all the interior walls except the south.[5]

PAVEMENT

The pavement was flagstone; there is evidence of a later foundation laid to receive mosaic.

4. Measurements.[3,6]

Main hall: 15.4 x 18 m.

North door: 1.90 m. wide.

East door: .85 cm. wide.

Walls: .90 cm. thick.

5. Orientation.

The bema, built against the south wall, determined the building's focal point, 180° south.[8] Since this is considered an unusual orientation for synagogues in this region, the suggestion has been made that the building was a school[6] (for a similar situation see Deir 'Aziz, G:2, IIIB-4).

6. Character and form: apse, niche, Torah Shrine, bema, chancel.

The raised bema was constructed of fine ashlar masonry. The steps, on either side, show signs of post holes and thresholds, indicating some form of enclosure. There is evidence of a genizah (?) cut into the bema's pavement.

7. Auxiliary rooms and/or structures.

The annexes and rooms surrounding the main hall have not been excavated.

8. Ornamentation.

The massive doorposts of the north entrance stand on carved bases. The doorposts are decorated with carved moldings and profiles separated by an astragal band. The lintel is decorated with a wreath tied with a Hercules knot and flanked by two pomegranates and amphorae. The eastern doorpost is decorated with a five-branched menorah and a peacock (?).
A three-branched menorah decorates a capital, and an eleven-branched menorah (or tree ?) is incised on a stone block. Several large capitals are decorated in a debased Ionic style, a simplification of Ionic capitals found at nearby Hebran and an elaboration of ones found at Gush Halav A (B:1, I-1), and 'Ammudim (B:2, I-1).[A]
Corinthian-type capitals crowning double corner pilasters are similar to ones found at Capernaum (B:3, I-1) and Chorozin (B:3, I-2), including the twisted rope molding around the neck. This molding also appears on half columns of the Temple of Dushara at Sî'.[A]

9. Coins, ceramics, and other artifacts found within the building complex.

   Unstratified finds of coins are dated from the end of the fourth century until the middle of the fifth.[6]

10. Inscriptions.

    An Aramaic inscription carved on a basalt cornerstone was found in secondary use in the abandoned Arab village. It is assumed to be from this building.

    (U)zzi made this square (?)[6]

12. Date.

    It has been postulated that the building was constructed in the first half of the third century, and continued in use until the middle of the fourth century, when it may have been destroyed by a fire.[6]

13. Bibliography.

   1. Urman, Dan. HA, 26 (1968), 6.

   2. Idem. HA, 34/35 (1970), 4.

   3. Idem. HA, 39 (1971), 8.

   4. Idem. HA, 41/42 (1972), 1.

   5. Idem. HA, 56 (1975), 2 f.

   6. Idem. "Golan." EAEh. 1976 ed.

   7. JSG, p. 84.

   8. Hüttenmeister, F. Antiken Synagogen. Vol. I, pp. 357-358.

AHMADIYYE

G:2, II-1

1. Name of site and map reference.

   Ahmadiyye, 'Amūdiya, Ahmadīya, Amudiyye, el-Hamedîyeh. 2160.2680 (2.3)

2. Survey of site.

   This small ruined village lies in a declivity at the western foot of another ruin called Shuweikeh; between the two ruins is a perennial spring used for irrigation. Schumacher visited the village in 1885 and reported that it consisted of twelve huts. He found several decorated basalt stones;[1] further finds were reported by the Israel survey team.[3]

8. <u>Ornamentation</u>.
   1. A Doric capital in secondary use was found.
   2. A lintel in secondary use is decorated with a nine-branched menorah flanked by a shofar and possibly an ethrog. [2]
   3. Found in the declivity was a stone decorated with an eagle with widespread wings, standing on a circular object. [1]
   4. Another stone found in the declivity is decorated with a part of a garland attached to a <u>bucranium</u> flanked by a bird and grape cluster. [1]
   5. A lintel is decorated with two seven-branched menorot. [2]
   6. A fragment of an architrave is decorated with an amphora, grape vine, and flowers. [1]

10. <u>Inscriptions</u>.
    A small fragment of an Aramaic inscription was carved on the architrave; its reading is unknown. [1]

12. <u>Date</u>.
    The architrave has been dated to the third century. [4]

13. <u>Bibliography</u>.

    1. Schumacher. <u>Jaulan</u>, pp. 70-72.

    2. Goodenough. <u>Jewish Symbols</u>. Vol. I. (1953), p. 222; Vol. III, ills. 577-578.

    3. <u>JSG</u>, #78, p. 269.

    4. Hüttenmeister. <u>Antiken Synagogen</u>. Vol. I, pp. 4-5.

BUTMIYYE
G:2, II-2

1. <u>Name of site and map reference</u>.
   Butmiyye, Butmiya, el-Butmiŷeh.
   2326.2616 (2.33)

2. <u>Survey of site</u>.
   The ruined village originally was built on a slightly elevated site that has a perennial spring and a large aqueduct. Schumacher found several decorated lintels; [1] further finds were reported by G. Reeg, who visited the ruins in 1975. [4]

8. <u>Ornamentation</u>.
   1. A lintel is decorated with four-leaf clover (?), spoked wheel, and several Greek characters. [1]
   2. A second lintel is decorated with what may be a ten-branched menorah (the drawing shows nine branches), flanked by two circles and several Greek characters. [1,2]

3. Rectilinear crosses and vine leaf ornaments are carved on another lintel.

4. A basalt doorpost, in secondary use, is decorated with a ten-branched menorah. There are five branches on one side and four branches on the other side of the menorah's central stem; it is flanked by ethrogs.[1]

12. <u>Date</u>.
The doorpost has been dated to the third-fourth centuries.[4]

13. <u>Bibliography</u>.

1. Schumacher. <u>Jaulan</u>, pp. 115-117.

2. Goodenough, E. R. <u>Jewish Symbols</u>. Vol. I, p. 222; Vol. III, ill. 586 (Khan Bandak).

3. <u>JSG</u>, #99, p. 274.

4. Hüttenmeister, F. <u>Antiken Synagogen</u>. Vol. I, pp. 77-78.

DĀBIYYE
G:2, II-3

1. <u>Name of site and map reference</u>.
Dābiyye, Dābīya, Dābbyie.
2184.2684 (2.36)

2. <u>Survey of site</u>.
The ruined village is located three km. northeast of Qisrin. The ruins surveyed by Dan Urman in 1968 were attributed to a synagogue.[1] The site was visited again in 1975 and a large ancient "public building" was reported found,[3,4] but it has not been excavated.

3. <u>Character and sections of the building as suggested by extant and identifiable remains</u>.
The "public building" is in the form of a rectangle.[3]
ENTRANCES
A door was in the middle of the east wall.
PAVEMENT
The pavement is made of basalt slabs.
Column bases, capitals and lintels were reported found inside the building.

8. <u>Ornamentation</u>.
A lintel, in secondary use in the village decorated with two seven-branched menorot is assumed to be from the "public building."[2]

12. <u>Date</u>.
   The ruins are dated to the third to fourth centuries. [2,5]
13. <u>Bibliography</u>.
   1. <u>JSG</u>, #73, p. 269.
   2. Urman, Dan. <u>HA</u> 41/42 (April, 1972), 1.
   3. <u>HA</u> 57/58 (April, 1976), 2.
   4. Saltz, Daniella. "Surveys, Salvage and Small Digs in Israel." <u>ASOR Newsletter</u> 10 (May, 1977), 1.
   5. Hüttenmeister, F. <u>Antiken Synagogen</u>. Vol. I, pp. 95, 524.

DABURAH
G:2, II-4

1. <u>Name of site and map reference</u>.
   Daburah, Dabbūra.
   2124.2725 (2.35)
2. <u>Survey of site</u>.
   The site is located on the north bank of the steep and rocky Nahal Gilbon (Wadi Daburah), on the western edge of the Golan plateau about 5 km. northeast of the Daughters of Jacob (<u>Benoth Ya'akov</u>) bridge over the Jordan River. Schumacher reported finding large unhewn building stones lying in heaps in the Arab village; he attributed them to ancient buildings, identity unknown. [1]   Z. Ilan has identified the ruins with Seleucia, one of the villages fortified by Josephus in the Golan. [9]   The site was surveyed in 1968 by S. Gutman, A. Druks, and Dan Urman; they reported finding many stones from a nearby "synagogue" reused in the village's modern dwellings. Ten fragments were carved with inscriptions [2] (see no. 10). The location of the "synagogue" is not known.
8. <u>Ornamentation</u>.
   1. A lintel (?) is decorated with two birds (vultures ?) with outspread wings, holding snakes in their beaks. A wheel, enclosing a stylised rosette (cross ?), is between the birds.
   2. A stone fragment is decorated with figures of a man and a child holding various objects including a basket in their arms.
   3. A stone fragment bears two winged figures (genii ?) flanking an amphora.
   4. A small stone fragment is decorated with a conch.

5. A broken lintel shows an eagle (vulture ?) with a single surviving wing, holding a small wreath in his beak. Below the wing is a horizontal fish, and next to it a vertical fish. A narrow band above the relief is inscribed with two Aramaic words: " . . . made this gate."

6. A large basalt lintel is decorated with a relief of two eagles (vultures ?) with outspread wings, holding snakes in their beaks. The snakes intertwine to form a plaited wreath tied with a Hercules knot at the bottom and two snake heads at the top. It bears a Hebrew inscription (see no. 10).

10. Inscriptions.

Fragments of six inscriptions have been recovered.[9] Numbers one to four are in Aramaic, number five in Aramaic and Greek, and number six in Hebrew.

1. " . . . made this gate." The term "gate" is also used at 'Ammudim (B:2, I-1).[7]

2. Two lines: " . . . [H]inanah . . . / May he be blessed."[7]

3. " . . . [s]on of Judah."[7]

4. "They made the house . . . May he be blessed."[7]

5. The following is inscribed on three stones found scattered in the village.[7]

> Eleazar the son of . . . made the
> columns above/ the arches and beams
> [may the blessing be upon him,]
> (Greek:) Isiktos built.

6. The basalt lintel (no. 6) contains this inscription, part of it within the wreath, the remainder flanking it:

> This is the school of the Rabbi/
> Eliezer ha-Qappar.

A scholar with this name lived towards the end of the second century C.E. at Lydda; another scholar with a similar name, bar Kappara, is mentioned in the Babylonian Talmud.[9] This is the first known synagogue inscription mentioning the name of a sage and the term Beth Midrash (school).[9]

11. Donors or patrons.

Inscriptions 1-5 name donors to the synagogue. Inscription 5 may refer to the artisan who made the columns, Isiktos, and the donor, Eleazar, possibly the son of Eliezer ha-Qappar.[9] Naveh has suggested that this inscription was on the synagogue's architrave.[11]

274 / Synagogue Architecture

12. <u>Date</u>.

   The relief carving and the Hebrew characters are considered to
   be similar to inscriptions at Capernaum (B:3, I-1) and
   Chorozin (B:3, I-2); thus the fragments have been dated to
   the third to fourth centuries.⁽⁹⁾ It has been theorized that
   the building was constructed in the second century.⁽¹⁰⁾

13. <u>Bibliography</u>.

   1. Schumacher. <u>Jaulan</u>, p. 117-118.

   2. <u>JSG</u>, #62, pp. 265-266.

   3. <u>HA</u> 30 (April, 1969), 1 f.

   4. <u>HA</u> 33 (1970), 11.

   5. <u>HA</u> 37 (1971), 2.

   6. Urman, Dan. "Dabburah." <u>Qad</u>. 4 (1971), 131-133.

   7. Idem. "Jewish Inscriptions from Dabura in the Golan."
        <u>Tarbiz</u> 40 (1970-1971), 399-408.

   8. Idem. <u>IEJ</u>, 22 (1972), 16-23.

   9. Ilan, Zev. "Daburah in the Golan: Archeological Remains
        and Identification." <u>Museum ha'Aretz</u> 13 (1971), 45-51.

   10. Urman, Dan. "Golan." <u>EAEh</u>. 1976 ed.

   11. Naveh, Joseph. Personal interview. May, 1977.

   12. Hüttenmeister, F. <u>Antiken Synagogen</u>. Vol. I, pp. 91-95.

ED-DĀNQALLE
G:2, II-5

1. <u>Name of site and map reference</u>.
   ed-Dānqalle, ad-Danqalla, Qādirīya, ed-Danqale, 'Edriya,
   Khan Bândak, Dannikleh.
   2154.2693 (2.40)

2. <u>Survey of site</u>.
   Schumacher surveyed this Turkoman village located 3.5 km.
   north of Qisrin in 1885. He reported finding ruins of ancient
   buildings south of the village. To the west of the village
   was a perennial spring set within an ancient semi-circular
   enclosure.⁽¹⁾
   Urman surveyed the site in 1972; he reported finding the ruins
   of an ancient building that he suggested may have been a synagogue. The ruins have not been cleared.⁽⁵⁾

3. Character and sections of the building as suggested by extant
and identifiable remains.
Two walls of the ancient building are extant; they are built
of basalt ashlars.[5]

4. Measurements.[5]
South wall: 14 m. long (surviving).
West wall: 19 m. long (surviving).

5. Orientation.
The building was aligned north-south.[5]

8. Ornamentation.
It is uncertain whether the decorated fragments described by
Schumacher came from the ruined building discovered by
Urman.[A]

1. A lintel, in secondary use, is decorated with two seven-
branched menorot.[1,2] One menorah stands on a tripod base;
the other has its base missing.

2. A broken lintel is decorated with a simple wreath tied in
a Hercules knot. The ribbons terminate in heart-shaped ivy-
leaves. To the right of the wreath is a spoked wheel.[1]

3. A stone fragment is decorated with a cross.[1]

4. A lintel fragment is decorated with a menorah.

10. Inscriptions.
A fragment of a lintel is inscribed in Aramaic:

> Blessed be . . . Halfso son . . . ,
> son of . . . [5]

12. Date.
The building has been dated in the third century.[6]

13. Bibliography.

1. Schumacher. Jaulan, p. 183.

2. Goodenough, E. R. Jewish Symbols. Vol. I, pp. 222-223;
   Vol. III, illus. 581 (Khan Bândak).

3. JSG, #70, p. 267.

4. Urman, Dan. HA 38 (1971), 2 f.

5. Idem. HA, 41/42 (April, 1972), 2.

6. Hüttenmeister, F. Antiken Synagogen. Vol. I, pp. 99-100.

'EN-NATOSH
G:2, II-6

1. Name of site and map reference.
   'En-Natosh, 'En-Naṣut.
   2151.2687 (2.48)

2. Survey of site.
   The ruined village is located about one km. southwest of
   ed-Dāqalle on a hill surrounded on three sides by valleys. A
   building identified as a synagogue was in the western section
   of the village. Urman surveyed the ruins in 1967/1968 and
   again in 1972.[1]

8. Ornamentation.
   Two stone slabs are decorated with reliefs of lions. A lintel
   was decorated with a seven-branched menorah.

12. Date.
    The decorated fragments are dated to the third to fourth
    centuries.[3]

13. Bibliography.

    1. Urman, Dan. HA 41/42 (1972), 2.

    2. Idem., HA 42 (1973), 3.

    3. Hüttenmeister. Antiken Synagogen. Vol. I, pp. 114-115.

KHIRBET ASALYIA
G:2, II-7

1. Name of site and map reference.
   Khirbet Asalyia.
   213.264

2. Survey of site.
   The site was surveyed in 1972; the ruins of a large building
   were reported.[1] No further information is available
   regarding its appearance.[A]

8. Ornamentation.
   1. A lintel is decorated with a Torah Shrine (?) flanked by
   two seven-branched menorot.
   2. A stone fragment depicts a menorah.
   3. A stone fragment is decorated with a "tree."

10. Inscriptions.
    A four-line Aramaic inscription was carved on a stone fragment;
    no translation is available.

13. Bibliography.

    1. Ben-Ari, M. and S. Bar-Lev. <u>HA</u> (July, 1976), 7.

KHIRBET ZAMIMRA
G:2, II-8

1. Name of site and map reference.   ʼ
    Khirbet Zamimra, Zumaimira, Zumēmira.
    2139.2614 (2.166)

2. Survey of site.
    The ruins of this village were discovered in 1968 by Claire
    Epstein.[3] They included the remains of a large "public
    building." The ruins were surveyed again in 1972 and at
    that time a basalt slab was recovered decorated with a
    menorah.[1]

3. Character and sections of the building as suggested by extant
    and identifiable remains.
    The structure is described as a "public building"; no further
    information is available.[3] The lower portions of a doorpost
    were uncovered near the building's west wall.[2]

5. Orientation.
    It has been postulated that the building's facade (entrance)
    determined its orientation, and that therefore the building
    was oriented west.[3]

8. Ornamentation.
    1. A fragment of stone is decorated with a column that rests
    on a base showing a crouching lion along its length.
    2. A basalt slab is carved with a seven-branched menorah
    flanked by a stylized ethrog and lulab.

13. Bibliography.

    1. Urman, Dan. <u>HA</u> 41/42 (April, 1972), 2.

    2. Idem. "Golan." <u>EAEh</u>. 1976 ed.

    3. Epstein, Claire. Personal interview. May, 1977.

    4. Hüttenmeister, F. <u>Antiken Synagogen</u>. Vol. I, pp. 517-518.

QUSBĪYA
G:2, II-9

1. Name of site and map reference.
   Qusbīya, el-Qusabiyyibe, Sulūqīya.
   2171.2645 (2.124)

2. Survey of site.
   The ruins are located about 1.3 km. southwest of Qusbīya
   al-Gadida near Salokia (2183.2652). Architectural fragments
   were found here during the 1972 survey of the region. [2]

8. Ornamentation.
   1. A basalt stone was carved with an eagle, now defaced.
   2. Fragments of a second eagle, minus its head, were found.
   3. A stone is carved with an eleven-branched menorah.
   Similar motifs were found at nearby Salokia (G:2, II-10).

12. Date.
    The fragments have been dated to the second-third centuries
    because of their similarity to reliefs found at Chorozin
    (B:3, I-2). [4]

13. Bibliography.

    1. JSG, #130, p. 280.

    2. HA 41/42 (1972), 2.

    3. HA 45 (1973), 1.

    4. Hüttenmeister, F. Antiken Synagogen. Vol. I, pp. 362-363.

SALOKIA
G:2, II-10

1. Name of site and map reference.
   Salokia.
   2183.2652 (2.124)

2. Survey of site.
   The site, surveyed by S. Bar-Lev in 1972, [1] is located by
   Qusbīya (G:2, II-9) in western Gaulanitis.

8. Ornamentation.
   S. Bar-Lev reported finding a basalt lintel, decorated with a
   relief of an eleven-branched menorah, and two large stone
   fragments, each carved with an eagle in relief. [1] Similar
   motifs were found at nearby Qusbīya (G:2, II-9).

13. Bibliography.

    1. Bar-Lev, S. HA, 45 (Jan., 1973), 1.

SANĀBER

G:2, II-11

1. **Name of site and map reference.**
    Sanāber, Sanābir.
    2129.2675 (2.134)

2. **Survey of site.**
    A basalt stone reported found at this site in 1976 is decorated
    with a seven-branched menorah.[2]

13. **Bibliography.**

    1. JSG, #76, p. 269.

    2. HA 57/58 (1976), 2.

    3. Hüttenmeister, F. Antiken Synagogen. Vol. I, p. 381.

YAHUDIYYE

G:2, II-12

1. **Name of site and map reference.**
    Yahudiyye, el-Yêhudîyeh, Ya'rabīya.
    2162.2604 (2.162)

2. **Survey of site.**
    Schumacher described the site as a large ruin situated on a
    narrow ridge about 220 yards wide near the Wadi el-Yêhudîyeh.
    Remnants of a wall with towers surround the ruin, suggesting
    that it may have been one of the cities in the Golan fortified
    by Josephus[1] (BJ II:274). To the north, the ridge widens to
    a plateau, upon which are the remains of various buildings
    built of large hewn basalt stone.[2] No information is
    available on individual buildings or their identification.[A]

8. **Ornamentation.**
    Capitals found in the debris were described as being in a
    combination of Ionic and Corinthian styles.[1] A stone
    decorated with a five-branched menorah was found at the site
    in 1968.[2,3]

12. Date.

The ruins are given a possible date in the third century. [4]

13. Bibliography.

1. Schumacher, G. Jaulan, pp. 270-272.

2. JSG, #102, p. 275.

3. HA 26 (1968), 6.

4. Hüttenmeister, F. Antiken Synagogen. Vol. I, pp. 482-487.

ED-DIKKE

G:2, IIIA-1

1. Name of site and map reference.

Ed-Dikke, ed-Dikkeh, ad-Dikkā, ed-Dikkih, ed-Dik.

2088.2593 (4.44)

Plan 32

2. Survey of site.

The site is located on the eastern bank of the Jordan River about 4 km. north of the river's entrance into the Sea of Galilee. Oliphant has described the ruins as lying on the barren slope of a hill. [2] Nearby is a stream with an ancient aqueduct and a ruined mill. [2] The site's modern name, Ed-Dikke, means "platform," a fitting name as the ruins are situated on a small elevation. They have been badly plundered by local inhabitants who used the material as a quarry for their modern buildings. [1,3]

Kohl and Watzinger cleared the ruins and included it in their study of Galilean synagogues. [1]

3. Character and sections of the building as suggested by extant and identifiable remains.

The building was constructed of well-dressed limestone ashlars. [1]

TERRACE/NARTHEX

A terrace (or narthex) that adjoined the west facade of the basilica was approached by two stairs on the north; its southern approach is unknown. [1]

PLAN

Only half of the main hall was cleared. [1] The rectangular hall was divided into a central nave and two side aisles by two longitudinal rows of columns, three per row; no indication of a stylobate has been found.

Uncovered near the western wall were the foundations of five
engaged pillars; these may have been piers used to support
arches between the wall and columns, or may have been intercolumnar arches.[6]

ENTRANCES

On the west side, a large central entrance was flanked by two
smaller lateral doors. An additional door was possible in
the south.[1,6]

BENCHES

Double tiered benches were along the north, east, and
south walls.

PAVEMENT

The pavement is flagstone.

4. Measurements.[1]

Exterior hall: 15.30 x 11.92 m.

Interior hall: 13.8 x 10.4 m.

5. Orientation.

The facade faced 90° west.[5]

6. Character and form: apse, niche, Torah Shrine, bema, chancel.

Kohl and Watzinger reported finding in the western area inside
the hall three blocks of an arch, together with its keystone
decorated with an eagle, now effaced.[1] A second stone, with
similar moldings, was found in secondary use in the village.
It is conjectured that the two arches were part of a screen
that stood inside the large central portal, blocking it.[1,4]
It is presumed that the screen functioned as part of a Torah
Shrine.[1,4] The arch could have been part of an architrave
(see no. 3).[6]

8. Ornamentation.

The ruins yielded numerous fragments of decorated stones, none
decorated with Jewish motifs. The basilica's door moldings
and lintel contain similar decorations to those at Kefar
Bar'am A (B:1, I-2), including the pulvinated frieze decorated
with a vine rinceau.[1] The lintel of the central portal is
decorated with a pair of genii (partially defaced) holding a
wreath; a second wreath behind one of the figures, may have
been held in her other hand.[1,4]

Fragments of window moldings are decorated with ivy leaves,
egg and dart patterns, grapevines, and meanders (the last
motif appears at Kefar Bar'am A).[1,4]

Fragments of double pilasters may have formed part of the
interior wall decoration.[1] Fragments of debased Ionic and

Corinthian capitals are considered similar in style to those found at Qisrin (G:2, I-2).[6]

12. Date.

The building has been considered to be contemporary to synagogues uncovered in neighboring Tetracomia and Tiberias (B:1, I-1, 2, 4, 5 and B:3, I-1, 2).[1] A possible third century date has been suggested.[5] See Kefar Bar'am A (B:1, I-2) and Capernaum (B:3, I-1) for problems associated with these early dates.

13. Bibliography.

1. Kohl and Watzinger, pp. 112-124.

2. Oliphant, L. "Explorations Northeast of Lake Tiberias and in the Jaulan." PEFQS (1885), 82-85.

3. Schumacher, G. Jaulan, pp. 120-123.

4. Goodenough. Jewish Symbols. Vol. I (1953), pp. 205-206. Vol. III, ills. 520-521, 524-528.

5. Hüttenmeister, F. Antiken Synagogen. Vol. I, pp. 103-105.

6. Avi-Yonah, Michael. "Synagogues." EAEh. 1978 ed.

GAMLA

G:2, IIIA-2

1. Name of site and map reference.

Gamla, Gamala, as-Salām.

2196.2567 (4.53a)

2. Survey of site.

The ruined village of Gamla, considered to be the Gamala mentioned in Josephus BJ IV:1 ff,[1,4] was discovered during the 1968 survey of the Golan. Mount Gamala, on whose slopes the village is built, is about 10 km. inland from the northeast shore of the Sea of Galilee. It has a high elongated ridge running north-south, with declivities turning downward, giving it the name "Gamala," camel's hump.

S. Guttman began excavating the village in 1970; he reported uncovering the city walls, which enclosed an area of about 180 dunams, a conduit from the Nahal Dailot to the "lower town," and two rock-cut cisterns in the "upper city."[1] In 1976 he reported the discovery of the "synagogue of the Zealots of Gamala," which he considers similar to those uncovered at Masada (F:IIIA-1) and Herodium (E:1, IIIA-2).[2] Foerster agrees, suggesting that the building belongs to a well-defined group of synagogues belonging to the Second Temple period:[5] Herodium, Masada, Migdal (B:3, IIIA-2), and Gamla. The evidence, however, does not support Guttman or Foerster's contention;[7] moreover, no evidence presently available identifies these buildings as synagogues. The structure, built low on the flank of the hill ("lower town" ?), has one wall contiguous with the city wall and another cut into bedrock.

3. Character and sections of the building as suggested by extant and identifiable remains.

The structure is built of finely hewn basalt ashlars.

COURT

A court is on the southwest side, adjacent to building.

PLAN

The building is rectangular; heart-shaped pillar bases, found in situ in two of the corners, suggest the building may have had an interior peristyle along all four of its walls.[A] However, the plan of the building has not been definitely determined.

ENTRANCES

A main central entrance on the southwest opened onto a short hallway that led into the main hall. Several other entrances were reached via stairways from a lower side street.[1]

BENCHES

Two tiers of benches were along the walls of the entry hall and along the east wall of the hall. Three tiers of benches are along the west wall, and four tiers of benches are on the wall opposite the main entrance. The top tier of the benches was a wide unplastered platform of pressed earth.

PAVEMENT

Basalt flags were laid only in the area of the possible peristyle; the center of the hall is pressed earth.

4. Measurements.

Main hall: 20 x 16 meters.[1]

Floor space: 10 x 12 meters.[2]

5. Orientation.

The building is aligned southwest-northeast. The entrance is on the southwest, suggesting that the facade was toward Jerusalem. This orientation does not conform to the buildings uncovered at Masada (F:IIIA-1), Herodium (E:1, IIIA-2), or Migdal (B:3, IIIA-2), with which this building has been compared.[1,5]

6. <u>Character and form: apse, niche, Torah Shrine, bema, chancel</u>.
It has been suggested that a large "closet" in the south wall
may have been used to store Torah Scrolls and other ritual
objects,[1] but there is no evidence to confirm this theory.[A]

8. <u>Ornamentation</u>.
A lintel, found near the main entrance, is decorated with a
geometric rosette. Other fragments of stone depict meanders,
rosettes, and vines.

9. <u>Coins, ceramics, and other artifacts found within building
complex</u>.
The entire ruins were littered with seige balls, believed to
have fallen when the town was under seige by the Romans.
Coins, dating from the first century B.C.E. to the first
century C.E. were reported found within the village.[1]

10. <u>Inscriptions</u>.
A three-line "Semitic" inscription was recently reported at
Gamla; it has not been published.[1]

12. <u>Date</u>.
The building has been dated to the Second Temple Period, and
was destroyed during the Roman seige of 68 C.E.[1,7]

13. <u>Bibliography</u>.

1. Guttman, S. HA (Oct., 1976), 6.

2. Mann, Sylvia. "Gamala: The Northern Masada." Jerusalem
   Post (Oct. 19, 1976).

3. Saltz, Daniella. "Surveys, Salvage, and Small Digs in
   Israel." ASOR Newsletter 10 (May, 1977), 1-2.

4. Epstein, Claire. Personal interview. May, 1977.

5. Foerster, G. "The Synagogues of Masada and Herodion."
   JJA 3/4 (1977), pp. 6-11.

6. Hüttenmeister, F. Antiken Synagogen. Vol. I, p. 524.

7. Chiat, Marilyn. "First Century Synagogues: Methodological
   Problems." Ancient Synagogues: Current Stage of
   Research. Edited by Joseph Gutmann. Brown Judaic
   Studies 22. Chico: Scholars Press, 1981, pp. 49-60.

BATRĀ
G:2, IIIB-1

1. <u>Name of site and map reference</u>.
Batrā, Bathyra.
2138.2568 (4.18)

2. Survey of site.

The ruins are on a cliff located 24.5 km. north of Hammat Gadara. The site was surveyed in 1968 by the Israel Archaeological Survey Society; a "synagogue" was reported found in the southern part of the site. [1]

3. Character and sections of the building as suggested by extant and identifiable remains.

The building identified as a synagogue was constructed of finely dressed stones. Fragments of an architrave and Ionic capitals were found in the debris. [1] The evidence is too inconclusive to make an attribution. [A]

5. Orientation.

The building is described as oriented to the west. [1,2]

8. Ornamentation.

Fragments of a stone were found that were carved with a wreath tied with a Hercules knot, Ionic capitals, and a torus decorated at both ends.

12. Date.

A possible third century date has been postulated. [2]

13. Bibliography.

1. Urman, D. "Golan." EAEh. 1976 ed.

2. Hüttenmeister, F. Antiken Synagogen. Vol. I, pp. 38-39.

BĒT AKKĀR
G:2, IIIB-2

1. Name of site and map reference.

Bēt Akkār, Bēt 'Akkār.

2355.2455 (4.22)

2. Survey of site.

The site is located in the eastern Golan, 26 km. northeast of Hammat Gadara. It was visited by Schumacher in 1885. He reported finding architectural fragments decorated with grapevines and amphorae, which he believed were of Jewish origin. [1] The identity and location of the building the fragments belonged to are unknown. [A]

13. Bibliography.

1. Schumacher, G. Across the Jordan (1866), pp. 53-60.

2. Hüttenmeister, F. Antiken Synagogen. Vol. I, p. 43.

DARDĀRA
G:2, IIIB-3

1. Name of site and map reference.
   Dardāra, al-Hašša, el-Khaskshe.
   2114.2576 (2.41)

2. Survey of site.
   A monumental rectangular building, oriented east-west was
   reported found at this site during the 1968 Survey of the
   Golan. Four to six courses of its north and south walls
   survive. It has been identified by the surveyors as a
   synagogue,[1,2] but the evidence is too inconclusive to make
   an attribution.[A]

13. Bibliography.

   1. JSG, #112, p. 277.

   2. Urman, Dan. "Golan." EAEh. 1976 ed.

   3. Hüttenmeister, F. Antiken Synagogen. Vol. I, p. 101.

DEIR 'AZIZ
G:2, IIIB-4

1. Name of site and map reference.
   Deir 'Aziz, Dēr 'Azīz, Dar Aziz.
   2170.2525 (4.42)

2. Survey of site.
   The site is located about 21 km. north of Hammat Gadara.
   Oliphant visited the site in 1885 and reported seeing a
   building a little way down the slope of a hill, on the north
   flank of the Wadi Shukeiyif; he identified the building as a
   synagogue.[1] Dan Urman surveyed the site again in 1972.[2]

3. Character and sections of the building as suggested by extant
   and identifiable remains.
   Oliphant reported the building's walls were extant, to almost
   3 m. in height.[1]
   ENTRANCES
   A single entry is in the middle of the east wall.

4. Measurements.
   Main hall: ca. 25 x 15 m.[3]
   Door lintel: 6 feet x 18 inches.[1]
   Door width: 4 feet x 6 inches.[1]

5. Orientation.
   The building is aligned north-south, with its main entrance
   on the east.[3]   Because of its unusual alignment, the building
   has been identified as a school rather than a synagogue (see
   Qisrin, G:2, I-2, for a similar situation).[3]

7. Auxiliary rooms and/or structures.
   A rectangular room, 10 x 2.5 m. was in the southeast corner
   of the building; it was roofed with long basalt slabs still
   in situ.[2,3]   Its function is not known.[A]

13. Bibliography.

    1. Oliphant, Lawrence. "New Discoveries." PEFQS (1886),
          pp. 77-78.

    2. JSG, #132, pp. 280-281.

    3. Urman, Dan. "Golan." EAEh. 1976 ed.

    4. Hüttenmeister, F. Antiken Synagogen. Vol. I, pp. 101-102.

EL-'ĀL

G:2, IIIB-5

1. Name of site and map reference.
   El-'Āl, al-'Āl, Eli-'Al.
   2200.2457 (4.6)

2. Survey of site.
   Oliphant describes El-'Āl as one of the largest villages in
   the Golan; it was built upon ancient ruins now all but
   obliterated by the modern town. A life-sized statue found
   lying in a yard in the village was of a woman, possibly Diana,
   clasping a quiver.[1]   The village was surveyed in 1972 by
   Dan Urman, who reported finding the ruin of a monumental
   building plus numerous architectural fragments.[2,3]   No
   description is available of the building's form, but the
   fragments are described as being decorated with motifs
   "typical of synagogues."[3]   The evidence is too inconclusive
   to make an attribution.[A]

13. Bibliography.

    1. Oliphant, Lawrence. PEFQS. (1885), p. 87.

    2. JSG, #181, pp. 287-288.

    3. Urman, Dan, "Golan." EAEh. 1976 ed.

    4. Hüttenmeister, F. Antiken Synagogen. Vol. I, pp. 8-9.

FĀKHŪRA
G:2, IIIB-6

1. Name of site and map reference.
   Fākhūra, Fāhūra, Pehura.
   2148.2674 (2.52)
2. Survey of site.
   The site is located 18.5 km. southwest of Quneitra. A
   threshold from an ancient building was recently reported
   here,[1] and identified as part of a synagogue.[1] The
   evidence is too inconclusive to make an attribution.[A]
13. Bibliography.

   1. JSG, #77, p. 269.

   2. Urman, Dan. "Golan." EAEh. 1976 ed.

   3. Hüttenmeister, F. Antiken Synagogen. Vol. I, p. 124.

HORVAT RAFĪD
G:2, IIIB-7

1. Name of site and map reference.
   Horvat Rafīd, ar-Rafīd, er-Rafid.
   2092.2624 (2.125)
2. Survey of site.
   The site is located about 500 meters east of the Jordan River,
   about 7 km. north of its entry into the Sea of Galilee; it
   should not be confused with ar-Rafid (2105.1675) or Rafid
   (2345.2625, G:2, IIIB-15). Schumacher visited the ruins in
   1890 and published several drawings of architectural fragments
   found there.[1] Sukenik surveyed the ruins in 1933 but did
   not find any evidence of a building foundation.[3]
8. Ornamentation.
   1. A fragment of a stone is ornamented with a pair of fish
   carved in relief; Sukenik believes they formed part of a
   zodiac.[3]
   2. A fragment of a stone is decorated with a shell framed by
   a guilloche, astragal, and egg and dart moldings and crowned
   by a gable. Figures of a standing bird flanked by two animals
   (lions ?) decorating the gable were effaced.[4]
   3. A small stone is carved with a shell within a guilloche.[4]
   4. Fragments of a debased Ionic capital, column base, and
   pedestal were found.

5. A fragment of a frieze depicts a vine scroll and two small amphorae.

12. Date.

The decorated fragments are considered to be contemporary with synagogues cleared in Galilee, dating to the second to fourth centuries.[1,5]

13. Bibliography.

1. Schumacher. ZDPV 13 (1890), 71-73.

2. Kohl, Watzinger, p. 2.

3. Sukenik, E. The Ancient Synagogue of El-Hammeh, pp. 91-93.

4. Goodenough, E. Jewish Symbols. Vol. I. (1953), p. 211, Vol. III, ills. 538-541.

5. Hüttenmeister, F. Antiken Synagogen. Vol. I, pp. 365-366.

HUHA
G:2, IIIB-8

1. Name of site and map reference.
Huha, Hōha.
2153.2556 (4.70a)

2. Survey of site.
The site, located near Gamla, was surveyed in 1975 by S. Bar-Lev and Z. Ilan,[1] who reported discovering portions of a building; its form was not reported.[1] The evidence is too inconclusive to make an attribution.[A]

8. Ornamentation.
Fragments of a frieze decorated with an eagle were found.[1]

12. Date.
The style of the frieze has been compared with reliefs found at Capernaum (B:3, I-1) and Chorozin (B:3, I-2), suggesting the building they decorated was contemporary.[1]

13. Bibliography.

1. Bar-Lev, S. and Zvi Ilan. HA 57/58 (April, 1976), 2.

2. Hüttenmeister, F. Antiken Synagogen. Vol. I, p. 525.

KAFR EL-MĀ
G:2, IIIB-9

1. Name of site and map reference.
   Kafr el-Mā, al-Mā.
   2272.2464 (4.80)

2. Survey of site.
   The site is located 13 km. northeast of Hammat Gadara. A
   stone found at this site was decorated with a cross and what
   appears to be "Trees of Life" (menorot ?).[1,2] See Burīqa,
   G:1, IIIB-1.
   It has been postulated that the stone decorated a synagogue[2]
   or a church.[3] The evidence is too inconclusive to make an
   attribution.[A]

13. Bibliography.

   1. JSG, #178, pp. 286-287.

   2. Urman, Dan. "Golan." EAEh. 1976 ed.

   3. Hüttenmeister, F. Antiken Synagogen. Vol. I, p. 245.

KAFR HĀRIB
G:2, IIIB-10

1. Name of site and map reference.
   Kafr Hārib.
   2121.2405 (4.81)

2. Survey of site.
   Architectural fragments described as "typical" of ancient
   synagogues were reported found here in 1970. The evidence is
   too inconclusive to make an attribution.[A]

13. Bibliography.

   1. JSG, #190, p. 289.

   2. Urman, D. "Golan." EAEh. 1976 ed.

   3. Hüttenmeister, F. Antiken Synagogen. Vol. I, p. 246.

KAFR NAFĀKH
G:2, IIIB-11

1. Name of site and map reference.
   Kafr Nafākh, Kafr Nafāh.
   2194.2742 (2.83)
2. Survey of site.
   The ruins of an ancient synagogue were reported at this
   site,[1,2] but the evidence is too inconclusive to make an
   attribution.[3,A]
13. Bibliography.

   1. JSG, #53, p. 264.

   2. Urman, D. "Golan." EAEh. 1976 ed.

   3. Hüttenmeister, F. Antiken Synagogen. Vol. I, p. 249.

KHIRBET DĀLĪYA
G:2, IIIB-12

1. Name of site and map reference.
   Khirbet Dālīya, Khirbet Daliyat.
   2190.2554 (4.37)
2. Survey of site.
   Ruins were discovered here during the 1968 survey of the Golan
   conducted by the Israel Archaeological Survey Society.
   Surveyors reported finding in the southeast portion of the
   site a "monumental" building oriented to the west.[1] The
   architectural fragments have been described as "typical" of
   ancient synagogues.[2] The evidence is too inconclusive to
   make an attribution.[2,A]
8. Ornamentation.
   1. A basalt lintel, 170 x 50 cm. was reported found near the
   building's east wall; it is decorated with three rosettes.[1]
   2. A basalt lintel, the same size as no. 1, was found west of
   the building. It bears a wreath of vine branches issuing from
   flanking amphorae, tied with a Hercules knot.[1]
13. Bibliography.

   1. Urman, D. "Golan." EAEh. 1976 ed.

   2. Hüttenmeister, F. Antiken Synagogen. Vol. I, p. 96.

LAWĪYA

G:2, IIIB-13

1. Name of site and map reference.
    Lawīya, Lawiyye, Lawieh, al-Lawiyeh, al-Lawīya.
    2140.2503 (4.97)

2. Survey of site.
    The site is located on a steep hillside that descends to the
    shore of the Sea of Galilee, about 18 km. north of Hammat
    Gadara. Oliphant reported finding the foundation of an ancient
    building, that he identified as a synagogue.[1] The ruins
    included three columns in situ, a cornice fragment and a
    carved block. However, Israeli surveyors were unable to
    locate the ruins.[2] The identity of the building (?) remains
    unknown.[3,A]

13. Bibliography.

    1. Oliphant, L. "New Discoveries." PEFQS (1886), 78.

    2. JSG, #141, p. 282.

    3. Hüttenmeister, F. Antiken Synagogen. Vol. I, p. 283.

MAZRA'AT QUNETIRA

G:2, IIIB-14

1. Name of site and map reference.
    Mazra'at Qunetira, Mzra'at Kuneitra, Mzra'at Qunetira.
    2229.2555 (4.103)

2. Survey of site.
    The site is located about 26 km. south of the modern Syrian
    town of Quneitra. Ze'ev Yeivin surveyed the ruins in the
    course of researching his dissertation. He conjectured the
    ancient village covered an area of about 45 dunams and had a
    population of about 4,500.[1] Urman surveyed the site in
    1967/1968 and reported discovering the ruins of a building
    that he suggests may have been a synagogue. The evidence is
    too inconclusive to make an attribution.[2,3,4]

13. Bibliography.

    1. Yeivin, Ze'ev. "Survey of Settlements in Galilee and
        Golan from the Period of the Mishnah in Light of the
        Sources." Diss. Hebrew University, 1971.

2. <u>JSG</u>, #122, p. 279.

3. Urman, Dan. "Golan." <u>EAEh</u>. 1976 ed.

4. Hüttenmeister, F. <u>Antiken Synagogen</u>. Vol. I, pp. 310-311.

RAFĪD

G:2, IIIB-15

1. <u>Name of site and map reference</u>.
Rafīd (not to be confused with Horvat Rafīd, G:2, IIIB-7).
2345.2625 (2.126)

3. <u>Character and sections of the building as suggested by extant</u>
<u>and identifiable remains</u>.
G. Schumacher reported finding the foundation of a building,
with "apses," in the southeastern portion of the site. The
plan indicates a single external semicircular apse. [1]
Schumacher identified the building as a "synagogue," [1] but
the evidence is too inconclusive to make an attribution. [A]

8. <u>Ornamentation</u>.
1. A basalt doorpost is decorated with a rectilinear cross.
2. A basalt lintel depicts two birds (doves ?) holding the
ribbons of a wreath in their beaks. [1]
3. Another lintel is decorated with three circles. [1]

12. <u>Date</u>.
The ruins have been dated to the second-third centuries. [3]

13. <u>Bibliography</u>.

1. Schumacher, G. <u>Jaulan</u>, pp. 226-229.

2. <u>JSG</u>, #97, pp. 273-274.

3. Hüttenmeister, F. <u>Antiken Synagogen</u>. Vol. I, pp. 366-367.

SAFŪRIYYE

G:2, IIIB-16

1. <u>Name of site and map reference</u>.
Safūriyye, Safūra, as-Safūrīya
2167.2395 (4.133)

2. <u>Survey of site</u>.
The site is located about 31 km. south of modern Quneitra.
The 1968 survey of this region records the discovery of a
"synagogue" at this site. [1,2] No further information is

available. The evidence is too inconclusive to make an attribution. [A]

13. Bibliography.

1. JSG, #196, p. 290.

2. Urman, Dan. "Golan." EAEh. 1976 ed.

3. Hüttenmeister, F. Antiken Synagogen. Vol. I, pp. 380-381.

SEQŪFĪYĀ
G:2, IIIB-17

1. Name of site and map reference.
   Seqūfīyā, Suqūfīyā, Skufiyyā, Squpiyye.
   2147.2452 (4.147)

2. Survey of site.
   The site is located 13 km. north of Hammat Gadara. A 1970 report records the discovery of the remains of a building with an interior colonnade; it is identified as a "synagogue."[1]   The evidence is too inconclusive to make an attribution. [3,A]

13. Bibliography.

1. JSG, #180, p. 287.

2. Urman, Dan. "Golan." EAEh. 1976 ed.

3. Hüttenmeister, F. Antiken Synagogen. Vol. I, pp. 420-421.

BATANAEA

G:3

At the time of Pompey's invasion of Palestine and Syria,
Batanaea was a sparsely populated region belonging to the
Ituraeans. Herod was given control of the territory and populated
it with Judaean and Babylonian Jews and Idumaeans (Avi-Yonah, The
Holy Land, pp. 82, 90). The territory was later transferred to
the Province of Syria and finally became part of Provincia Arabia
(Ibid., p. 112; Smallwood, Jews, p. 533).

Architectural fragments decorated with Jewish motifs, and a
building identified as a synagogue, have been uncovered in the
ancient Jewish village of Naveh. In the village of Tafas, located
south of Naveh, a Greek inscription was found that has been
attributed to a synagogue or a place of worship of "Jewish-
Christians." (See: Tafas, G:3, II-1.)

NAVEH

G:3, I-1

1. Name of site and map reference.
    Naveh, Nawâ, Nawe, Nave.
    247.255 (-.122)
2. Survey of site.
    The ancient Jewish village of Naveh is located 45 km. east-
    northeast of Tiberias. The town receives several mentions
    in rabbinic literature, particularly in regard to the Jewish
    Patriarch's control of several prosperous nearby estates
    (T Sheb. 4:8-66). Schumacher visited the village and
    published several drawings of stones decorated with Jewish
    motifs.[1] The site was visited in 1936 by L. A. Mayer and
    A. Reifenberg, who reported finding the ruins of an ancient
    building that they identified as a broadhouse type syna-
    gogue.[3] No plan or further information is available.
6. Character and form: apse, niche, Torah Shrine, bema, chancel.
    Mayer and Reifenberg describe a niche raised 2.2 m. above the
    pavement in one of the broadhouse building's walls; it was
    flanked by two pillars and surmounted by an upward radiating
    conch.[3,4,6]

8. <u>Ornamentation</u>.

Many ancient stones found in secondary use in the village are decorated with Jewish motifs. Two lintels are decorated with inhabited meanders (see Kefar Bar'am A, B:1, I-2 and Horvat Rimmon E:4, I-3). In the center of one lintel is a seven-branched menorah; its central branch appears to support a garland (?).[6]

A second building (described by Dalman as a "Jewish house")[2] has a beautifully carved lintel over its entrance. In the center of the lintel is a wreath framing a shell flanked by two seven-branched menorot.[7]

Three other fragments are decorated with menorot, often flanked by lulabs and shofars.

10. <u>Inscriptions</u>.

A fragmentary three-line Aramaic inscription was carved on a stone reused in the east wall of the modern mosque.

> . . . [s]on of Yudan/ . . . and son
> of his brother (or "son of Ahawa,"
> a given name)/ . . .
> . . . shrine.[4]

The name Eleazar <u>bar</u> Yudan also occurs in an inscription at Kefar Bar'am A (B:1, I-2). It may refer to the same individual, an architect and builder from Naveh.[7]

11. <u>Donors and patrons</u>.

The son of Yudan who may have been the actual builder of the synagogue.[7]

12. <u>Date</u>.

The broadhouse building has been dated to the third or fourth centuries, because of the style of the meander decoration and the form of the inscription, both considered similar to those of Kefar Bar'am A.[3,8]

13. <u>Bibliography</u>.

1. Schumacher. <u>Across the Jordan</u>, pp. 169-174.

2. Dalman. <u>PJB</u>, 9 (1913), p. 59.

3. Mayer, L. and A. Reifenberg. "Synagogue at Nawa in the Hauran." <u>BJPES</u>, IV (1936), 1-8.

4. Braslawsky, I. "A Hebrew-Aramaic Inscription at Nawe." <u>BJPES</u>, IV (1936), 8-12.

5. Klein, S. "The Synagogue at Naveh (Nawe)." <u>BJPES</u> IV (1936), 76-78.

6. Goodenough, E. R. _Jewish Symbols_. Vol. I, pp. 236-237, Vol. III, ills. 617-625.

7. Amiran, Ruth. "A Fragment of an Ornamental Relief from Kefar Bar'am." _IEJ_ 6, 4 (1956), 239-245.

8. Hüttenmeister, F. _Antiken Synagogen_. Vol. I, pp. 336-339.

TAFAS
G:3, II-1

1. Name of site and map reference.

   Tafas, Tipasa (?)

   2505.2385 (-.150)

2. Survey of site.

   The site is located 51 km. east of the city of Tiberias, and south of Naveh. Charles Fossey has published a Greek inscription found at this site.[1]

10. Inscriptions.

    The three-line Greek inscription is inscribed on a lintel.

    > Jacob and Samuel and their father
    > Clematios have erected this synagogue.[1,3,5,6]

    The suggestion has been made that the inscription came from a Jewish-Christian place of worship.[4] It has also been identified as a synagogue inscription, on the basis of literary and archaeological evidence (see Naveh, G:3, I-1), that attest to a Jewish community existing in the region of Batanaea.[6] The names Jacob and Samuel are common Jewish names; the latter occurs again in a synagogue inscription from Gerasa A (G:11, I-1).[5] There is no reason to attribute the lintel to a Jewish-Christian house of worship.[A]

11. Date.

    The inscription has been dated to the fourth century.[6]

13. Bibliography.

    1. Fossey, Charles. "Inscription de Syrie." _Bull. de Corr. Hell._ 21 (1897), 46 f.

    2. Idem. _REJ_ 36 (1898), 140.

    3. Klein, _Corpus, Inscr._, p. 104.

    4. Alt, A. "Ein Denkmal des Juden-Christentums in Ostjordanland." _PJB_ 25 (1929), 89-95.

    5. Frey. _CIJ_, #861.

6. Lifshitz. <u>Donateurs</u>, #63.

7. Hüttenmeister, F. <u>Antiken Synagogen</u>. Vol. I, pp. 433-434.

HIPPOS
G:4

Hippos (Aramaic: Susita) was a city founded by the Seleucids
on a high hill overlooking the eastern shore of the Sea of
Galilee. It was given the Greek name Hippos (horse), preceded by
the dynastic name Antiochia. The city became part of the Roman
Decapolis and was later made part of Herod's kingdom. After
Herod's death it became part of the province of Syria (Smallwood,
Jews, pp. 108-110). Although Hippos was considered outside the
halakhic boundaries of Eretz Israel it still had a large minority
Jewish population (Ibid., p. 357).

No verified synagogue ruins have yet been uncovered within
the territorial boundaries of Hippos, but architectural fragments
decorated with Jewish motifs have been found at Apheck. Umm
el-Kanâtir has long been considered the site of a synagogue;
however, the evidence is too inconclusive to allow for a certain
attribution.

APHECA
G:4, II-1

1. Name of site and map reference.
   Apheca, Fīq, Fīk, Afeq.
   2164.2425 (4.2)

2. Survey of site.
   The large village of Apheca is located 11 km. north-northeast
   of Hammat Gadara. It was built on both sides of the Wadi
   Fīk, which flows down over several basalt terraces before
   becoming a broad stream in the valley below. In 1885, the site
   was visited by Schumacher, who reported finding many architectural fragments strewn over the area and in secondary use. [1]

8. Ornamentation.
   1. A small basalt column is decorated with a seven-branched
   menorah. [1,2]
   2. A basalt lintel depicts a circle enclosing a menorah
   (tree ?) flanked by an ethrog and shofar. [2]
   3. A stone fragment bears a five-branched menorah.
   4. Another stone fragment is decorated with a nine-branched
   menorah.

5. A debased Ionic capital is similar to the one found at Qisrin (G:2, I-2).

10. Inscriptions.
A fragmentary inscription was carved on the small basalt column below the menorah:

I, Judah the hazan . . .[3]

The term hazan (a synagogue functionary) occurs one other time in a Palestinian synagogue inscription, at 'Ammudim (B:2, I-1), and possibly at En-Gedi (E:4, I-1).

Several stone fragments were inscribed with Kufic and Greek letters; their translations are unavailable.[5]

12. Date.
The fragments have been dated to the second to third centuries.[6]

13. Bibliography.

1. Schumacher, G. Jaulan, pp. 136-143.

2. Goodenough, E. Jewish Symbols. Vol. I. (1953), p. 221. Vol. III, ills., 579-580.

3. Avigad, N. "An Aramaic Inscription from the Synagogue at Umm el-Amed in Galilee." Bulletin Rabinowitz, III (1960), 62.

4. JSG. #187, pp. 288-289.

5. Urman, Dan. "Golan." EAEh. 1976 ed.

6. Hüttenmeister. Antiken Synagogen. Vol. I, pp. 2-3.

KHISFIN
G:4, IIIB-1

1. Name of site and map reference.
Khisfin, Hisfin.
2265.2507 (4.70)

2. Survey of site.
The site is located 23 km. northeast of Hammat Gadara. The Israel Department of Antiquities identifies the ruins of a building found at this site as a church;[1,3] Saller has identified it as a synagogue.[2] A lintel of the building is set with a Greek inscription placed within a wreath.[1] The evidence is too inconclusive to make an attribution.[A]

13. Bibliography.

1. Israel Department of Antiquities and Museums. Archives.
   Jerusalem: Israel Museum.

2. Saller, S. Second Revised Catalogue, #84.

3. JSG. #150, p. 283.

4. Hüttenmeister, F. Antiken Synagogen. Vol. I, pp. 175-176.

UMM EL-KANÂTIR
G:4, IIIB-2

1. Name of site and map reference.
   Umm el-Kanâtir, Umm al-Qanātir, Umm al-Kanatar.
   2195.2506 (4.157)

2. Survey of site.
   The site is located on the eastern slopes of a wadi on a level
   plain or terrace, directly beneath the upper ledge of a rocky
   cliff. Beyond the terrace is a steep descent to the bottom of
   the wadi; the site is difficult to reach and easily defended.
   The path down to the wadi leads to a spring that flows from the
   rocks into an ancient trough walled over by two arches built
   of basalt blocks set without mortar.[1,2] A stone slab, found
   near to the spring, is decorated with an image of a lion.[2]
   About 50 m. north of the spring are the ruins of a large
   rectangular building. The building was surveyed and partly
   cleared in 1905 by Kohl and Watzinger, who included it in
   their study of Galilean synagogues.[3]

3. Character and sections of the building as suggested by extant
   and identifiable remains.
   The structure was built of large basalt stones set without
   mortar.

   NARTHEX
   A narthex in front of the south facade is raised three steps
   above ground level. It had two columns, possibly carrying a
   pediment, crowned with capitals carved in an unusual basket
   style.[3]

   PLAN
   A basilica is divided by two longitudinal rows of columns
   (five columns each) on the west and east and joined on the
   north by a transverse colonnade (two columns), to form a
   central nave surrounded on three sides by aisles. The column
   bases rest on a stylobate.

ENTRANCES

The main entrance is in the middle of the south wall. A side entrance on the west opens onto the aisle.

4. Measurements.

Main hall: 18.8 x 13.8 (?) m.

South door: 1.55 m. wide.

West door: 1.63 m. wide.

5. Orientation.

The building's axis is north to south; its facade is on the south.[8] It should be noted that in all the sources, except Hüttenmeister, the building's axis is in error, owing to a misplaced arrow in Kohl and Watzinger's plan.

8. Ornamentation.

Two decorated stones were found in front of the facade: a relief of an eagle,[2,5] and the forequarters of a lion.[2,5] Fragments of other architectural decoration found in the ruins include a large triangular slab cut in the shape of an arch and decorated with moldings;[2] a fragment of a niche and window frame decorated with a vine scroll and grape clusters, and an eagle with widespread wings; and fragments of a cornice decorated with an egg and dart molding.[2]

12. Date.

The date attributed to the building by some scholars is the fifth century,[3,4] a dating based on the unusual basket capital of the narthex that is considered to be Byzantine in style.[3,4] A somewhat earlier date has also been proposed, in the so-called "transition" period.[6]

13. Bibliography.

1. Oliphant, L. "Exploration Northeast of Lake Tiberias and in the Jaulan." PEFQS (1885), pp. 89-91.

2. Schumacher, G. Jaulan, pp. 260-265.

3. Kohl, Watzinger. Synagogen Galilaea, pp. 125-134.

4. Sukenik, E. The Ancient Synagogue of El-Hammeh, pp. 85-87.

5. Goodenough, E. R. Jewish Symbols. Vol. I. (1953), p. 206. Vol. III, ills. 530-534.

6. Avi-Yonah, M. "Synagogue Architecture in the Late Classical Period." In Jewish Art, p. 70.

7. JSG, #148, p. 283.

8. Hüttenmeister, F. Antiken Synagogen. Vol. I, pp. 465-468.

TRACHONITIS
G:5
AURANITIS
G:6
DIUM
G:7

These three territories lie beyond the geographic boundaries of this handbook; they were gentile lands with little if any Jewish population (Smallwood, Jews, p. 86). Dium became one of the cities of the Decapolis; and the other two cities became part of the kingdom of Herod the Great, remaining under the control of his dynasty until the death of his grandson Agrippa II (Ibid. and Avi-Yonah, Holy Land (1977), p. 81). Dium was transferred in 106 C.E. from the province of Syria to Arabia, and Auranitis and Trachonitis were annexed to Syria (Avi-Yonah, pp. 110 and 112). Except for Dium, the territories remained without municipal status and were essentially an area of small villages (Jones, Cities, p. 289). Several of the villages, such as Philippopolis, Maximianopolis, and Constantia, all in Trachonitis, were raised to the status of colonies with their own eras and were given the right to strike coins (Ibid., p. 285).

Diocletian was responsible for the transfer of Auranitis, Trachonitis, and Batanaea from the province of Syria to Arabia, in compensation for Arabia's loss of the southern part of its territory to Palestine (Smallwood, p. 533). This region has been surveyed and described in publications by H. C. Butler (Howard Crosby Butler, Publications of the American Archaeological Expeditions to Syria in 1899-1900 (New York: Century Co. & Princeton Univ. Press). Idem, Publications of the Princeton University Expeditions to Syria in 1904, 1905 and 1909, (Leiden: Brill). Idem, Early Churches. No Jewish evidence has yet come to light.

GADARA

G:8

Gadara was originally the capital of the district of
Galaaditis (Gilead) and part of the Seleucid kingdom. It was
captured by the Hasmonean king Alexander Jannaeus but after the
arrival of Pompey was transformed into one of the cities of the
Roman Decapolis (Josephus, AJ XIV:75). The territory later
became part of Herod's kingdom; after his death it was annexed
to Syria (Smallwood, Jews, pp. 28-29).

Evidence of Jewish occupation has been found at two sites in
Gadara: Hammat Gadara and Beth Yerah. In addition, two stones
decorated with menorahs were given the provenance of Gadara,
although they were reported found in Tiberias.

BETH YERAH

G:8, I-1

1. Name of site and map reference.

   Beth Yerah, Khirbet al-Karek, Khirbet Karak.

   2041.2359 (4.30)

   Plan 33

2. Survey of site.

   The ancient town is located on the southwest tip of the Sea
   of Galilee, 8 km. southeast of Tiberias.

   Roman baths were excavated here in 1944 and again in the 1950s.
   During the latter clearance, a Roman fort and synagogue were
   uncovered. [1-6] The baths, fort, and synagogue are located
   about 50 meters south of a Byzantine church. [7]

   The fort, dated to the second to third century, was in use
   until the fourth or fifth centuries, when a bath was built
   atop its walls. The fort was in the form of a walled quad-
   rangle about 60 meters square; square towers stood in each
   of its corners and two additional towers flanked its main
   southern entrance. [5]

   The later bath had two sections: a frigidarium and a hypocaust
   cellar. Much of the bath was paved with marble slabs, but
   colored and gilt tesserae stuck to plaster indicate that the
   walls, or a dome, were decorated with mosaic. The baths may
   have been destroyed in the seventh century. [6]

305

A large apsidal basilica found within the fort's enclosure
(later identified as a synagogue) may originally have been
built as a civil basilica. The excavator, P. Bar-Ardon,
reports that Roman buildings under the enclosure have not as
yet been investigated.[5]

3. <u>Character and sections of the building as suggested by extant
    and identifiable remains</u>.

    PORTICO (?)

    An entrance was cut into the north wall of the enclosure and a
    shallow stone tank was placed in front of it. A long narrow
    portico, or colonnade, may have run parallel with the north
    wall, which was directly in front of the basilica's facade.

    PLAN

    The basilica was divided by two longitudinal rows of columns
    (four ? per row) into a central nave and flanking aisles.

    ENTRANCES

    Possibly three entrances were in the facade wall, on the north.

    PAVEMENT

    The pavement was mosaic.

4. <u>Measurements</u>.

    Main hall: 38 x 20 m.[5]

    37 x 22 m.[9]

    37 x 23 m.[8]

    Auxiliary rooms: ca. 8 x 10 m.[5]

5. <u>Orientation</u>.

    An apse faces 150° south-southeast; Jerusalem is more to the
    west.[10]

    See Hammat Gadara (G:8, I-2) for information regarding the
    orientation of Transjordan synagogues. In antiquity Beth
    Yerah was east of the Jordan River.

6. <u>Character and form: apse, niche, Torah Shrine, bema, chancel</u>.

    A semicircular apse projects off the basilica's southeast
    wall.

7. <u>Auxiliary rooms and/or structures</u>.

    Rooms adjoin the basilica to the south and west. A complicated
    system of water channels passed through the corners of these
    rooms.[5]

8. <u>Ornamentation</u>.

    Only fragments of the basilica's mosaic pavement survive.
    They include an incomplete representation of a man and a
    horse, and a plant described as a "stylized ethrog tree."[1]
    A column base is incised with a seven-branched menorah,
    flanked by a shofar, ethrog, and incense shovel.

9. <u>Coins, ceramics, and other artifacts found within building complex</u>.

Pottery has been dated to the fourth and fifth centuries.[5]

12. <u>Date</u>.

The synagogue has been dated to the end of the fifth century or the beginning of the sixth.[8] It apparently coexisted with the Byzantine church built 50 meters to its north.[A]

13. <u>Bibliography</u>.

1. Bar-Ardon, P. "Beth Yerah." <u>IEJ</u>, 1 (1950/1951), 250.

2. Idem. <u>IEJ</u>, 2 (1952), 222.

3. Idem. <u>IEJ</u>, 4 (1954), 128.

4. Idem. <u>IEJ</u>, 8 (1958), 62.

5. Idem. "A Possible Fortified Synagogue at Beth Yerah." <u>International Congress of Roman Frontier Studies</u>, VII (1971), p. 185.

6. Maisler, B., M. Stekelis and M. Avi-Yonah. "The Excavations at Beth Yerah (Khirbet el-Kerek) 1944-1946." <u>IEJ</u>, 2, 4 (1952) 218-229.

7. Delougaz, P., R. C. Haines. <u>A Byzantine Church at Khirbat al-Karak</u>, pp. 56-57.

8. Yeivin, Sh. <u>A Decade of Archaeology in Israel, 1948-1958</u>. Istanbul, 1960.

9. Hestrin, Ruth. "Beth Yerah." <u>EAEh</u>. 1975 ed.

10. Hüttenmeister, F. <u>Antiken Synagogen</u>. Vol. I, pp. 72-73.

HAMMAT GADARA
G:8, I-2

1. <u>Name of site and map reference</u>.

Hammat Gadara, el-Hamme, al-Hamma, El Hama, eh-Hammeh, Tell Bâni.

2125.2321 (4.64)

Plan 34

2. <u>Survey of site</u>.

Hammat Gadara is located 7.5 km. east-southeast of the Sea of Galilee. The synagogue ruin is on Tell Bâni, a mound that rises to a height of about 26 meters above the level of the Plain of el-Hamme. Schumacher visited the site and reported finding the remains of several buildings.[4] The synagogue ruins were discovered in 1932 and excavated by E. L. Sukenik on behalf of Hebrew University, Jerusalem.

The synagogue was built on the crest of the mound, toward the west. It was part of a larger complex of rooms and annexes surrounded by a wall 32.5 meters long.[1]

3. <u>Character and sections of the building as suggested by extant and identifiable remains</u>.

The structure is built of basalt; its masonry work is of inferior quality.

PLAN

Two longitudinal rows of columns (four per row) were joined on the north by a transverse colonnade (two columns) that divided the interior into a central nave, surrounded on three sides by aisles. Two angled L-shaped plastered columns are <u>in situ</u> in the northeast and northwest corners. The columns, without bases, are sunk into sockets below the pavement level.[1]

ENTRANCES

On the east, the main entrance opens into the main hall from an adjoining passage (see no. 7). Additional doors opened from adjoining annexes (see no. 7).

BENCHES

Low benches set against the hall's interior walls were built atop the mosaic pavement.[1]

ROOF

Flat and convex earthenware roof tiles and semicylindrical ridge tiles found in the debris are considered similar to those uncovered at Beth Alpha (B:4, I-1).[1]

PAVEMENT

The pavement is mosaic.

4. <u>Measurements</u>.[1]

Building complex: 32.5 m. east-west along south wall.
ca. 29.0 m. east-west along north wall.
ca. 17.0 m. north-south along east wall.
ca. 23.5 m. north-south along west wall.

Main hall: ca. 13 m. square
13 m. x 13.9 m.[7]
14.35 x 13 m.[3,5]

Bema: 4.55 m. wide x 1.2 m. deep.
Apse: 4.55 m. wide x 2.10 m. deep.
Vestibule: 6.90 x 3.50 m.
Forecourt: 5.45 x 3.50 m.

5. Orientation.
    The apse faces 185° south.[1] The southern orientation of the
    synagogue is considered exceptional for Transjordan.[2] The
    synagogue at Gerasa A (G:11, I-1) faces west; however, the
    synagogue at Beth Yerah (G:8, I-1) also faces toward the
    south.[A] The problem regarding the building's orientation is
    compounded by the fact that the terrain favors a westward
    orientation.[A]

6. Character and form: apse, niche, Torah Shrine, bema, chancel.
    BEMA
    Placed against the south wall is a bema raised two steps above
    the hall pavement. To its east (and possibly the west) is a
    depression intended to receive a chancel screen pillar;
    continuous with it is a long groove for the screen. Fragments
    of the screen were reported found in this area of the hall.[1]
    APSE
    On the south was an internal, rectangular apse with rounded
    corners on its southeast and southwest, flanked by chambers.
    The east chamber was completely enclosed; the west was entered
    through the west aisle and west corridor. The apse pavement
    was sunk 1.8 meters below the bema's level and is paved with
    mosaic.

7. Auxiliary rooms and/or structures.
    1. A narrow corridor adjoined hall's west wall; its southern
    end was partitioned off by a diagonal wall.
    2. A narrow passage east of the main hall was originally
    divided into a forecourt and vestibule, and is separated from
    a four-room annex by a narrow court aligned north-south. The
    narrow passage opens onto the main hall.
    3. Four-room annex: Two of its rooms adjoin the east wall
    of the main hall. The larger southern room opens directly
    into the sanctuary's east aisle. Benches were built against
    its south, west, and east walls. The smaller of the two rooms
    has no direct access into main hall. The annex's other two
    rooms are east of the narrow court.

8. Ornamentation.
    The vestibule and main hall were paved with mosaic.[1] The
    vestibule has a checker-work pattern of lozenges (#311)
    framing flowers. On the east aisle, squares (four per row)
    frame a pattern of five rows of circles (#431) enclosing
    pomegranates. The pavement of the west aisle has been almost
    totally destroyed but appears to have been similar to the

vestibule's; it has a fragment of a <u>tabula ansata</u> set into it. The north aisle too was almost totally destroyed but appears to be similar to the west aisle.

The nave is divided into three panels separated by a narrow band of guilloche (#194). An elaborate border consisting of a crowstep band, guilloche (#199), and wave-crest (#190) frames the entire composition.[1,7,9]

1. The north panel is an elaborate geometric pattern of lozenges, squares, and rectangles. A <u>tabula ansata</u> containing an inscription is slightly west of the pavement axis; a matching one may have been on the east (see no. 10).

2. On the center panel, lozenges frame flowers of pomegranates. Two inscriptions, within a single <u>tabula ansata</u>, are set in the panel's southern border (see no. 10).

3. On the south panel in the center of a white field is a wreath tied with a ribbon that frames an inscription (see no. 10). The wreath is flanked by two lions; their bodies are in profile and their heads, with tongues protruding, face the viewer. Next to each lion is a cypress tree.

Also found were fragments of marble screens:[1,7,9] a panel decorated with a seven-branched menorah set within a wreath; and a panel decorated with a shell or rosette set within a wreath, inscribed with Greek letters (see no. 10).

9. <u>Coins, ceramics, and other artifacts found within building complex</u>.

Five hundred coins were found near the synagogue; of those, 22 are Byzantine, mainly Justin II (565-578). The oldest are Hellenistic.[1]

Two rings were found in the complex, one inscribed with the legend: "O Christ help Andrew." The other was deeply incised with an eagle, lion, and serpent.[1]

Fragments of glass oil lamps and a Byzantine oil lamp decorated with a cross design were also reported uncovered.[1]

10. <u>Inscriptions</u>.

Four Aramaic inscriptions were set in the mosaic pavement.

1. The inscription was set within the wreath in the south panel (not extant).[1]

> And remembered be for good/ Kyris Hoples
> and Kyra/ Protone, and Kyris Sallustius/
> his son-in-law, and <u>Comes</u> Phroros his son/
> and Kyris Photios his son-in-law, and
> Kyris/Haninah his son -- they and their
> children -- / whose acts of charity are
> constant everywhere/ [and] who have given
> five denarii/ [of] gold. May the King of
> the Universe bestow the blessing/ upon
> their work. Amen. Amen. Selah.

The term comes (count) also appears at Ramat Aviv (C:3, IIIA-1).
2. and 3.   These lines are side by side within a single tabula
ansata set in the central panel. They have four lines each;
parts are missing. (1)

> And r[emembered be for] good Rab Tanhum
> the Levite, the s[on of Hal]lipha, who
> has donated one tremissis; and remembered
> be for good Monikos of Susitha (?), the
> Sepphorite/ and [Kyros Pa]tricius of
> [Ke]phar 'Aqabyah, and Yose the son of
> Dositheus, of Capernaum, who have, all
> three, donated three scruples. May the
> King/ of the Un[iverse best)ow the
> blessing upon their work. Amen! Amen!
> Selah! Peace! And remembered be for
> good Yudan . . . of . . . who has donated
> three (?);/ and remembered be for good the
> people of Arbela who have donated of their
> cloths. May the King of the Universe
> bestow blessing upon their work. Amen!
> Amen! Selah!

> And remembered be for good Kyrios Leontios
> and Kyra Kalonike, [who have donated . . .
> denarii in ho]nor of the synagogue./ May
> the King of the Universe bestow blessing
> upon his work. Amen. Amen. Selah.
> Peace. And remembered be for good one
> woman/ Anatolia, [who has donate]d one den-
> arius in honor of the synagogue. May the
> King of the Universe bestow blessing upon
> her work./ Amen. Amen. [Selah] Peace.
> [And remembered be for good the "wakeful"
> (or inhabitants of the town)] who have
> donated one tr[em]issis.

4.   In the north panel, the upper right hand corner is missing;
the inscription reads:

> [And remembered for] good be Ada, the son
> of Tanhum/ the son of [Moni]kos, who has
> contributed one tremissis, and Yose,/ the
> son of Qarosah (?) and Monikos, who have
> contributed [one] half denarius toward
> th[is mosai]c. May theirs be/ the
> blessing. Am[en. Sel]ah. Peace.

Two fragmentary Greek inscriptions inscribed on parts of a
marble screen refer to the "sons of Paregorious."(1)

11. Donors or patrons.

Hammat Gadara's famed hot springs attracted visitors from all
over. Many Jewish visitors, who may have benefited from the
spring's curative powers, made large donations to the
community's synagogue, as did the family named in inscription
1. The title comes denoted officials or civilians of some

standing, usually heads of town councils.[1] With the
exception of the name "Haninah" all other names in inscription
1 are Greek or Latin.

The "cloths" mentioned in inscription 2 may have been donated
for the paroketh, the curtain that traditionally hung before
the Torah Shrine[1] (see Beth She'an A, B:4, I-2). The name
"Kyrios Leontios," in inscription 3, occurs again in a house
uncovered in Scythopolis (see p. 133).

12. Date.

The synagogue complex has been dated no earlier than the fourth
century and no later than the first half of the fifth.[1] This
date is based on the existence of an apse, the style of mosaic
pavement, the use of Greek titles (outlawed for Jews in 433),
and the units of currency mentioned in the inscriptions. A
later date, the middle of the sixth century, has also been
proposed because of the minimal use of figurative motifs.[6,7]
It is unknown when the Christian objects were deposited in
the ruins.[A]

The synagogue appears to have been destroyed by a fire.[1]

13. Bibliography.

1. Sukenik, E. The Ancient Synagogue of El-Hammeh.

2. Idem. Ancient Synagogues, pp. 81 f.

3. Archives. British Mandatory Government. Jerusalem.
   Rockefeller Museum.

4. Schumacher, G. Jaulan, pp. 149-160.

5. Avi-Yonah, M. "Mosaic Pavements in Palestine." QDAP,
   II (1932), 159.

6. Idem. QDAP IV (1934), 188.

7. Idem. "Hammat Gader." EAEh. 1976 ed.

8. Frey. CIJ, #856-860.

9. Goodenough, E. Jewish Symbols. Vol. I. (1953), pp. 239-
   241. Vol. III, ills. 626-630.

10. Hüttenmeister, F. Antiken Synagogen. Vol. I, pp. 152-158.

GADARA

G:8, II-1

1. Name of site and map reference.

Gadara, Umm Qeis, Umm Qēs.

2140.2290 (4.53)

2. Survey of site.

Situated 10 km. southeast of the southern shore of the Sea of Galilee, Gadara was the capital of the territory and a city of the Roman Decapolis. The city is mentioned in the Babylonian Talmud in reference to "Shizzpar, the head of Geder" (RH 22a), and the philosopher Oenomaus of Gadara ("ha-Gardi"), who was a friend of Rabbi Meir (Lam. R., Proem 2; Hag. 15b).

Many traces of the ancient city remain, including a colonnaded street paved with basalt, two theaters, a necropolis with sarcophagi, and a large area of tumbled stones and column drums. [5]

8. Ornamentation.

1. A stone, now at the Louvre, was found built into a modern house in Tiberias; according to the occupant, the stone was found at Gadara. [1] Measuring approximately 38 x 86 cm., the stone is decorated with a wreath tied with a Hercules knot, inside of which is a burning seven-branched menorah standing on a tripod base flanked by a lulab and shofar. In each of the stone's four corners is a rosette. [2,3]

2. Another stone, also decorated with a menorah, is in the Hospice of the Franciscan Fathers in Jerusalem. Its provenance is unknown, but it too was reported found in Tiberias; [4] but it may be from Gadara. [6]

13. Bibliography.

1. Dussaud, Rene. Les Monuments Palestiniens et Judaïques (Paris, 1912), p. 87.

2. Schumacher, G. Northern Aylun (1890), pp. 46 ff.

3. Idem. The Jaulan (1888), pp. 146-190.

4. Goodenough, E. R. Jewish Symbols. Vol. I, pp. 219, 225; Vol. III, illus. 574, 592.

5. Harding, C. Lankester. The Antiquities of Jordan. rev. ed. (London, 1967), p. 56.

6. Hüttenmeister, F. Antiken Synagogen. Vol. I, pp. 125-6.

ABILA/CAPITOLIAS
G:9

The territorial extent of this city is not known from any
ancient sources; therefore its boundaries can only be conjectured.
Abila was one of the cities refounded by Pompey and may have been
made part of the Decapolis (Avi-Yonah, The Holy Land, p. 81).
Jews apparently had moved to this region during the period it was
under Hasmonean control (Josephus, BJ I:104; AJ XIII:391-394).
    The city has yet to be excavated; however, fortifications,
temples, a theater, and a basilica are reported among its ruins
(Avi-Yonah, Gazetteer, p. 25). No Jewish evidence has yet come
to light.

PELLA
G:10

Pella was founded and settled by Macedonian veterans of the
campaigns of Alexander the Great, who bestowed upon their new
foundation the name of their general's birthplace. For a short
period, Pella was part of the Hasmonean kingdom, until it was
returned to gentile control by Pompey and made part of the
Decapolis (Josephus, BJ I:155-157; Pliny, NH V:74). The city was
very Hellenized in culture and openly hostile to Jews, although
it offered Jewish Christians refuge when they fled Jerusalem in
70 C.E. (Eusebius, Eccl. Hist. 3.5, 3-4).
    Pella receives mention in the Jerusalem Talmud regarding
clean and unclean localities. A visiting rabbi was informed that
Pella's hot springs (probably Hammat-Pella, 207.219) were considered within Eretz Israel, possibly indicating the city was not.
(Robert Houston Smith, Pella of the Decapolis, Wooster, 1973,
60, pp. 57-58.) No archaeological evidence has been uncovered
in the territory attesting to a Jewish settlement.

GERASA
G:11

A Jewish community was established in the Hellenistic city
of Gerasa during the time it was under Hasmonean control (Josephus,
BJ II:480). Jews remained there, apparently unmolested, until
the reign of Justinian. Gerasa experienced two periods of prosperity: The first occurred in the first two centuries of the
Common Era, the second in the fifth and sixth centuries. It then
fell into an irreversible decline in the late sixth century and
was finally abandoned.

The city has an enormous amount of archaeological evidence
attesting to its great wealth first under Roman domination and
then later as a center for Christianity (Kraeling, Gerasa).

Gerasa has one verified synagogue site, within the city
itself; it was transformed into a church sometime before 530/531.
Little is known of its appearance, except that it had some
affinities to Capernaum (B:3, I-1, column bases), and a mosaic
pavement illustrating a biblical text.

It has been suggested that architectural material reused in
the building of Hadrian's arch in the city of Gerasa may be from
an earlier "Jewish building"; however, the evidence is too meager
to support such a conclusion.

GERASA A
G:11, I-1

1. Name of site and map reference.
   Gerasa, Jerash, Ğaraš.
   2340.1878 (-.54)
   Plan 35

2. Survey of site.
   The synagogue/church stands on very high ground that falls
   steeply away to the south. It is west of the Temple of
   Artemis, half-way between the temple's enclosure and the city
   wall. The synagogue ruins have been occupied by a succession
   of buildings, making it almost impossible to determine its
   exact phases of construction.[8] The synagogue was cleared in
   1929 by R. W. Hamilton on behalf of Yale University and the

British School of Archaeology in Jerusalem. Three principal
phases of construction were distinguished (see no. 12):[8]
1. An atrium at the east side of the site was erected in the
third or fourth century.
2. The synagogue is west of the atrium.
3. A few centimeters above the synagogue's pavement are the
remains of a church built in 530-531. Further west was another
court.

3. <u>Character and sections of the building as suggested by extant
and identifiable remains</u>.

ATRIUM

The atrium is not aligned with the synagogue or church and
may be from an earlier building (a synagogue ?) on the site.[8]
It was in the form of a square court, with porticoes on its
four sides; the columns of the porticoes rested on square
pedestals that were set on stylobates. The pedestals are
considered similar to those at Capernaum (B:3, I-1).[8] The
columns are crowned with Corinthian-style capitals and carry
stone architraves.

PAVEMENT

The pavement is made of flagstone.

SYNAGOGUE

NARTHEX

West of the atrium was a wide flight of stairs that ascended
to a narthex that opened onto a hall. Part of the synagogue,
the narthex lies under the apse of the later church. There
is evidence that three doorways opened from the narthex into
the synagogue's main hall.

PLAN

Two longitudinal rows of columns, resting on octagonal bases
(four of the original seven per row are <u>in situ</u>), divide
the interior of the synagogue into a central nave and side
aisles.

BENCHES

Masonry benches were set along the hall's north and south
walls.

PAVEMENT

The narthex and main hall were paved with mosaic.

CHURCH

The synagogue was converted into a church by changing its
orientation: The narthex was transformed into an apse and
chancel. The church pavement was raised on the west to
obliterate the synagogue's bema.

4. Measurements. [8]
   Narthex: 13.40 x 4 m.

5. Orientation.
   According to the position of its pavement, the synagogue was
   oriented 290° west. [12]

6. Character and form: apse, niche, Torah Shrine, bema, chancel.
   In the southwest corner of the synagogue hall is a rock that
   rises above the pavement level; it has been suggested that the
   synagogue's bema was built atop this rock. [8]
   In front of the church's west door (added when the building
   was transformed into a church) are two columns. Between them
   and the west wall are the foundations of a small chamber
   projecting from the building. It has been suggested that this
   was the synagogue's apse; the chamber's mosaic pavement,
   however, is similar to that of the church. [8]

8. Ornamentation.
   NARTHEX
   The synagogue's narthex was paved its entire width with an
   elaborate mosaic pavement.
   The border of the pavement is inhabited by a wide variety of
   realistically portrayed animals, birds, flowers, and plants.
   The animals move right to left cross the top border and in
   the opposite direction on the bottom. Directly opposite what
   was the central entrance into the synagogue is a menorah
   flanked by a lulab, ethrog, shofar, and "small box."
   In the field of the mosaic, the figures are placed so as to
   be seen as the worshipper entered the narthex from the east.
   The panel illustrates the narrative of Noah and his family
   leaving the ark after the flood. To the left are Shem and
   Japheth, but only their heads and Greek names survive; above
   them is the dove with the olive branch. Much of the panel
   is filled with animals grouped in three rows: birds, beasts,
   and creeping things.
   NAVE
   Only a fragment of the pavement, by the fourth pedestal,
   survives. It has a portion of a dentilled border and a
   broad guilloche band (#197). The north aisle is paved in a
   diaper pattern, interrupted by an inscription set within a
   tabula ansata.
   In the apse (?), the field is similar to that of the north
   aisle of SS. Peter and Paul. It is enclosed within a guilloche
   border. [7] The field consists of a series of scalloped

squares divided diagonally by single foils and filled with a
scale pattern enclosing flowers.

9. **Coins, ceramics, and other artifacts found within building**
    complex.
    Lamps were uncovered that are dated to the fifth or sixth
    centuries and bowls dated to the fourth or fifth centuries.[2]

10. **Inscriptions.**
    1. On the north aisle, a five-line Aramaic inscription is
        set within a **tabula ansata**, to be read as one faces east.[4]

    > Peace upon all/ Israel Amen Amen/
    > Selah Phinehas son of/ Baruch,
    > Jose son of/ Samuel, and Judan son
    > of/ Hezekiah.

    2. In the narthex, a Greek inscription in two columns is set
        on either side of ritual objects; it is to be read as one
        faces east.[10]

    > . . . to the most Ho[ly] Place. Amen.
    > Amen, Selah. Peace to the synagogue.

11. **Donors or patrons.**
    The names mentioned in the first inscription are conjectured
    to be associated with an atelier of Aramaic-speaking mosaicists
    imported by Gerasa's hellenistic Jewish community.[4] The
    Greek inscription commemorates one of the congregants.

12. **Date.**
    The atrium has been dated to the third or fourth centuries.[8]
    It has been postulated that the synagogue pavement was laid
    sometime in the first half of the fifth century, except for
    the north aisle, which was probably added about a half a
    century later.[7] The synagogue has been dated to the fifth
    century;[1] however, a fourth-fifth century date has been
    proposed for the pavement.[11,12]
    The synagogue was converted into a church sometime before
    530/531; this is the date given in an inscription set in
    the church pavement.

13. **Bibliography.**

    1. Crowfoot, J. and R. Hamilton. "The Discovery of a
        Synagogue at Jerash." PEFQS (1929), pp. 211-219.

    2. Crowfoot. PEFQS (1930), p. 40.

    3. Barrois, A. "Découverte d'une synagogue a Djerash." RB,
        XXXIX (1930), 259-265.

4. Sukenik, E. "Note on the Aramaic Inscription at the Synagogue at Gerasa." PEFQS (1930), pp. 48-49.

5. Idem. The Ancient Synagogue at Beth Alpha, pp. 27, 51-56.

6. Idem. Ancient Synagogues, pp. 35-37, 77.

7. Biebel, F. M. In Gerasa, pp. 318-323.

8. Crowfoot, J. In Gerasa, pp. 234-239.

9. Frey. CIJ, #866-867.

10. Goodenough, E. R. Jewish Symbols. Vol. I. (1953), pp. 180 f., 259 f. Vol. III, illus. 450, 656.

11. Applebaum, S. "Gerasa." EAEh. 1976 ed.

12. Hüttenmeister, F. Antiken Synagogen. Vol. I, pp. 126-130.

GERASA B
G:11, IIIB-1

1. Name of site and map reference.
Gerasa, Jerash, Ğaraš.
234.287 (-.54)

2. Survey of site.
G. Dalman reported acquiring at Gerasa a gilt glass seal on which was engraved a seven-branched menorah.[1] Gilt glass has been found in Jewish tombs in Rome and Palestine; it has not been found decorating any synagogue.[A] A. Detweiler found some architectural fragments in the fill of the Roman arch honoring Hadrian; he suggests that it came from an earlier Jewish building, possibly a synagogue, destroyed during the first Jewish revolt.[2] Nevertheless, no evidence indicates that the fragments should be attributed to a synagogue.[3,A]

8. Ornamentation.
The fragments from Hadrian's arch include a metope decorated with an amphora, a metope decorated with a standing bird, and a capital carved with a pronged device, which the excavator suggests formed part of a menorah.[2]

13. Bibliography.

1. Dalman, G. PJB, XII (1917), 36.

2. Detweiler, A. H. "Some Early Architectural Vestiges from Jerash." BASOR, 87 (Oct., 1942), 10-17.

3. Hüttenmeister, F. Antiken Synagogen. Vol. I, p. 128.

PHILADELPHIA

G:12

Philadelphia, the southernmost city of the Roman Decapolis, was located near the border with Bostra (238.152). The city was never part of the Hasmonean kingdom, but rather was controlled by their rivals, the Nabataeans (Avi-Yonah, The Holy Land, p. 63). The Nabataeans surrendered the cities of Damascus, Canatha, and Philadelphia to the Romans, who incorporated them into the Decapolis (Pliny, NH V:74).

The modern city of Amman has all but covered ancient Philadelphia. Butler surveyed the region in the early twentieth century, and recently the Jordanian government has allowed some excavation. No evidence of a Jewish community has come to light.

HESHBON

G:13

Heshbon, a famed biblical site, is recorded by Eusebius (Onom. 84:4) as being 20 Roman miles east of the Jordan River, across from Jericho. To the west was Peraea; the village of Nebo (Fasga, 219.131), named on the famed Moabite stone, and Mount Nebo, alleged site of Moses' tomb, are located 9.6 km. west of the city of Heshbon (Avi-Yonah, The Holy Land, pp. 177-178).

Heshbon is included in Josephus' list (AJ XIII:397) of cities in Jewish control during the reign of the Hasmonean king, Alexander Jannaeus. During the time of Herod the Great, the city became a military colony settled by veterans (AJ XV:294-295).

Although Josephus records Jews living in Heshbon, no archaeological evidence of their settlement has been uncovered.

MEDEBA

G:14

Medeba (Madaba) is a biblical site named on the famed
Moabite stone, the stele of Mesha, King of Moab, dated 850 B.C.E.

Ten churches have been uncovered in the city including one
paved with a mosaic map of ancient Palestine, the famed Medeba
map, preserved in the city's modern Greek Orthodox Church.   No
evidence of a Jewish occupation of the territory has been
uncovered.

PERAEA

G:15

The Romans never urbanized Peraea, transforming it instead,
as they did its neighbor Jericho across the Jordan, into an
imperial estate. It was composed of three toparchies: Julias
(Livias), Abila (Khirbet el-Kafrein), and possibly Gadara (Gedar).

Josephus notes the arrival of many Jews into the territory
following its capture by the Hasmonean king Alexander Jannaeus
(BJ IV:413-418; 439); however, no archaeological evidence has
been uncovered of their settlement.

AEROPOLIS
G:16

Aeropolis was located in biblical Moab, east of the Dead Sea.
For a brief period it belonged to the Hasmonean monarchy, but it
soon became part of the Nabataean kingdom.

A building uncovered near a temple dedicated to Diocletian
and Maximian in Rabbath Moab (Aeropolis) has been identified by
F. Zayadine as a synagogue. This identification is based on the
building's orientation toward the west and a quote from the
writings of the fifth century monk Bar-Sauma, who reportedly
destroyed the synagogue in Rabbath Moab. The western orientation
is not unknown in fourth century Syrian churches; this fact,
coupled with the fantastic quality of the monk's description,
made the building's attribution uncertain.

RABBAT MOAB
G:15, IIIB-1

1. Name of site and map reference.
    Rabbat Moab, Aeropolis, er-Rabba.
    220.076
    Plan 36

2. Survey of site.
    About 50 meters west of the town's ancient colonnaded street
    are the remains of a Roman temple that contained two Latin
    dedications, one to Diocletian and one to Maximian.[1] South
    of the temple is another building whose apse is discernible.
    The building was initially identified as a Byzantine church,
    but its western orientation has led F. Zayadine to conclude
    that it was a synagogue.[1] (See no. 5.) There is, at
    present, no evidence to support this attribution.[A]
    A small church was uncovered east of the temple; its apse is
    oriented toward the east.[1]

3. Character and sections of the building as suggested by extant
    and identifiable remains.
    PLAN
    Although no remains of a colonnade survive, it is believed
    that the interior of the building was divided into a central
    nave and side aisles by two rows of columns.[1]

327

ENTRANCES

One large door was in the center of the east wall and a
smaller one to its south. On the west, doors at the end of
each aisle opened into chambers flanking the apse (see no. 6).

4. <u>Measurements</u>.[1]

Main hall: 37 x 20 m. (external).

5. <u>Orientation</u>.

The focal point of the basilica is to the west, and this
orientation has led to the building's identity as a
synagogue.[1] Jerusalem, technically, is to the northwest;
however, see Hammat Gadara (G:8, I-2) for discussion of the
orientation of Transjordan synagogues.[A] Churches facing
west are not unknown; examples are the fifth century church
at Ba'albek, the "Great Church" at Antioch, and the famed
Cathedral of Tyre.[A]

6. <u>Character and form: apse, niche, Torah Shrine, bema, chancel</u>.

The west end of the basilica has an arrangement similar to
that of several Syrian churches, including the Bishop
Genesius at Gerasa: a triply divided east end consisting of an
apse between side chambers.[A] For an example and discussions
of a tripartite arrangement in a synagogue, see Rehov (B:4,
I-5).

12. <u>Date</u>.

The building was allegedly built at the same time the nearby
temple was abandoned, the second quarter of the fourth century.
It was destroyed in the fifth century.[1]

13. <u>Bibliography</u>.

1. Zayadine, Fawzi. "Deux Inscriptions Grecques de Rabbat
      Moab (Aeropolis)." <u>Annual of the Jordan Department
      of Antiquities</u> 2 (1970), 71-72.

TABLES

Tables

The following tables are collations of data documented in the handbook. They follow the order of the 13 data entries. Numbers 1 and 13 are omitted. Number 2 is based on data from all the handbook entries. Numbers 3 through 7 are based on category I sites; numbers 8 through 12 on category I and II. No tables are provided for numbers 9 and 12; in their place are brief explanations of why tables were not possible for these two particular categories.

Roman numerals following a handbook number refer to a building's stages of construction; Arabic numerals refer to the number of objects, for example, niches.

Samaritan evidence is not included, except for those synagogues of questionable Samaritan attribution.

TABLE 1

NO. 2:   SURVEY OF SITE

Region	Cat. I	Cat. II	Cat. IIIA	Cat. IIIB
A. Phoenician cities	0	2	0	3
B. Galilee	18	17	4	18
C. Coastal cities	3	7**	2	1
D. Samaria	0	0	0	1
E. Judaea	6**	6	2	3
F. Limes Palaestina	3	1	1	0
G. East of Jordan	6	15	3	21
Total	36	48	12	47

* for each Samaritan site.

TABLE 2

NO. 3: CHARACTER AND SECTIONS OF THE BUILDING AS SUGGESTED
BY EXTANT AND IDENTIFIABLE REMAINS (FORM)

Basilica with three colonnades	Basilica with two colonnades	Broadhouse with columns	Broadhouse without columns	Other
B:1, I-2	B:1, I-1	B:1, I-3	E:4, I-2	B:4, I-3
B:1, I-4	B:1, I-5(II-III)	B:1, I-5(I)	E:4, I-4	B:4, I-6
B:2, I-1	B:2, I-2	G:2, I-2(?)	G:3, I-1(?)	C:9, I-1
B:3, I-1	B:2, I-3			E:2, I-1
B:3, I-2	B:3, I-3			E:4, I-1
B:3, I-4(I)	B:4, I-1			
G:8, I-2	B:4, I-2			
	B:4, I-4			
	B:4, I-5			
	*C:2, I-2			
	E:4, I-3			
	F:1, I-1			
	F:4, I-1			
	F:4, I-2			
	G:8, I-1			
	G:11, I-1			
Total 7	16	2 1?	2 1?	5

* Could be considered a broadhouse; see Table 6, Measurements.

TABLE 3

NO. 3: CHARACTER AND SECTIONS OF THE BUILDING AS
SUGGESTED BY EXTANT AND IDENTIFIABLE
REMAINS (COURT AND NARTHEX)

Court	Narthex	Both
B:2, I-2	B:1, I-2	B:3, I-3(II-III)
B:3, I-1	B:1, I-4	B:4, I-1
B:3, I-2*	B:4, I-1	B:4, I-4
B:3, I-3*	B:4, I-2(II)	B:4, I-5(III)
B:3, I-4	B:4, I-4	E:4, I-2
B:4, I-1	B:4, I-5(III)	E:4, I-4
B:4, I-3	C:2, I-1	F:4, I-2
B:4, I-4	E:4, I-1	G:2, I-1
B:4, I-5(III)	E:4, I-2	
E:4, I-2	E:4, I-3(II)	
E:4, I-4	E:4, I-4	
F:4, I-2	F:4, I-2	
G:2, I-1	G:2, I-1	
	G:8, I-1(?)	
	G:11, I-1	
Total 13	14 1?	8

* Have terraces.

TABLE 4

NO. 3: CHARACTER AND SECTIONS OF THE BUILDING AS SUGGESTED
BY EXTANT AND IDENTIFIABLE REMAINS (ENTRANCES)

Single entrance	Double entrance	Triple entrance
B:1, I-1	E:4, I-1(I)	B:1, I-2
B:1, I-3		B:1, I-4
B:1, I-5		B:2, I-1
B:4, I-4(?)		B:2, I-2
C:2, I-1		B:3, I-1
C:2, I-2		B:3, I-2
E:2, I-1		B:3, I-3(?)
F:4, I-1		B:3, I-4(IV)
G:2, I-1(?)		B:4, I-1
G:2, I-2		B:4, I-2
G:8, I-2		B:4, I-3
		B:4, I-5
		C:9, I-1
		E:4, I-1(II)
		E:4, I-2
		E:4, I-3
		E:4, I-4
		F:1, I-1(?)
		F:4, I-2
		G:8, I-1(?)

Total   9
           2?
	1	17
		   3?

TABLE 5

NO. 3: CHARACTER AND SECTIONS OF THE BUILDING AS SUGGESTED
BY EXTANT AND IDENTIFIABLE REMAINS (ACCESSORIES)

	Benches	Chair of Moses	Genizah	Gallery
	B:1, I-1	B:3, I-1(?)	B:1, I-1(?)	B:1, I-3
	B:1, I-2	B:3, I-2	B:1, I-3(?)	E:4, I-4
	B:1, I-3	B:3, I-3	B:4, I-4	
	B:1, I-4	E:4, I-1	B:4, I-5	
	B:1, I-5		C:2, I-1(?)	
	B:2, I-1		F:1, I-1(?)	
	B:3, I-1		G:2, I-2	
	B:3, I-2			
	B:3, I-4			
	B:4, I-1			
	B:4, I-3			
	B:4, I-4(?)			
	B:4, I-5			
	E:4, I-1			
	E:4, I-2			
	E:4, I-4			
	G:2, I-2			
	G:8, I-2			
	G:11, I-1			
Total	18 1?	3 1?	3 4?	2

TABLE 6

NO. 4:   MEASUREMENTS

Synagogue (Largest - Smallest)	Length x Width (Meters)	Ratio
G:8, I-1	38 x 25	1.52
C:9, I-1	30 x 26	1.15
B:2, I-2	28 x 15	1.87
B:1, I-4	27.4 x 13.6	2.01
B:3, I-1	24.4 x 18.65	1.31
B:3, I-2	22.8 x 16.7	1.37
F:4, I-2	21.0 x 14.8	1.42
B:4, I-5	19.0 x 17.0	1.12
B:3, I-4 (IV)	19 x 15	1.27
F:1, I-1	19 x 15	1.27
B:2, I-1	18.8 x 14.1	1.33
B:1, I-1	18.2 x 17.8	1.02
B:1, I-2	18.1 x 13.9	1.30
C:3, I-1	18 x 9	2.0
B:4, I-2	17.0 x 14.2	1.20
B:4, I-4 (II)	16 x 14	1.14
B:1, I-5 (III)	16 x 11.5	1.39
E:4, I-1 (I)	15.5 x 10	1.55
*G:2, I-2	15.4 x 18.0	1.17
B:3, I-4	ca. 14 x 13	1.08
E:4, I-1 (II)	13.5-16 x 12.5	1.18
*E:4, I-2	13.3 x 21.30	1.60
G:8, I-2	13 x 13	1
F:4, I-1	13 x 10	1.30
E:4, I-3 (II)	13.5 x 9.5	1.42
B:4, I-1	12.4 x 10.8	1.15
E:2, I-1	12.2 x 7.0	1.74
B:3, I-3	12.0 x 12.0	1
B:4, I-6	11.3 x 10.6	1.07
*B:1, I-3	11 x 15	1.36
*C:2, I-2	10.16 x 10.70	1.05
*E:4, I-4	9 x 16	1.78
B:4, I-3	7 x 7	1
B:2, I-3	? x 15.7	?

* Broadhouses

TABLE 7

NO. 5: ORIENTATION

Facade toward Jerusalem	Apse, niche toward Jerusalem	Other
B:1, I-1	B:1, I-3	B:2, I-3
B:1, I-2	B:1, I-5 (I)	B:4, I-2
B:1, I-4	B:3, I-3 (II)	B:4, I-6
B:1, I-5	B:3, I-4 (III-IV)	C:2, I-2
B:2, I-1	B:4, I-1	C:9, I-1
B:2, I-2	B:4, I-4	E:2, I-1
B:3, I-1	B:4, I-5	G:2, I-1
B:3, I-2	C:2, I-1	G:2, I-2
B:3, I-3 (I)	E:4, I-1	
	E:4, I-2	
	E:4, I-3	
	E:4, I-4	
	F:1, I-1	
	F:4, I-1	
	F:4, I-2	
	G:8, I-1	
	G:8, I-2	
	G:11, I-1 (?)	
Total 9	18	8
	1?	

TABLE 8

NO. 6: CHARACTER AND FORM: APSE, NICHE, TORAH
SHRINE, BEMA, CHANCEL (APSE)

	Internal apse	External apse	Semi-circular apse	Other shape apse
	B:3, I-4 (IV)		B:3, I-4 (IV)	
	G:8, I-2	B:4, I-1	B:4, I-1	G:8, I-2
		B:4, I-2	B:4, I-2	
		B:4, I-4	B:4, I-4	
		F:1, I-1	F:1, I-1	
		F:4, I-1	F:4, I-1	
		G:8, I-1	G:8, I-1	
Total	2	6	7	1

TABLE 9

NO. 6: CHARACTER AND FORM: APSE, NICHE,
TORAH SHRINE, BEMA, CHANCEL

Niche(s)	Bema	Chancel	Torah Shrine
B:2, I-2	B:1, I-3	B:3, I-3 (II)	B:1, I-1
B:3, I-3 (II)	B:1, I-5 (I-II)	B:4, I-2 (III)	B:1, I-3
B:3, I-4 (III)	B:2, I-2	B:4, I-4 (III)	B:1, I-4
E:2, I-1 (6)	B:3, I-4 (IV)	B:4, I-5 (III)	B:1, I-5 (IIA)
E:4, I-1	B:4, I-1	C:9, I-1 (?)	B:3, I-1
E:4, I-2 (3)	B:4, I-4	E:4, I-1 (II)	
	B:4, I-5	F:1, I-1	
	E:4, I-2	G:8, I-2	
	E:4, I-3 (?)		
	E:4, I-4 (2)		
	F:1, I-1		
	G:2, I-2		
	G:8, I-2		
Total 6	12 1?	7 1?	5

TABLE 10

NO. 7:   AUXILIARY ROOMS AND/OR STRUCTURES*

Within complex	Isolated	Auxiliary room(s) other than court or narthex
B:1, I-3	B:1, I-1	B:1, I-1
B:3, I-4	B:1, I-2	B:1, I-2
B:2, I-2	B:1, I-4	B:1, I-3
B:4, I-2	B:3, I-1	B:1, I-4
B:4, I-3	B:3, I-2	B:2, I-2
C:9, I-1	B:4, I-1	B:4, I-1
E:4, I-1 (?)	E:4, I-2	B:3, I-2
E:4, I-3		B:3, I-3
E:4, I-4		B:4, I-4
F:4, I-2		B:4, I-1
G:2, I-2		B:4, I-3
G:8, I-1		C:9, I-1
G:8, I-2		E:4, I-1
		E:4, I-2
		E:4, I-3
		E:4, I-4
		F:4, I-2
		G:2, I-2
		G:8, I-2
Total 12	7	19

* The area around many synagogues has not been excavated.

TABLE 11

NO. 8:   ORNAMENTATION (MOSAIC, RELIEF)

Relief	Mosaic	Both	Other	3D
A:1, II-1	A:1, II-1(?)	A:1, II-1(?)	B:1, I-3	B:1, I-2
B:1, I-1	A:2, II-1	B:2, I-3	B:2, I-2	B:3, I-3
B:1, I-2	B:2, I-3	E:4, I-2	B:4, I-5	B:3, I-1
B:1, I-3	B:2, II-5		C:2, I-1	B:3, I-2
B:1, I-5	B:2, II-6		C:2, I-2	
B:1, II-1	B:4, I-1			
B:1, II-3	B:4, I-2			
B:1, II-4	B:4, I-3			
B:1, II-6	B:4, I-4			
B:1, II-7	B:4, I-5			
B:2, I-1	B:4, I-6			
B:2, I-2	C:2, I-1			
B:2, I-3	C:9, I-1			
B:2, II-1	E:2, I-1			
B:2, II-3	E:4, I-1			
B:2, II-4	E:4, I-2			
B:3, I-1	E:4, I-4			
B:3, I-2	F:1, I-1			
B:3, I-3	F:4, I-1			
B:3, II-1	F:4, I-2			
B:3, II-2	G:8, I-1			
B:3, II-3	G:8, I-2			
B:4, II-1	G:11, I-1			
C:2, I-1				
C:1, I-2				
C:7, II-1				
C:8, II-1				

TABLE 11: Continued

	Relief	Mosaic	Both	Other	3D
	C:9, II-1				
	E:4, I-2				
	E:4, I-3				
	E:4, II-1				
	E:4, II-2				
	G:2, I-1				
	G:2, I-2				
	G:2, II-1				
	G:2, II-2				
	G:2, II-3				
	G:2, II-4				
	G:2, II-5				
	G:2, II-6				
	G:2, II-7				
	G:2, II-8				
	G:2, II-9				
	G:2, II-10				
	G:2, II-11				
	G:2, II-12				
	G:3, I-1				
	G:4, II-1				
	G:8, II-1				
Total	49	24	2 1?	5	4

TABLE 12

NO. 8:   ORNAMENTATION (FIGURATIVE/NON-FIGURATIVE)

Figurative	Non-figurative	Both	Mutilated
A:2, II-1	A:1, II-1	B:1, I-2	B:1, I-2
B:1, I-1	B:1, I-2	B:1, I-3	B:1, I-5
B:1, I-2	B:1, I-3	B:1, I-5	B:1, II-6
B:1, I-3	B:1, I-5	B:1, II-6	B:3, I-1
B:1, I-5	B:1, II-1	B:2, I-1	B:3, I-2
B:1, II-3	B:1, II-6	B:2, I-2	B:3, II-3
B:1, II-4	B:1, II-7	B:2, I-3	B:4, I-6
B:1, II-6	B:2, I-1	B:2, II-3	B:4, II-1
B:2, I-1	B:2, I-2	B:3, I-1	F:4, I-2
B:2, I-2	B:2, I-3	B:3, I-2	G:2, II-9
B:2, I-3	B:2, II-1	B:3, I-4	G:3, I-1
B:2, II-3	B:2, II-3	B:3, II-3	G:8, I-1
B:3, I-1	B:2, II-4	B:4, I-1	
B:3, I-2	B:2, II-6	B:4, I-3	
B:3, I-4	B:3, I-1	B:4, I-6	
B:3, II-2	B:3, I-2	B:4, I-4	
B:3, II-3	B:3, I-3	C:9, I-1	
B:4, I-1	B:3, I-4	E:4, I-1	
B:4, I-3	B:3, II-1	F:1, I-1	
B:4, I-4	B:4, II-3	F:4, I-2	
B:4, I-6	B:4, I-1	G:2, II-1	
C:2, I-2	B:4, I-2	G:2, II-4	
C:9, I-1	B:4, I-3	G:2, II-6	
E:4, I-1	B:4, I-4	G:2, II-8	
E:4, I-4	B:4, I-5	G:2, II-9	
F:1, I-1	B:4, I-6	G:2, II-10	
F:4, I-2	C:2, I-1	G:3, I-1	
G:2, II-1	C:2, I-2	G:8, I-1	
G:2, II-4	C:7, II-1	G:8, I-2	
G:2, II-6	C:8, II-1	G:11, I-1	
G:2, II-8	C:9, I-1		
G:2, II-9	E:2, I-1		
G:2, II-10	E:4, I-1		
G:3, I-1	E:4, I-2		
G:8, I-1	E:4, I-3		

TABLE 12:   Continued

Figurative	Non-figurative	Both	Mutilated
G:8, I-2	E:4, I-4		
G:11, I-1	E:4, II-1		
	E:4, II-2		
	F:1, I-1		
	F:4, I-1		
	F:4, I-2		
	G:2, I-1		
	G:2, I-2		
	G:2, II-1		
	G:2, II-2		
	G:2, II-4		
	G:2, II-5		
	G:2, II-6		
	G:2, II-7		
	G:2, II-8		
	G:2, II-9		
	G:2, II-10		
	G:2, II-11		
	G:2, II-12		
	G:3, I-1		
	G:8, I-1		
	G:8, I-2		
	G:8, II-1		
	G:11, I-1		
Total 38	61	30	12

TABLE 13

NO. 8:   ORNAMENTATION (MOTIFS)

Eagles*	Genii**	Lions+	Peacocks++	Zodiacs§
B:1, I-1	B:1, I-2	B:1, I-2	B:4, I-3	B:4, I-1
B:1, I-2	B:1, II-4	B:1, I-5	C:2, I-2	B:2, I-2(?)
B:2, I-3	B:1, II-6	B:2, I-1	C:9, I-1	B:2, I-3.(?)
B:3, I-1	B:3, I-1	B:2, I-3	E:4, I-1	B:3, I-4
G:2, II-1		B:3, I-1	F:1, I-1	C:2, I-2
G:2, II-4		B:3, I-2		F:4, I-2
G:2, II-9		B:3, I-4		
G:2, II-10		B:4, I-1		
		B:4, I-5(I)		
		C:9, I-1		
		F:1, I-1		
		F:4, I-2		
		G:2, II-6		
		G:2, II-8		
		G:8, I-2		
Total 8	4	15	5	4 2?

---

*   Eagles are all in relief, except B:2, I-3, in relief and mosaic.

**   Genii are all in relief.

\+   Lions: five in relief, seven in mosaic, three are 3-dimensional.

\+\+   Peacocks are all in mosaic.

§   Zodiacs are all in mosaic except for the questionable find at B:2, I-2.

TABLE 14

NO. 8: ORNAMENTATION (JEWISH MOTIFS)

Shofar	Lulab	Ethrog	Torah Shrine	Menorah
B:1, II-7	B:1, II-7	B:1, II-7	B:1, II-7	A:1, II-1
B:3, I-1	B:2, II-1 (?)	B:2, II-1 (?)	B:3, I-1	B:1, I-3
B:3, I-4	B:3, I-4	B:3, I-4	B:3, I-2	B:1, I-5
B:3, II-1	B:3, II-1	B:3, II-1	B:3, I-4	B:1, II-7
B:4, I-1	B:4, I-1	B:4, I-1	B:3, II-1	B:2, I-3
B:4, I-2	B:4, II-1	B:4, I-3	B:4, I-1	B:2, II-1
B:4, I-4	C:2, I-2	B:4, II-1	B:4, I-2	B:2, II-3
B:4, I-6	C:7, II-1	C:2, I-2	C:7, II-1	B:2, II-4
C:7, II-1	C:8, II-1	C:8, II-1	E:4, I-4	B:3, I-1
C:2, I-2	E:2, I-1	C:9, II-1	F:4, I-1	B:3, I-2 (?)
C:8, II-1	E:4, I-2	E:4, I-2	F:4, I-2	B:3, I-3
C:9, II-1	F:1, I-1	F:1, I-1	G:2, II-7	B:3, I-4
E:2, I-1	G:2, II-8	G:2, II-1		B:3, II-1
E:4, I-2	G:3, I-1	G:2, II-2		B:3, II-2
F:1, I-1	G:4, II-1	G:2, II-8		B:3, II-3
F:4, I-1	G:8, I-1	G:3, I-1		B:4, I-1
G:2, II-1	G:8, II-1	G:4, II-1		B:4, I-2
G:3, I-1	G:11, I-1	G:8, I-1		B:4, I-3
G:4, II-1		G:11, I-1		B:4, I-4
G:8, I-1				B:4, I-5
G:8, II-1				B:4, I-6
G:11, I-1				B:4, II-1
				B:4, II-2
				B:4, II-3
				C:2, I-1
				C:2, I-2
				C:8, II-1
				C:9, II-1
				E:2, I-2
				E:4, I-1
				E:4, I-2
				E:4, I-3
				E:4, I-4
				E:4, II-1
				E:4, II-2

TABLE 14: Continued

Shofar	Lulab	Ethrog	Torah Shrine	Menorah
				F:1, I-1
				F:4, I-1
				F:4, I-2
				G:2, I-2
				G:2, II-1
				G:2, II-2
				G:2, II-3
				G:2, II-5
				G:2, II-6
				G:2, II-7
				G:2, II-8
				G:2, II-9
				G:2, II-10
				G:2, II-11
				G:2, II-12
				G:3, I-1
				G:4, II-1
				G:8, I-1
				G:8, I-2
				G:8, II-1
				G:11, I-1
Total 22	17 1?	18 1?	12	55 1?

9. Coins, Ceramics, and Other Artifacts Found Within Building Complex.

    As the handbook indicates, few synagogues have been excavated in a stratigraphic manner, thus a great deal of the evidence has not been accurately documented. The exceptions are Gush Halav A (B:1, I-1), Khirbet Shema' (B:1, I-3), Meron (B:1, I-4), the on-going excavations at Capernaum (B:3, I-1) and Nabratein (B:1, I-5), and several other sites recently (or currently) excavated. Unfortunately, in the case of the latter examples the data have not been fully published making any conclusions regarding inter-pretations premature. For example, the small lamp decorated with a cross found at En-Gedi (E:4, I-1), or the ring inscribed with the legend "O Christ help Andrew" found at Hammat Gadara (G:8, I-2), have not been adequately explained. When, at some future date, the data are documented, it will shed additional light on the study of synagogues; however, the material obtained by means other than stratigraphic, is lost to the scholar. Kraabel, Meyers and Strange's publications on Khirbet Shema', Meron, and Meyers on Gush Halav A, indicate the important information that can be obtained by accurately assessing these finds. This entry is included in the handbook, in spite of the paucity of evidence, to alert the scholar to a shortcoming in synagogue documentation, and indicate the advantages of such research.

TABLE 15

NO. 10:   INSCRIPTIONS (TYPES)

Donative	Commemorative	Salvation*	Builder[+]	Other
B:1, I-1	B:1, I-5	B:1, II-2	B:1, I-2	B:4, I-5
B:1, II-1	B:2, I-2	B:1, II-3	B:1, I-4	C:2, I-1
B:1, II-5	B:2, II-5	B:1, II-4	B:1, II-1	E:4, I-1
B:2, I-1	B:3, I-4	B:2, II-5	B:1, II-6	G:2, II-4
B:2, I-2	E:2, I-1	B:2, II-6	B:4, I-1	
B:2, II-2	G:1, II-5	B:3, I-2	B:4, I-2	
B:2, II-4		B:3, II-1	B:4, I-3	
B:2, II-5		B:3, II-3	C:6, II-1	
B:3, I-1		B:4, I-2	G:2, II-4	
B:3, I-2		B:4, I-3	G:3, I-1	
B:3, I-4		C:6, II-1	G:11, I-1 (?)	
B:4, II-1		C:7, II-1		
B:4, I-1		C:2, I-1		
B:4, I-3		C:8, II-1		
B:4, I-5		C:9, I-4		
C:2, I-1		C:9, II-1		
C:2, I-2		E:4, I-1		
C:8, II-1		E:4, I-2		
C:9, I-1		E:4, I-4		
C:9, II-1		E:4, II-1		
E:1, II-1		F:1, I-1		
E:4, I-1		F:1, II-1		
E:4, I-2		F:4, I-1		
E:4, I-4		F:4, I-2		
E:4, II-1		G:8, I-2		
F:1, I-1				

TABLE 15:   Continued

	Donative	Commemorative	Salvation*	Builder[+]	Other
	F:4, I-2				
	G:2, I-1				
	G:2, I-2				
	G:2, II-4				
	G:3, I-1				
	G:3, II-4				
	G:8, I-2				
Total	33	6	25	10 1?	4

* Usually begins with: "Remember be for good . . ."

[+] The term 'made' usually refers to a donor, however these refer to an actual artisan who worked on the building.

TABLE 16

NO. 10:   INSCRIPTIONS (ARAMAIC, HEBREW, GREEK)

Aramaic	Hebrew	Greek
B:1, I-1	B:1, I-2	B:2, I-1
B:1, I-4	B:1, I-5	B:2, II-5
B:1, II-1	B:1, II-1	B:2, II-6
B:1, II-2	B:1, II-3	B:3, I-1
B:1, II-4	B:1, II-6	B:3, I-4
B:1, II-5	B:2, I-2	B:3, II-1
B:2, I-1	C:7, II-1	B:3, II-3
B:2, II-2	C:2, I-1	B:4, I-1
B:2, II-4	C:2, I-2	B:4, I-2*
B:2, II-5	C:8, II-1	B:4, I-3
B:2, II-6	C:9, II-1	B:4, II-1
B:3, I-1	E:2, I-1	B:4, II-3
B:3, I-2	E:4, I-1	C:7, II-1
B:3, I-4	E:4, I-4	C:2, I-1
B:3, II-1	F:4, I-1	C:8, II-1
B:3, II-3	G:2, II-4	C:9, I-1
B:4, I-1		C:9, II-1
B:4, I-3		E:2, I-1
B:4, I-5		G:2, II-4
C:2, I-2		G:8, I-1
C:6, II-1		G:11, I-1
E:4, I-1		
E:4, I-2		
E:4, I-4		
E:4, II-1		
F:1, I-1		
F:1, II-1		

TABLE 16: Continued

	Aramaic	Hebrew	Greek
	F:4, I-1		
	F:4, I-2		
	G:2, I-1		
	G:2, I-2		
	G:2, II-1		
	G:2, II-4		
	G:2, II-5		
	G:2, II-7		
	G:3, I-1		
	G:4, II-1		
	G:8, I-1		
	G:11, I-1		
Total	39	16	21

* This site also has a Samaritan inscription.

TABLE 17

NO. 11:   DONORS OR PATRONS

Individual(s)	Community	Anonymous
B:1, I-1	B:4, I-3	B:4, I-3
B:1, I-2	C:2, I-1	C:7, II-1
B:1, II-1	E:2, I-1	E:2, I-1
B:1, II-2	E:4, I-1	E:4, I-4
B:1, II-4	E:4, I-4	F:4, I-1
B:1, II-5	F:1, I-1	
B:1, II-6	F:4, I-1	
B:2, I-1	F:4, I-2	
B:2, I-2		
B:2, II-2		
B:2, II-4		
B;2, II-5		
B:2, II-6		
B:3, I-1		
B:3, I-2		
B:3, I-4		
B:3, II-1		
B:4, I-1		
B:4, I-5		
C:2, I-1		
C:2, I-2		
C:6, II-1		
C:8, II-1		
C:9, I-1		
C:9, II-1		
E:1, II-1		
E:2, I-1		

TABLE 17: Continued

	Individual(s)	Community	Anonymous
	E:4, I-1		
	E:4, I-2		
	E:4, I-4		
	E:4, II-1		
	F:1, I-1		
	F:1, II-1		
	F:4, I-2		
	G:2, I-1		
	G:2, I-2		
	G:2, II-4		
	G:2, II-5		
	G:3, I-1		
	G:3, II-1		
	G:4, II-1		
	G:8, I-2		
	G:11, I-1		
Total	43	8	5

12. Date

As discussed earlier (p. 5), the dates of
most Palestinian synagogues are uncertain. Kohl and Watzinger
proposed the dates for the so-called "early" Galilean type
synagogues, and these have been accepted by many scholars as the
criteria for dating other ruins which they consider to be similar.
However, recent and ongoing excavations at Capernaum (B:3, I-1),
Gush Halav A (B:1, I-1), Khirbet Shema' (B:1, I-3) and Meron
(B:1, I-4) have underscored the need for a new evaluation of
dating procedures. Only three synagogues have dates mentioned
in inscriptions: Beth Alpha (B:4, I-1), Gaza A (C:9, I-1) and
Nabratein A (B:1, I-5). Except for Gaza, the other two dates
appear to commemorate renovations to already existing buildings.

The dates, as suggested by archaeologists and scholars in
the field, appear to cluster around two periods: the third to
fourth centuries and the fifth to sixth. Twelve synagogues are
given the span of the third to sixth centuries; they are: Gush
Halav A (B:1, I-1), Nabratein A (B:1, I-5), Capernaum (B:3, I-1),
Chorozin (B:3, I-2), Hammat Tiberias A (B:3, I-3), Hammat
Tiberias B (B:3, I-4), Beth She'an A (B:4, I-2), Maoz Hayyim
(B:4, I-4), Rehov (B:4, I-5). En-Gedi (E:4, I-1), Eshtemoa
(E:4, I-2) and Khirbet Sūsīya (E:4, I-4). It must be cautioned,
however, that not all these dates are universally accepted.

The reason often proposed to explain the temporary termina-
tion of synagogue construction in the mid-fourth century is the
supposed Jewish revolt in 352 against Emperor Gallus which
resulted in the destruction of many Jewish communities in the
north (see Beth She'arim, B:2, I-2).

GLOSSARIES

Often Used Hebrew Terms

'Aggadah, haggada | (lit. "saying") The non-legal contents of the Talmud and Midrash, especially legends, stories, homilies and exposition of Scripture.

Amora'im | The title of rabbis in the Talmudic period (3-6th C).

Bema, bimah | A platform in the synagogue on which stands the desk from which the Torah is read.

Beth | House.

Diaspora | Collective term for all Jewish communities outside Palestine.

Darom (daromas) | South; southern Judaea.

Ethrog, etrog | Citron; one of the "four species" used on Sukkot.

Ga'on | Title of the heads of the Rabbinic academies in Babylonia and Palestine from the 6-11th C.

Genizah | (lit. "storing") A place for storing books or ritual objects which have become unuseable; often used as the synagogue's "treasury."

Halakah | (lit. "going") Law, legal ruling; used specifically for legal material in the two Talmudim and in subsequent Rabbinic literature.

Har | Mountain.

Horvat, Khirbet (Arabic) | Ruin.

Kefar, Kfar | Village.

Lulab, lulav | Palm branch; one of the "four species" used on Sukkot.

Ma'amad | The name given to the delegations of the 24 districts, into which Palestine was divided, who represented the populace at the Temple service in a weekly rotation.

Menorah, menorot (pl.) | Candelabrum; seven-branched oil lamp used in the Tabernacle and Temple.

Midrash | (lit. "searching") Rabbinic method of exegesis; works in which expositions in the Midrashic manner are collected.

Miqvah, mikveh	(lit. "collection of water") A pool or bath of clear water, immersion in which renders an individual ritually clean.
Mishnah	The first collection of Jewish Law arranged in 6 orders, forms the basis for the Talmud.
Nahal	Dry stream.
Nahar	River.
Negeb, negev	South; arid area of Palestine.
Ner Tamid	(lit. "eternal light") Burns perpetually in synagogues as a symbolic reminder of the Temple menorah.
Sanhedrin	The assembly of ordained scholars which functioned in Palestine both as a supreme court and as a legislature from before 70 C.E. until 425 C.E.
Shephelah	Southern part of Palestine's coastal plain.
Shofar	A ram's horn, or of any ritually pure animal except the cow, blown on the High Holidays and other important occasions.
Talmud	An extensive commentary on the Mishnah; two editions, the Babylonian and the Jerusalem.
Tanna'im	The sages of the first and second centuries C.E. whose teachings are incorporated in the Mishnah.
Tell	An ancient mound in the Middle East composed of remains of successive settlements.
Torah	(lit. "teaching") The first section of the Jewish Bible; contains the five Books of Moses: the Pentateuch.

Often Used Architectural Terms

Acroterium	Blocks on the lower edges of the pediment to support statuary or decoration.
Adytum	The inner sanctuary of a temple.
Anta (antae, pl.)	A pilaster or jamb which terminates the side wall of a temple; usually has a base and capital different from those of adjacent columns.
Apodyterium	Dressing room of a bath.
Apse	A curved recess, often semi-circular, projecting from a building.
Architrave	The beam or lowest division of the entablature extends from column to column.
Ashlar	Rectangular block of hewn stone.
Astragal	Convex molding; e.g. the bead and reel.
Atrium	An outer court, often with a colonnade, the center area open to the sky.
Attic base	Two large rings of convex molding of which the upper ring has a smaller diameter than the lower, and between the two rings a spreading concave molding. The lower end of the shaft terminates in a roundel, above which is a vertical fillet followed by a sharp inward curve.
Bucranium	An ox-head or ox-skull in relief used as decoration often combined with garlands, or rosettes.
Caldarium	The hot bath.
Cardo	The main north - south street.
Cavea	Auditorium.
Cella	Principal room of a temple. See naos.
Cenotaph	A funerary monument to a person buried elsewhere.
Chancel	Area for clergy in church; usually separated from nave by a screen.
Colonnade	A row of columns supporting an entablature.
Crepis	Stepped outer edges of a temple platform.
Decumanus	Main east - west road.

Distyle	Having two columns; porches described as 'distyle in antis,' i.e. two columns between antae.
Entablature	Comprises the architrave, frieze and cornice, supported by a colonnade.
Fascia	Band usually in the architrave.
Frieze	The decoration of the middle division of the entablature.
Frigidarium	Cold water bath.
Guilloche	Two or more intertwining bands with circular spaces in the center. A form of interlace.
Lintel	A horizontal timber or stone that spans an opening.
Naos	Principal room of a temple. See cella.
Narthex	A long, usually arcaded, porch forming an entrance into a public building (see portico).
Nave	The wide central aisle of a basilica.
Nymphaeum	Roman pleasure houses, usually with flowers, running water and statues.
Odium	A small theater.
Opisthodomus	An open porch, often a duplicate of the pronaos, usually with no door leading into the temple's cella.
Palaestra	Gymnasium.
Pediment	Triangular piece of wall above the entablature; fills in and supports the sloping roof. "Gable-roof."
Peripteral	A building with an outer colonnade; full height of building and covered by the same roof.
Peristyle	The colonnade around the inside of a court or room; rarely used for an external colonnade.
Portico	Porch; usually colonnaded with a roof supported on one side by columns (see narthex).
Pronaos	Porch or ante-room of a temple.
Propylaeum	A major gateway before a temple complex.
Prostyle	Columns in front of antae.
Pulpitum	Stone screen in church to shut off choir from nave.

Pulvinated	A convex frieze.
Scaena	The walls of the stage building of a theater.
Stylobate	Continuous base supporting a row or rows of columns.
Temenos	A sacred prcinct in which stood a temple or sanctuary.
Tholos	A circular building.
Triclinium	A dining room with three couches.
Voussoir	One of the wedge-shaped blocks making up an arch.

LISTS OF ABBREVIATIONS

Abbreviations of Often Used Sources

Abel, Geógraphie.
 Abel, Le P. F.-M. Geógraphie de la Palestine. 2 vols. Paris:
 J. Gabalda, 1933.

Avi-Yonah, Gazetteer.
 Avi-Yonah, Michael. Gazetteer of Roman Palestine. Monographs
 of the Institute of Archaeology, Qedem 5. Jerusalem: Hebrew
 University, 1976.

Avi-Yonah, Holy Land.
 Avi-Yonah, Michael. The Holy Land: From the Persian to the
 Arab Conquests, A Historical Geography. Rev. ed. Grand Rapids:
 Baker Books, 1966.

Boethius, Ward-Perkins, Roman Architecture.
 Boethius, Axel and J. B. Ward-Perkins. Etruscan and Roman
 Architecture. Middlesex: Penguin Books, 1970.

Butler, Early Churches.
 Butler, H. C. Early Churches in Syria. Edited and completed
 by E. Baldwin Smith. Amsterdam: Adolf Hakkert, 1969.

Butler, Syria.
 Butler, H. C. Syria: Publications of the Princeton University
 Archaeological Expeditions to Syria in 1904-1905 and 1909.
 Div. II, Section A, Parts 1-7. Leyden: Brill, 1914, 1919.

Clermont-Ganneau, ARP.
 Clermont-Ganneau, Charles. Archaeological Researches in
 Palestine During the Years 1873-1874. Vol. II. London:
 Palestine Exploration Fund, 1896.

Clermont-Ganneau, RAO.
 Idem. Receuil d'Archéologie Orientale. 8 vols. Paris, 1888-
 1924.

Conder, SWP.
 Conder, C. R. and H. H. Kitchener. The Survey of Western
 Palestine: Memoirs of the Topography, Orography, Hydrography
 and Archaeology. London: 1881-1883.

Goodenough, Jewish Symbols.
 Goodenough, E. R. Jewish Symbols in the Greco-Roman Period.
 13 vols. New York: Pantheon, 1953-1965.

Guérin, DGHA.
 Guérin, V. Description Géographique, Historique et Archéologique de la Palestine. 7 vols. Paris, 1868-1880.

Hüttenmeister, Antiken Synagogen.
 Hüttenmeister, Frowald and Gottfried Reeg. Die Antiken
 Synagogen in Israel. 2 vols. Wiesbaden: Reichert, 1977.

Jones, Cities.
 Jones, A. H. M. The Cities of the Eastern Roman Provinces.
 2nd ed. Oxford: Clarendon Press, 1971.

JSG
  Kochavi, M. ed. Judaea, Samaria and the Golan: Archaeological
  Survey 1967-1968. Jerusalem: Carta, 1972.

Klein, Corpus Inscr.
  Klein, Samuel. Judisch-Palastinisches Corpus Inscriptionum.
  Wien-Berlin, 1920.

Kohl and Watzinger.
  Kohl, H. and C. Watzinger. Antike Synagogen in Galilaea.
  Leipzig: J. C. Hinrichs', 1916. Rpt. Jeru.: Kedem, 1973.

Kraabel, NCE
  Kraabel, A. Thomas. "Synagogues, Ancient," New Catholic
  Encyclopedia: Supplement 1967-1974 (1974) 436-439.

Krautheimer, Early Christian.
  Krautheimer, Richard. Early Christian and Byzantine Architecture. 2nd ed. Middlesex: Penguin, 1975.

Masterman, Studies.
  Masterman, E. W. G. Studies in Galilee. Chicago: Univ. of
  Chicago Press, 1909.

Meyers, Meron.
  Meyers, Eric, James F. Strange, Carol Meyers. Excavations at
  Ancient Meron, Upper Galilee, Israel 1970-72, 1974-75, 1977.
  Meron Excavation Project, Volume III. Cambridge: The American
  Schools of Oriental Research, 1981.

Meyers, Shema'.
  Meyers, Eric, A. T. Kraabel, J. F. Strange. Ancient Synagogue
  Excavations at Khirbet Shema', Upper Galilee, Israel. 1970-
  1972. The Annual of the American Schools of Oriental Research.
  Vol. XLVII. Durham: Duke Univ. Press, 1976.

Orni, Geography.
  Orni, Efraim and Elisha Efrat. Geography of Israel. 2nd rev.
  ed. Jerusalem, 1966.

Ovadiah, Corpus.
  Ovadiah, Asher. Corpus of the Byzantine Churches in the Holy
  Land. Bonn:Hanstein, 1970.

Rabinowitz, Bulletin.
  Louis Rabinowitz Fund for the Exploration of Ancient Synagogues.
  3 vols. Jerusalem, 1949, 1951, 1960.

Reeg, Antiken Synagogen.
  Hüttenmeister, Frowald and Gottfried Reeg. Die Antiken Synagogen in Israel. 2 vols. Wiesbaden: Reichert, 1977.

Rénan, Mission.
  Rénan, E. Mission de Phénicie. Paris, 1864.

Saller, Catalogue.
  Saller, J. Second Revised Catalogue of Ancient Synagogues of
  the Holy Land. Jerusalem: Franciscan Press, 1972.

AIMA
  Repertoire Graphique de Décor Géometrique dans la Mosaïque
  Antique. Association Internationale pour l'Etude de la
  Mosaïque Antique. Paris, 1973.

Schumacher, Jaulan.
    Schumacher, G. The Jaulan. London, 1889. Rpt. Jeru.: 1976.

Smallwood, Jews.
    Smallwood, E. Mary. The Jews Under Roman Rule. Leiden: Brill, 1976.

Sukenik, Ancient Synagogues.
    Sukenik, E. L. Ancient Synagogues in Palestine and Greece. London: Oxford Univ. Press, 1934.

SWP
    Conder, C., H. Kitchener. The Survey of Western Palestine. 3 vols. London: Oxford Univ. Press, 1881-1883. Rpt. Jerusalem, 1970.

SWP, Jeru.
    Warren, Charles, C. Conder. The Survey of Western Palestine, Jerusalem. London, 1884.

SWP, SP
    Survey of Western Palestine: Special Papers. London, 1881.

Abbreviations: Encyclopedias

EAEh
   Encyclopedia of Archaeological Excavations in the Holy Land.
   4 vols. London, 1975-1979.

EJ
   Encyclopedia Judaica. 16 vols. Jerusalem, 1973.

IDB
   Interpreters Dictionary of the Bible (1962). S.v. "Synagogues,"
   by I. Sonne, 477.

IDBS
   Supplement, 1972, s.v. "Synagogue," by Eric Meyers.

PW
   Pauly Wissowa. Real Encyclopadie der Klassischen Altertums-
   wissenschaft. S.v. "Synagogen," vol. IV A, 2.

TD
   Theological Dictionary of the New Testament. Eng. ed. (1971)
   S.v. "Synagogue," by W. Schrage.

PE
   Princeton Encyclopedia of Classical Sites. Princeton, 1976.

RA
   Archives of the British Mandatory Government, Palestine.
   Rockefeller Museum, Jerusalem.

Abbreviations of Ancient Texts and Sources

Onom.
Eusebius of Caesarea. Onomasticon der Biblischen Ortsnamen.
Ed. by E. Klostermann, Leipzig, 1904.

Frey, CIJ.
Frey, P. J.-B. Corpus Inscription Judaicarum. Vol. II.
Rome, 1952.

Jos.
Josephus Flavius. Loeb edition.
AJ   Antiquities Judaicae
AP   Contra Apionem
BJ   Bellum Judaicum
Vit.   Vita

Lifshitz, Donateurs.
Lifshitz, B. Donateurs et Fondateurs les Synagogues Juives.
Cahiers de la Revue Biblique, VII, 1967.

Philo.
Philo Judaeus. Loeb edition.
    In. Flacc.   In Flaccum
    Leg.   Legatio ad Gaium
    Quod Omnis   Quod Omnis Probus Liber Sit.

Pliny. Gaius Plinius Secundus. Loeb edition. NH Natural History.

Abbreviations: Journal and Bulletins

AASOR	Annual of the American Schools of Oriental Research
ADAJ	Annual of the Department of Antiquities of Jordan
AJA	American Journal of Archaeology
'ATIQOT	'Atiqot, Journal of the Israel Department of Antiquities
BA	The Biblical Archaeologist
BASOR	Bulletin of the American Schools of Oriental Research
BIES	Bulletin of the Israel Exploration Society, continuing:
BJPES	Bulletin of the Jewish Palestine Exploration Society
CNI	Christian News from Israel
EI	Eretz Israel: Archaeological, Historical and Geographical Studies, published by the Israel Exploration Society
HA	Hadashot Arkheologiyot: Agaf Ha-'Atiqot Veha-Muse'onim (author's name when provided)
HUCA	Hebrew Union College Annual
IEJ	Israel Exploration Journal
JAOS	Journal of the American Oriental Society
JBL	Journal of Biblical Literature
JJA	Journal of Jewish Art
JJPES	Journal of the Jewish Palestine Exploration Society
JPOS	Journal of the Palestine Oriental Society
JZWL	Jüdische Zeitschrift für Wissenschaft und Leben
LA	Liber Annus: Studii Biblici Franciscani
PEFA	Palestine Exploration Fund Annual
PEQ	Palestine Exploration Quarterly, continuing:
PEFQSt	Quarterly Statement of the Palestine Exploration Fund
PJB	Palästinajahrbuch des Deutschen evangelischen Institute für Altertumswissenschaft des Heiligen Landes zu Jerusalem
QAD	Qadmoniot: Quarterly for the Antiquities of Eretz-Israel and Bible Lands
QDAP	Quarterly of the Department of Antiquities in Palestine

RB	Revue Biblique
REJ	Revue des études juives
TARBIZ	A Quarterly Review of the Humanities
YEDIOT	Continuation of BIES (1962-1967)
ZDMG	Zeitschrift der Deutschen morgenländischen Gesselschaft
ZDPV	Zeitschrift der Deutschen Palästina-Vereins

Abbreviations of Tractates of the Talmud
(Source: The Babylonian Talmud, ed. I. Epstein)

*Ab.	Aboth	RH	Rosh Hashanah
*'Ar.	'Arakin	Sanh.	Sanhedrin
'A.Z.	'Abodah Zarah	Shab.	Shabbath
BB	Baba Bathra	Sheb.	Shebi'ith
*Bek.	Bekoroth	Shebu.	Shebu'oth
Ber.	Berakoth	Shek.	Shekalim
Bez.	Bezah	Sot.	Sotah
Bik.	Bikkurim	Suk.	Sukkah
BK	Baba Kamma	Ta'an	Ta'anith
BM	Baba Mezi'a	*Tam.	Tamid
Dem.	Demai	*Tem.	Temurah
*'Ed., 'Eduy.	'Eduyyoth	Ter.	Terumoth
'Er., 'Erub.	'Erubin	*Toh.	Tohoroth
Git.	Gittin	?Toho.	v. Toh.
Hag.	Hagigah	*TY	Tebul Yom
Hal.	Hallah	*'Uk	'Ukzin
Hor.	Horayoth	*Yad.	Yadayin
*Hul.	Hullin	Yeb.	Yebamoth
*Kel.	Kelim	Yom.	Yoma
*Ker.	Kerihoth	*Zab.	Zabim
Ket.	Kethuboth	*Zeb.	Zebahim
Kid.	Kiddusin		
Kil.	Kil'ayim		
*Kin.	Kinnin		
Ma'as.	Ma'asroth	BT	BABYLONIAN TALMUD
Mak.	Makkoth	JT	JERUSALEM TALMUD
*Maks.	Makshrin		(Yerushalmi,
Meg.	Megillah		Palestine)
*Me'il.	Me'ilah		
*Men.	Menahoth	Mish.	MISHNAH
*Mid.	Middoth	Tosaph.	TOSAPHOTH
*Mik.	Mikwa'oth	Tos.	Tosefta
MK	Mo'ed Katan		
M.Sh.	Ma'aser Sheni	* Not in Jerusalem Talmud	
Naz.	Nazir		
Ned.	Nedarim		
*Neg.	Nega'im		
Nid.	Niddah		
*Oh.	Oholoth		
'Or.	'Orlah		
*Par.	Parah		
Pe.	Pesahim		

MAP AND PLANS

City-territories in Palestine. Atlas of Israel.

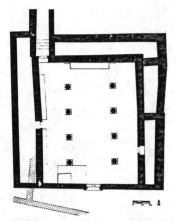

1. Gush Halav A.

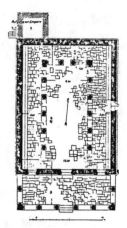

2. Kefar Bar'am A.

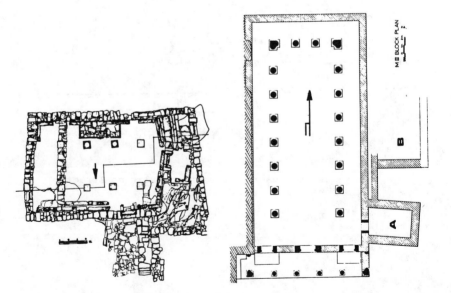

3. Khirbet Shema'.

4. Meron.

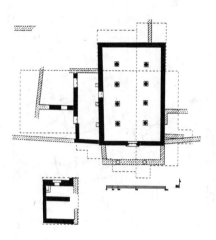

5. Nabratein A.

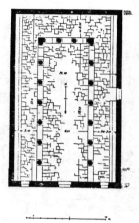

6. 'Ammudim.

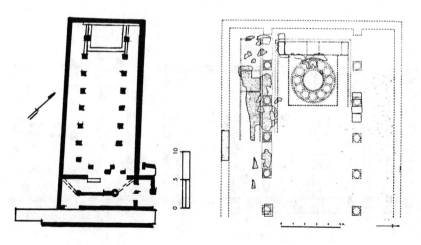

7. Beth She'arim.

8. Japhia.

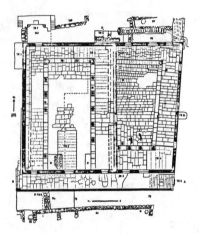

9. Capernaum.

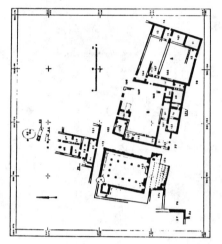

10. Chorozain.

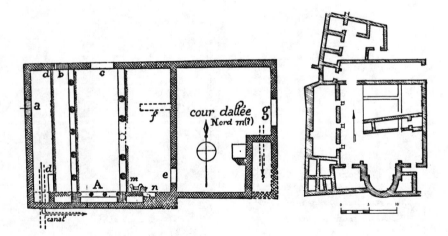

11. Hammat Tiberias A.

12. Hammat Tiberias B.

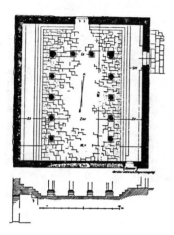

13. Arbela.

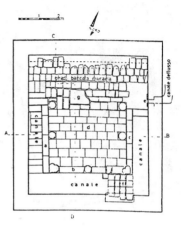

14. Migdal.

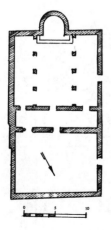

15. Beth Alpha.

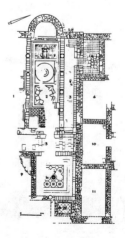

16. Beth She'an A.

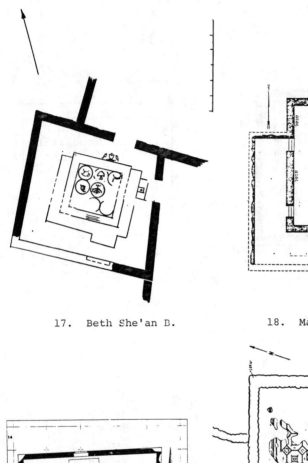

17. Beth She'an B.

18. Ma'oz Hayyim.

19. Rehov.

20. Tel Menora.

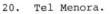

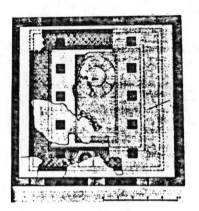

21. Husifah.

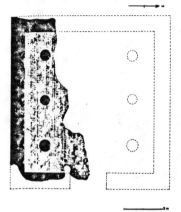

22. Ramat Aviv.

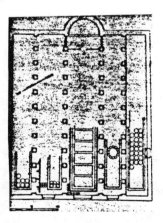

23. Gaza.

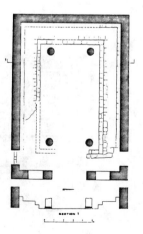

24. Herodium.

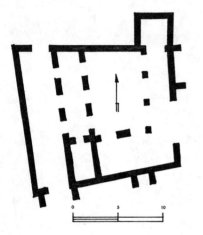

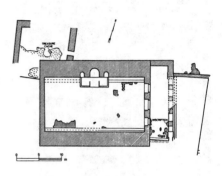

25. En-Gedi.

26. Eshtomoa.

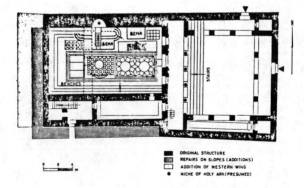

27. Khirbet Sūsīya.

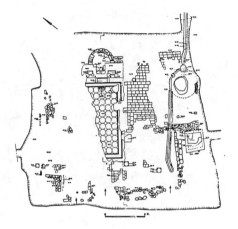

28. Ma'on.

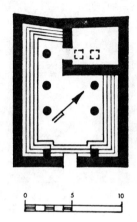

29. Masada.

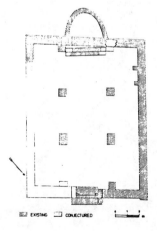

30. Jericho.

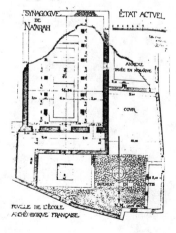

31. Na'aran.

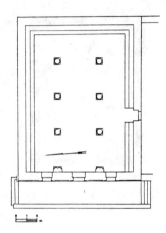

32. Ed-Dikkeh.

33. Beth Yerah.

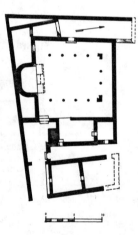

34. Hammat Gadara

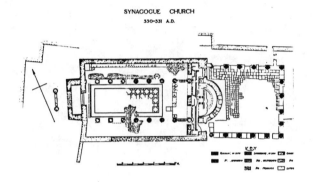

35. Gerasa.

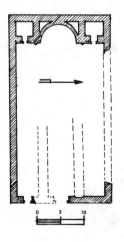

36. Rabbat Moab

INDICES

Index of Place Names (Alphabetical)
         * Samaritan
        ** Possibly Samaritan

Index of Place Names (Numerical)

C:2, I-1	Caesarea	153-158
C:2, I-2	Husifah	158-161
C:2, IIIA-1	Khirbet Semmâka	161-163
C:2, IIIB-1	Khirbet Dūbil	163-164
C:3, IIIA-1	Ramat Aviv	165-167
C:6, II-1	Horvat Habrā	171-172
C:6, II-2	Jamnia	172-173
C:7, II-1	Azotus Mesogaeus/Hippenus	175-176
C:7, II-2	Azotus Mesogaeus	177
C:8, II-1	Ascalon	179-181
C:9, I-1	Gaza A	183-186
C:9, II-1	Gaza B	187-188
C:9, II-2	Gaza C (Samaritan)	188-189
D:2, IIIB-1	Shiloh	197-198
E:1, II-1	Jerusalem	201-202
E:1, IIIA-1	David'a Tomb	203-204
E:1, IIIA-2	Herodium	204-207
E:2, I-1	Huldah	209-211
E:2, II-1	Kefar Bilu	211-212
E:2, II-2	Na'aneh	212-213
E:3, I-1	Salbit	215-217
E:3, II-1	Emmaus	218
E:4, I-1	En-Gedi	219-224
E:4, I-2	Eshtemoa	224-228
E:4, I-3	Horvat Rimmon	228-230
E:4, I-4	Khirbet Sūsiya	230-235
E:4, II-1	Beth Guvrin	235-237
E:4, II-2	Horvat Kishor	237
E:4, IIIB-1	Horvat Karmil	238
E:4, IIIB-2	Horvat Midras	238-239
E:4, IIIB-3	Khirbet 'Aziz	239
F:1, I-1	Ma'on	243-247

Index of Biblical and Talmudic Passages

IV. Tosefta   (Page)

    Sheb. 4:8-66   (Naveh)   295

    Meg. 4:22   (Beth She'an A)   128

    Meg. 4:22   (Caesarea)   153

    Meg. 4:22   (Eshtemoa)   224

    Meg. 4:22   (Herodium)   204

    Meg. 4:22   (Masada)   248

V.   Palestinian Talmud

    Ber. 3:6a   (Caesarea)   153

    Ber. 4:27d   (Emmaus)   218

    Sheb. 9:2   (Meron)   37

    Shab. (passim)   (Caesarea)   153

    Yom. 7:1   (Jerusalem)   201

    Meg. 3:1   (Jerusalem)   201

    Yeb. 2:5   (Nabratein A)   41

    Sot. 7:1   (Caesarea)   153

    Sot. 7:7-8   (Jerusalem)   201

VI. Babylonian Talmud

    Shab. 116a, 152a   (Caesarea)   153

    Shab. 147b   (Emmaus)   218

    R.H. 22a   (Hammat Gadara)   307

    Hag. 15b   (Hammat Gadara)   307

    Ket. 105a   (Jerusalem)   201

    Men. 85a, 85b   (Chorozain)   97

VII. Other Midrashim

    Lam. R. Proem 2   (Hammat Gadara)   307

Index of Ancient Sources